SOVIET POLITICS

SOVIET POLITICS

RUSSIA AFTER BREZHNEV

Edited by Joseph L. Nogee

PRAEGER SPECIAL STUDIES • PRAEGER SCIENTIFIC

New York • Westport, Connecticut • London

Library of Congress Cataloging in Publication Data

Main entry under title:

Soviet politics.

Includes index.
1. Soviet Union—Politics and government—
1953–   —Addresses, essays, lectures.   I. Nogee,
Joseph L.
DK286.5.S683   1985   947.085′3   84-26289
ISBN 0-275-90148-3 (alk. paper)
ISBN 0-275-91652-9 (pbk.: alk. paper)

Library of Congress Catalog Card Number: 84-26289
ISBN: 0-275-90148-3
ISBN: 0-275-91652-9 (ppbk)

First published in 1985

Praeger Publishers, 521 Fifth Avenue, New York, NY 10175
A division of Greenwood Press, Inc.

Printed in the United States of America

The paper used in this book complies with the Permanent
Paper Standard issued by the National Information Standards
Organization (Z39.48-1984).

10 9 8 7 6 5 4 3 2

Published and Distributed by the
Praeger Publishers Division
(ISBN Prefix 0-275)
of Greenwood Press, Inc.,
Westport, Connecticut

CONTENTS

INTRODUCTION

Introduction

Amid the many uncertainties about Soviet politics, one fact stands out: the 1980s are a period of transition. Abroad and at home the ruling Soviet oligarchy is faced with the need to overcome problems that have been developing for years. In nearly every major foreign policy arena Moscow is groping for the solutions to problems that will bring it some kind of a stable, successful outcome. Since the collapse of detente, relations with the United States have reverted to a state of hostility reminiscent of the cold war. An arms race, not at all to its liking, proceeds in both the European theater and at the strategic level. A long-term modus vivendi has yet to be worked out with China. Indeed, in Asia the Soviet Union is faced with the continuing antagonism of Japan as well as China. Moscow's domination of Eastern Europe, shakened by the Polish revolution in 1980, is still challenged by forces pressing for greater autonomy, notwithstanding the suppression of Solidarity. In Afghanistan, after almost half a decade of combat against primitive resistance forces, victory continues to elude the Red Army. In the Third World generally Moscow in recent years has encountered as many setbacks as it has made advances.

If successes elude the Soviet leadership in foreign policy, they are stymied even more by domestic problems. Under the guidance of Leonid Brezhnev the Soviet economy stagnated for years. The industrial growth rate at the beginning of the 1980s was the lowest in the postwar years. Sluggish agricultural production has become a chronic problem. Consumer goods remain in short supply and much of what is available is of abysmally poor quality. Absenteeism, alcoholism, bribery, indifference to work standards, and theft of government property have become the most obvious signs of what Seweryn Bialer refers to as the "rot that has set in within Soviet society."[1] For years now the country has been immobilized in a state of corruption, economically, socially, and politically. At all levels of Soviet society there is a widespread recognition of the need for reform. Individually, none of these problems can be considered as threatening the stability—let alone survival—of the Soviet system, but collectively they constitute a crisis of major proportions.

Overlapping this programmatic and structural crisis is the fact the Soviet Union is undergoing a change of leadership. It is experiencing what political scientists refer to as a political succession. It is in fact the combination of the need to change policies, structures, and leaders at the same time which gives to contemporary Soviet politics its extraordinarily dynamic character. This is not the first time that the Soviet Union has been in the grip of a political crisis resulting from the need to cope with major domestic and foreign problems while simultaneously selecting a new political leadership. In the 1920s following the death of Lenin, and in the 1950s following the death of Stalin, the Soviet system was faced with comparable challenges. In these prior occasions the results in terms of new leaders and new policies took years to work themselves out. The current crisis has been years in the making and will almost certainly require several years to resolve. Few analysts are bold or incautious enough to predict the specific outcomes of this process, though most tend to agree with Timothy Colton on the improbability of fundamental change.[2]

In every generation the Soviet political system has experienced a struggle for succession accompanied by pressures for radical changes in domestic and foreign policy. Even in the relatively short history of the Soviet regime this pattern has become too clear to be the product of simple historical accident. The roots of this pattern are in the political system. Part of the explanation for the recurring crises in political succession lies in the fact that the Soviet political system lacks a constitutional procedure to govern the process of leadership change. We do not know when there will be a change of leadership in the Soviet Union, what factors determine who the new leaders will be, nor what the range of powers the new leaders will possess. Thus every change in leadership in the Soviet Union has come as a surprise, not only to those outside the country, but to the Soviet people as well.

The highest political office in the Soviet system is that of general secretary of the Communist party. This position is identified with the Soviet leader not because of party statutes or law but simply because since the Stalin period the recognized leader of the Soviet regime has been identified with that office.[3] Beginning with the Brezhnev administration the leader has additionally assumed the offices of president (chairman of the Presidium of the Supreme Soviet) and chairman of the Defense Council. But it is the office of general secretary or head of the party that is critical. A major feature of that office, which complicates the problem of political succession, is the lack of a fixed term for the incumbent. To date four leaders— Lenin, Stalin, Brezhnev, and Andropov—held power until their death, and two—Malenkov and Khrushchev—were removed by coups.[4] Nor are there fixed terms for the other members of the central party organs (the Politburo and Secretariat) who share power with the leader. Nikita Khrushchev attempted to limit the terms for party leaders, but even his modest reforms were abolished by Brezhnev.

Also, there are no clear guides as to the scope of powers possessed by the party leader. They range all the way from the dictatorial powers exercised by Stalin to the collective leadership of the post-Khrushchev period. Not only have different leaders wielded power in different degrees, the scope of most leaders' powers has changed over time. The general practice has been for the leader to accumulate more power over time as his position within the oligarchy became more secure. And the best strategy for enhancement of the leader's security has been to secure the promotion within the party bureaucracy, particularly in the Central Committee, Politburo, and Secretariat, of individuals loyal to the leader personally or sympathetic to his policies.

In theory, leadership of the party is collective, not individual. In practice it has been both at different periods of time. Perhaps a more accurate way of assessing the power relationship between the designated leader and his colleagues is to view it as falling somewhere along a continuum, with one-man rule at one end and equal collegiality at the other end. Stalin came closest to absolute one-man rule, whereas Brezhnev, Andropov, and Chernenko represent a more shared leadership. The long-term trend has been toward a more collective leadership.

Finally, the succession process is complicated because of the lack of recognized procedures to mark the process of change. In practice every succession has involved a political struggle involving individuals and bureaucratic and institutional interests in which many of the rules were developed in an ad hoc manner. Few features of Soviet politics have been as enigmatic as the game of political succession.

One significant difference between the current political succession and previous ones is that it will involve a generational change. During Brezhnev's 18-year tenure there were almost no promotions of young men into the ruling oligarchy. Indeed, at the Twenty-Sixth Party Congress in 1981, for the first time in party history there was not a single change made in the composition of either the Politburo or the Secretariat. When Brezhnev died, a month short of his 76th birthday, there were 14 full members of the Politburo of whom one was in his eighties, seven in their seventies, four in their sixties, and only two in their fifties. Yuri Andropov, who became general-secretary at age 68, made a few changes in the leadership, but at his death the Politburo remained a gerontic group. When Chernenko assumed power in February 1984 at the age of 72 the average age of the Politburo was 67. Furthermore, since the late 1970s every party leader has suffered from serious health problems. In his later years Brezhnev was so infirm that he was able to work only a few hours a day. Through most of his brief tenure Andropov suffered from kidney failure, so that in the last six months of his rule he made no public appearances. Konstantin Chernenko, reportedly suffering from emphysema, is believed not to be in very robust condition.

Soviet politics is thus in a state of transition. Major changes of leadership are inevitable, though they may come slowly. There is a widespread recognition of the need for reform, though the forces opposed to reform, located principally in the party bureaucracy, are powerful and determined. The paradox confronting Soviet politics is reflected in the choice of party leaders since Brezhnev; Yuri Andropov was apparently selected because of his reputation as a strong leader who would get the country moving again. It was expected that he could reverse the stagnation and decline that had occurred under Brezhnev. Yet Andropov was replaced by the very person who was believed to be his rival for the office, a man who was Brezhnev's closest protege. There is little in Chernenko's long career as a party bureaucrat that would suggest an inclination or capacity to bring about major changes in Soviet society. In any event, like Andropov, Chernenko is almost certainly only a transitional leader.

To assess the state of Soviet politics in this period of transition a group of Soviet scholars was invited to examine a particular aspect of Soviet politics that reflected their individual research interests. Not every facet of Soviet politics is covered in this collection, but every essay covers an important feature of Soviet politics or the Soviet political system.

The political succession now taking place, according to Robert Donaldson, began with Aleksei Kosygin's retirement in October 1980 and will not be completed until Chernenko's successor is chosen. This leadership change differs from previous successions in that it will mark the first generational change since the Great Purge of the 1930s. Donaldson argues that the composition of the leadership is important for policy making. The post-Brezhnev leadership will be younger, better educated, molded by the reformism of the Khrushchev period, and probably more committed to change than their predecessors. Although one cannot predict what policies they will pursue, Donaldson recommends that Western leaders try to develop contacts with those coming to power, if that is possible.

George Breslauer applies the analytical framework he developed in *Khrushchev and Brezhnev as Leaders: Building Authority in Soviet Politics* to the Andropov administration. He makes an important distinction between the tasks of a leader in accumulating power and building authority. The former is necessary to obtain office, the latter to legitimize holding office. Among the techniques discussed by Breslauer in authority building are (1) demonstrating skill in problem solving, (2) building charisma, (3) establishing one's indispensability as a leader, and (4) intimidating rivals. Andropov was selected as general secretary in order to get the country moving after the long malaise under Brezhnev. Breslauer speculates that Andropov's reforms were limited in scope because he needed to move slowly to overcome opposition.

Ellen Mickiewicz examines the role of the media in the Soviet political system. She contends that a vital function of the media is political socialization, that is, to change the ethical and moral outlook of the population to bring it in line with what authorities call the New Soviet Man. The media are important also in mobilizing the population to meet production goals. Making extensive use of survey data, Mickiewicz shows that the media are less than successful in their socialization mission. For example, the more educated the Soviet citizen is, the more likely he or she is to be critical of the content of Soviet media. Soviet efforts to propagandize the public with a single official point of view often offends more than it convinces, though on questions involving international relations, which are covered by the central media, there is a high degree of interest and confidence among the public. The local press on the other hand, which often presents a distorted view of life, has produced a widespread alienation among the reading public.

Roman Kolkowicz looks at the relationship between the military and the Communist party. He argues against the widely held model which views the military as a compliant tool of the party, thoroughly subordinated and without any institutional conflicts with the party. In fact, Kolkowicz demonstrates that the military in the Soviet Union has become virtually a state within a state. Since Stalin the military has come to play an increasingly larger role in Soviet politics, particularly as an arbiter among contenders during periods of leadership change. Brezhnev in particular supported the military with enormous resources siphoned away from the civilian economy. Kolkowicz contends that the military and the party have become thoroughly interdependent.

Robert Sharlet shows how Yuri Andropov attempted to use the law as an instrument for reform and social engineering. Corruption under

Brezhnev had reached a point where justice had become in effect a "cash commodity." Andropov had hoped to get the economy moving by the use of legal pressures and by purging corrupt officials. Sharlet shows how the criminal codes introduced in January 1983, by enlarging the domain of crimes and by increasing punishment, seek to impose a more rigorous discipline in Soviet society.

Alfred Meyer, in looking at the impact of ideology on Soviet politics, finds that Marxism in the Soviet Union is dead, an empty shell into which Soviet leaders can put any meaning they may wish. It is no guide to action. The only unbreakable law of Soviet ideology is the maintenance of total control over the minds and activities of all its citizens, and, as Meyer notes, that is hardly an ideology. The real Soviet ideology, Meyer believes, is the religion of progress, modernization, science, rationality, and entrepreneurship. He offers the provocative thought that "Soviet ideology is a carbon copy of Americanism." But he qualifies the argument by describing Soviet thinking as "substitute Americanism" because of its emphasis on the state rather than on the individual. Supplementing those elements borrowed from the United States is a nationalism the roots of which are in traditional Russia.

Darrell Hammer writes about a problem little understood in the West, the resurgence of Russian nationalism in the Soviet Union. He describes two distinct expressions of this nationalism: (1) the "Russophiles," a group of writers who emerged in the 1960s who advocate cultivation of the Russian culture and support for the Russian Orthodox Church. Some in this group are anti-Bolshevik, oriented toward village as opposed to urban life, oppose modernization, and are not inclined to support Soviet imperialism; (2) the "National Bolsheviks" who stress the greatness of the Russian state and are prepared to support the Bolshevik state as an expression of Russian nationalism. They tend to glorify the military and to support Soviet imperialism. Of these two tendencies the latter is clearly more compatible with the regime than the former. However, Hammer points out that both Andropov and Chernenko opposed the idea of Russian nationalism. That does not mean that under some circumstances the regime might not be tempted to exploit Russian nationalist feelings for its own purposes, as Stalin did in World War II.

Dan Jacobs and Theresa Hill in their analysis of Soviet nationality problems attempt to dispel the "myth" of the homogeneity of the Soviet masses. The multitude of diverse peoples that make up Soviet society pose continuing problems for the regime, including difficulty in organizing economic reform and in creating the New Soviet Man. Jacobs and Hill argue that the goal of Soviet policy is the eradication of national differences and assimilation into Russian culture. The means by which this is done include promotion of the Russian language, intermarriage, population migration, education, urbanization, and modernization. Their assessment is that the government has had some success but many failures in their nationality policies. A major problem considered here (and in the Hammer chapter) is the impending demographic change when the non-Russians will begin to outnumber the Russians. At best, the authors argue, the nationality problem will be managed, not solved.

Karl Ryavec focuses on one of the central problems of the Soviet system today: the inefficiency of the economy and the need for reform. The heart of the problem is the bureaucratic, centralized mechanism of decision making and administration. He examines several alternative possibilities for reform that range from marginal changes in the present system to radical transformation. He discusses the several obstacles to reform and concludes that up to this time there have been only words rather than action. Surveying part of the Soviet literature on economic change, he describes the views of several Soviet writers on the need for reform.

Joseph Nogee stresses the continuity in foreign policy under the leadership of the three most recent general secretaries. The post-detente phase of high East–West tension began in the latter years of Brezhnev's administration. His successors inherited several serious foreign policy problems which have yet to be resolved. In East–West relations the most serious problem is the collapse of arms control talks. Moscow's failure to stop the U.S. deployment of Pershing II and cruise missiles in Europe is a major foreign policy failure. Moscow abandoned efforts to negotiate with the United States until after the U.S. presidential election.

The authors of the essays in this volume were invited to present their ideas at a conference in Houston organized by the Center for Public Policy at the University of Houston, University Park. The conference was entitled "Soviet Politics Under Andropov" and met in Houston on March 2–3, 1984. Cosponsors of the conference were the National Strategy Information Center and the Southwestern Regional Program in National Security Affairs. Those who participated in the formal proceedings of the conference were Vernon Aspaturian, Robert Donaldson, Paul Gregory, Darrell P. Hammer, Theresa Hill, Dan Jacobs, Christopher Jones, Donald R. Kelley, Henry A. Kissinger, Roman Kolkowicz, Alfred G. Meyer, Ellen Mickiewicz, R. Judson Mitchell, Victor Mote, Joseph L. Nogee, John P. Robertson, Karl Ryavec, Robert Sharlet, John Spanier, Adam Ulam, Ivan Volgyes, and Peter Zwick. Although the authors of the essays in this vol-

ume benefited from the discussion and comments of the conference, the responsibility for the findings in this volume are solely those of each author.

I would like to thank Dr. Thomas H. Mayor, director of the Center for
Public Policy and dean of the College of Social Sciences, Mary Alice
Doyle, director of operations for the center, and Dr. William P. Snyder,
director of the Southwestern Program in National Security Affairs for the
financial support and organizational effort which made possible the Houston conference. The Center for Public Policy at the University of Houston,
University Park, provided support during the summer for me to edit the entire manuscript, for which I am grateful. Finally I would also like to thank
Dotty Breitbart and David Stebbing of Praeger Publishers who helped produce a more readable manuscript.

Joseph L. Nogee
Houston, June 1984

NOTES

1. Seweryn Bialer, "The Political System," in *After Brezhnev, Sources of
Soviet Conduct in the 1980s,* Robert F. Byrnes, ed. (Bloomington, IN: Indiana
University Press, 1983), p. 48.

2. Timothy J. Colton, *The Dilemma of Reform in the Soviet Union* (New
York: Council on Foreign Relations, 1984), p. 58.

3. Georgii Malenkov, a transition leader, maintained his power as prime
minister. Nikita Khrushchev had the title of "First Secretary."

4. Lenin was politically incapacitated by a stroke in 1922, but he did not die
until 1924.

1

POLITICAL LEADERSHIP AND SUCCESSION: THE PASSING OF THE BREZHNEV GENERATION

Robert H. Donaldson

In the 65 years before Leonid Brezhnev's death in November 1982, the Soviet Union had had only three real leadership successions: the struggle for leadership following the illness and death of Vladimir Lenin, from which Joseph Stalin emerged victorious; the succession to Stalin, in which Nikita Khrushchev ultimately prevailed; and the succession to Khrushchev, which was unlike the others because it began with a coup d'etat rather than with the death of the incumbent leader.

It is thus particularly striking that in the space of 15 months, from November 1982 to February 1984, the Soviet Union had two successions, with a third clearly not far away. Not only were the Andropov and Chernenko successions close in time, but they were also different from the earlier ones in significant ways. To best understand the meaning of these two successions and the coming succession to Chernenko, we should view them not as separate cases but as *stages* in the post-Brezhnev succession.

The significance of recent Soviet leadership changes resides not alone in the death of two general secretaries of the Communist Party of the Soviet Union (CPSU) in less than two years (the phenomenon highlighted in the press) but in a much more profound changing of the Kremlin guard. In fact, a large cluster of positions at the top of the Soviet hierarchy will by the end of the 1980s be occupied not just by new individual officeholders but by a whole new political generation—the first thoroughgoing generational change in the Soviet Union since the Great Purge of the late 1930s.

To put in perspective this unusual state of affairs, it is useful to consider how many political generations have come and gone in other countries in the period since the 1930s. In the United States, for example, no president since Harry Truman had attained national political visibility prior to the late 1940s or early 1950s. Similarly, most of the politicians currently active at top levels in West European countries attained their initial high-level posts no earlier than the early 1960s. Even in China, most of the present members of the top leadership (with the notable exception of Deng Xiaoping) have not been politically prominent at the national level for as long as a quarter-century.

Because of the peculiar length of the tenure in high-level positions that the generation of Leonid Brezhnev, Aleksei Kosygin, Mikhail Suslov, Andrei Gromyko, and Dimitri Ustinov has had, and because of the high average age of this leadership group, the current leadership change in the Soviet Union is truly a profound generational passage. In this sense, the process can indeed be seen as a prolonged multistage transition, which began at the very beginning of the decade with Kosygin's retirement in October 1980 and Suslov's death in February 1982, and which has continued with the deaths of Brezhnev in November 1982 and Andropov in February 1984.

LEADERSHIP POLITICS AND POLICYMAKING

But, it can be asked, even in this broader sense of changing leadership and succession, what difference does it really make who leads or which generation is in power? Isn't the Soviet Union a political entity whose basic direction is fixed by its ideology, economic system, geopolitical situation, and historical traditions? And, above all, isn't it subject to an enormous faceless bureaucracy directing a military–industrial complex that has been described by Alfred Meyer as "USSR, Incorporated"?[1]

Indeed, political leadership *can* make a difference, and even individual personality can have a major impact on policy overtones. This is so in part precisely because political power is so concentrated and centralized in the top institutions of the CPSU. To treat Soviet policy as emanating from a faceless elite is to neglect the close interrelationship between intra-elite politics and policy making, and the very strong role played by the former in the shaping and rationalization of the latter. In fact, rather than being simply a calculated response to external stimuli on the part of a monolithic political structure, both domestic and foreign policies in the Soviet Union are more accurately perceived as emerging from the interaction of decision makers representing a variety of personal and institutional perspectives who are involved in the simultaneous resolution of a number of domestic and foreign issues. Policy decisions are often shaped by the contests for influence among individuals and factions, thus raising the Kremlinologist's question of *kto-kogo*? (who is prevailing over whom?). Few students of Soviet history would seriously argue that it made little difference for the country whether Stalin prevailed over Trotsky and Bukharin, whether Khrushchev emerged triumphant over Malenkov and Beria, or whether Brezhnev succeeded in staving off the challenges of Shelepin and Shelest.

By no means do all policy conflicts in the Soviet Union pose a direct threat to the position of the general secretary of the Communist party, or even threaten to shake up the membership of the Politburo. Policy formulation can be more or less divisive and more or less sensitive. In some cases, the leader's policies can be successfully questioned, challenged, and even vetoed, without forcing the leader to vacate his office. But since there is no time limit on the campaign for office in the Soviet Union, and since political power is neither institutionalized nor stable, there is always the possibility that power struggles can be directly transformed into challenges to the power of a particular member of the top leadership. On major issues, disagreements over policy may require changes in the membership of the Politburo in order for one course rather than another to be implemented.

Not since the time of Stalin has a single member of the Politburo been able to dictate the terms of every policy, ignoring the challenge of both rivals and experts, and removing those who refuse to bend to his will. No longer is it possible for the analyst to assume that every policy implemented in the Soviet Union is simply the product of the dictator's will. Rather, even in the periods when there has been a recognizable *primus inter pares,* he has found it necessary to delegate some responsibility and modify some of his initiatives because of either actual or anticipated opposition. Under Brezhnev the CPSU Politburo evolved as a body composed of the chiefs of the major institutions and interest groups of the country, where policies were debated and decisions arrived at through a style that favored cautious consensus building rather than dramatic innovation. And because the members of the Politburo were so similar in age and in political experience, their attitudes and policy choices will likely prove to be distinctively different from those of the successor generation. To put it more precisely, the fact that these leaders came to political maturity in the middle of the Stalin era, with most of them rising to positions of command in their thirties as the result of the liquidation of their elders, probably makes their outlook different from that of the men whose political careers were started in the time of de-

Stalinization and Sputnik. Finally, the leaders' political style, whether the Politburo members are able to resolve policy questions through consensus or whether conflict and controversy are the norm, can have great impact both on the stability of the regime and on its ability to overcome the inertial drift and immobilism that has settled in over much of the past decades.

THE INSTITUTIONAL CONTEXT
OF SOVIET SUCCESSION

It is helpful at this point to examine the institutional context in which leadership change occurs in the Soviet Union—in particular, the role played by the CPSU Central Committee, the Secretariat, and the Politburo, as well as the top institutions of the Soviet state, including the military organizations.

In theory, major decisions on policy and leadership in the CPSU are made by the Party Congress, to which delegates are elected from party organizations throughout the country. In practice, the Congress merely hears and rubber stamps decisions already made by the ruling oligarchs. But this has not always been the case. Under Lenin, and as late as 1930, the Party Congress was the scene of serious debate on domestic and foreign policy and international revolutionary strategy, as well as on leadership issues. In the 1920s, during the succession struggle between Stalin and Trotsky, the Party Congress was often a forum of important discussions and voting. But as it grew larger and met less frequently, the Party Congress also became more and more a creature of its executive organs, which technically were responsible to it. Between 1930 and 1952 it met only three times; in 1952, the party statutes were changed to abandon the fiction of annual meetings and require meetings of the Congress only once every four years. In 1966, the interval between meetings was officially extended to five years.

At the end of its session, the Party Congress elects the Central Committee, the body charged with directing party policy between sessions of the Congress. Originally a compact body that met with some frequency and served as a principal arena of debate on policy, the Central Committee was enlarged and packed by Stalin. Its authority diluted, it met only rarely during the last years of his life. Current party rules require that it meet at least twice a year. Still it rarely engages in full-scale consideration of foreign policy questions, and only when the Politburo is divided does it play a real deliberative role. Rather, it usually serves as a sounding board and legitimizer of the policies and personnel decisions presented for its unanimous approval by its Politburo.

The Central Committee currently consists of over 400 full and nonvoting (candidate) members, including the leading officials of the central party organizations, the major bosses of regional and city party organs, the editors of the main newspapers and journals, leading scientists, academicians, and managers, the top personnel of the armed forces and police, trade union and mass organization officials, the top officials of the central and regional government bodies, as well as a few token workers and peasants.

Members of the Central Committee are truly the power holders of the Soviet political system. But this is because they hold leading offices in party and state organizations rather than because of any function the Central Committee itself regularly performs. That body can best be thought of as the place in the Soviet system "where the elite meet," as well as the recruitment pool from which the next generation of top leaders will be drawn.

The Politburo (called the Presidum from 1952 to 1966) is the chief decision-making body in the Communist party. Under Stalin, it came first to dominate the Party Congress and the Central Committee, and then to be dominated by the dictator himself. For over a quarter of a century, Stalin exercised true one-man rule in the Soviet Union, personally making all major decisions, including those in the realm of foreign policy. Having to consult no one allowed Stalin to act quickly and to reverse his course abruptly. But his secretive and suspicious style, and his demonstrated willingness to exterminate any actual or potential dissenter, stifled the process of gathering and assessing information and led to distortions of perception and policy that occasionally did great harm to the interests of the Soviet Union.

No leader since Stalin has been able to amass the kind of personal power that he had, and the Politburo, though its members are not in fact equal in power, now functions more as a collective body. It is the one political organization in the Soviet Union where a vote really means something. Under Brezhnev it apparently met at least once a week, and it operated more often by consensus than by majority rule, with divisive issues occasionally being referred for further deliberation rather than forced to a vote.[2]

The Politburo in recent years has consisted of between a dozen and sixteen full members and six to eight nonvoting members. Included in its ranks are half a dozen or so of the Central Committee secretaries, in addition to the general secretary; the first secretaries of the major republic and urban party organizations; and the top officials of the Council of Ministers and the Supreme Soviet. (See Table 1 for a list of the members as of June, 1984.) In 1973 full voting status was conferred on the ministers of defense and foreign affairs and the chief of the secret police (KGB). This was widely interpreted at the time as an action to ensure formal representation of these leading foreign and defense policy officials on the top decision-making body in the Party.

There is evident functional specialization among the top Soviet leaders, and not all members of the Politburo are equally involved in deliberations on particular policy matters. Some issue arenas are evidently referred to subcommittees for discussion. One of the most important committees is the Defense Council, chaired by the general secretary and including in its membership the chairman of the Council of Ministers, the chairman of the Presidium of the Supreme Soviet, the Central Committee secretary in charge of defense affairs, the minister of defense, and a few other top civilian and military leaders.[3]

The other top party organ is the Secretariat, which is responsible for formulating the issues and alternatives which will constitute the agenda of the Politburo. The Secretariat is responsible for supervision of the implementation of Politburo decisions and for the gathering of information on the activities of party and state bodies. In addition, it exercises together with that body the control over appointments and removal of personnel (including those in the foreign policy arena) in the party bureaucracy, the government, and key institutions in society. The party members who receive these jobs are expected to function as the eyes and ears of the party, as well as its voice in communicating party desires and mobilizing individuals and groups behind the goals of the party.

The number of party secretaries typically ranges between nine and eleven, and several simultaneously sit on the party Politburo. Each secretary has a functional specialization and is responsible for the guidance of one or more of the Secretariat's departments or committees. The general secretary has, since Stalin's time, been able to translate his dominance of the Secretariat into a role as *primus inter pares* in the Politburo itself and, ultimately, the top Soviet spokesperson on both foreign and domestic policy matters. Not since Stalin, however, has a general secretary been able to add and remove members of top party bodies over the objections of a majority of his Politburo colleagues.

Table 1. Membership in the CPSU Politburo, June 1984

Member	Year of birth	Year elected to current Politburo status	Current Position (and year assumed)
Full Members			
K.U. Chernenko	1911	1978	General secretary, Central Committee; chairman, Presidium of the Supreme Soviet (1984)
G.A. Aliyev	1923	1982	First deputy chairman, Council of Ministers (1982)
M.S. Gorbachev	1931	1980	Secretary, Central Committee (1978)
V.V. Grishin	1914	1971	First secretary, Moscow City Party Committee (1967)
A.A. Gromyko	1909	1973	Minister of foreign affairs (1957); first deputy chairman, Council of Ministers (1983)
D.A. Kunayev	1912	1971	First secretary, Kazakhstan Central Committee (1964)
G.V. Romanov	1923	1976	Secretary, Central Committee (1983)
V.V. Shcherbitskiy	1918	1971	First secretary, Ukraine Central Committee (1972)
M.S. Solomentsev	1913	1983	Chairman, Party Control Commission (1983)
N.A. Tikhonov	1905	1979	Chairman, Council of Ministers (1980)
D.F. Ustinov*	1908	1976	Minister of defense (1976)
V.I. Vorotnikov	1926	1983	Chairman, Russian Republic Council of Ministers (1983)
Candidate Members			
V.N. Chebrikov	1923	1983	Chairman, KGB (1983)
P.N. Demichev	1918	1964	Minister of culture (1974)
V.I. Dolgikh	1924	1982	Secretary, Central Committee (1972)
V.V. Kuznetsov	1901	1977	First deputy chairman, Presidium of the Supreme Soviet (1977)
B.N. Ponomarev	1905	1972	Secretary, Central Committee (1961)
E.A. Shevardnadze	1928	1978	First secretary, Georgia Central Committee (1972)

*Ustinov died December 20, 1984.
Source: Compiled by the author.

A primary point that emerges from the foregoing analysis is that there still is, after 67 years, no top constitutional or statutory basis for determining that the general secretary of the CPSU will be the "head" of the Politburo or Defense Council or that he will or will not also hold the title of Soviet "president"—the chief of state. Indeed, the party's formal leadership norms stress democratic centralism and a collective style of leadership rather than the "personal rule" (limited, not dictatorial, but still *primus inter pares*) that recent Soviet general secretaries have exercised.

Nor is there a settled constitutional means by which the Soviet Union replaces its top leader. When a Canadian prime minister retires or a U.S. president dies or resigns, either an heir is already designated or a process is carefully prescribed whereby one is selected. There is no orderly succession to a designated heir in the Soviet Union, and indeed, no top Soviet leader has ever managed to set up arrangements to pass power on to his preferred heir, if he has had one.

Still, prior to Brezhnev's death, Western experts thought they had inferred from previous successions, as well as from their knowledge of the Soviet system, some general informal guidelines or norms that seemed to operate in favoring certain candidates for the top job. In 1975 Grey Hodnett laid down 13 personal and institutional "qualifications" for a full-term general secretary,[4] and in 1979 Professor Judson Mitchell wrote about basic "functional requirements" of the party that seemed to call for three elements of career experience in a successful candidate for the succession: "command in the field," "service at the center," and "experience in industry and agriculture."[5] What is most interesting about the two successors to Brezhnev is that they both lacked two of these three elements, as well as at least six of Hodnett's 13 qualifications.

THE SUCCESSORS TO BREZHNEV

We now turn to an examination of precisely why the successions to Brezhnev appear to be deviant and what significance that has for the system and its future. The first fact to be noted is that when Brezhnev died at age 75 he was about the same age as the other Politburo members who had the "right" mix of qualifications to succeed him, whereas when Stalin and Khrushchev left their colleagues, they were 10 to 15 years older than most of their potential successors. This deviation in the Brezhnev case is, as the Soviets are fond of saying, "not accidental." Having been one of the conspirators (indeed, the "heir apparent") who forced Khrushchev into premature and unwilling retirement, Brezhnev acted in his last 10 years in power precisely as though he were determined that history would not be repeated. No logical successor was to be found precisely because Brezhnev (and, one presumes, his elderly colleagues as well) determined that there should *not* be one.

It is important to realize, however, that this did not result from a situation, often erroneously depicted, of a stable oligarchy growing old together, with virtually no change in top ranks over a long period. Indeed, there were frequent changes in Brezhnev's Politburo in his last decade, initially resulting from policy struggle or from his efforts to force out actual or potential rivals for his post. The immobility at the top of the Soviet leadership was more apparent than real. What one does see is a steadily aging leadership, on the average, but many of the faces (besides the top four—Brezhnev, Kosygin, Suslov, and Kirilenko) were continually changing. Of the 15 full Politburo members of 1971, only six remained in 1980, and this before the recent wave of deaths. Clearly, circulation occurred, but it was not generational; ousted politicians were replaced by men the same age or older.

After 1980, the changes were chiefly actuarial rather than political. Nine members of the top elite, including the top five, have died (or retired, as in Kirilenko's case). Today, only one member of the Politburo (Demichev, an alternate) remains from 1964. None of the full members who were in central party or government positions in 1971 is still in the leadership. Demonstrably, change has occurred, but the leadership is still essentially a gerontocracy, averaging almost 67 years even after the eight deaths of the early 1980s. This, then, is a picture of a group of leaders deliberately shunting aside the "young Turks."

Moreover, below the very top leadership level, Brezhnev had adopted a policy of "stability of cadres" that virtually guaranteed that those leaders who were a decade or so younger would not obtain the range of experiences that would ideally "qualify" them for the top positions. Judson Mitchell has elaborated on this phenomenon by noting the compartmentalization of the Soviet elite that has resulted from the decline in the practice of shifting personnel among institutions or between regions or from regions to the center.[6] Brezhnev undoubtedly won much political support among incumbent officeholders for this policy. As Seweryn Bialer has put it, "If Khrushchev brought the Soviet elite the gift of security of life, Brezhnev assured it security of office."[7] All told, over 90% of the members of the 1976 Central Committee who were still alive in 1981 were reelected, an unprecedented degree of stability at that level of the Soviet leadership.

THE ANDROPOV SUCCESSION

Given that there was no logical successor to Brezhnev in 1982, why then did Yuri Andropov succeed to the post of general secretary of the CPSU? Indeed, there is considerable irony in this outcome, for if Brezhnev had died a year earlier (before Suslov's death and the resulting vacancy that allowed Andropov to leave his position as head of the KGB) or if he had died four months later, after Andropov's kidneys had failed in February 1983, Andropov probably would not have succeeded. Clearly luck played a role, but so did good planning. Andropov was reportedly able to use the KGB to spread rumors that tended to discredit both his rivals and members of Brezhnev's family. He moved surely and swiftly in securing Suslov's position in the CPSU Secretariat for himself, thus positioning himself for the impending vacancy at the head of that body. Three other men also had dual membership in the Secretariat and Politburo at the time of Brezhnev's death, but one (Kirilenko) was already politically moribund and another (Gorbachev) was thought to be too junior. Andropov managed to turn the obvious role of his remaining rival (Konstantin Chernenko) as Brezhnev's spear carrier into a liability for the preferred heir, capitalizing on his own greater "line" experience and personal reputation, and especially on his greater experience in foreign affairs. His supporters even spread rumors in the West that Andropov was a "closet liberal" and fan of Western music, whiskey, and pop fiction, including the works of Jacqueline Susann.

Having achieved the top spot, Andropov consolidated his power very quickly. He was able to do this in part precisely because there was no obvious strong rival for the leadership. He made some useful alliances: with Geydar Aliyev, the former KGB and party chief of Azerbaidzhan, who was transferred to the first deputy's spot in the Council of Ministers; with supporters of the retired second secretary, Andrei Kirilenko; and even, in a sense, with Chernenko himself. Further confirmation of the absence of a strong challenge to his authority came when he succeeded to the presidency in June 1983, at a time when his health was already obviously failing. By that time, Andropov had launched several policy initiatives, and he was beginning to upset some applecarts. During his brief tenure as general secretary, a number of officials, at both the central and regional levels, were dismissed or retired, including 44 of the 300-plus surviving members of the 1981 Central Committee. Most of the beneficiaries of these changes were men considerably younger than their predecessors. This significant departure from earlier practice suggests that the long-postponed generational change in Soviet leadership was beginning under Andropov's sponsorship, and it also helps to explain the apparent nervousness among Andropov's aged surviving colleagues when they were forced to choose at his death between Chernenko and a much younger man (Mikhail Gorbachev).

THE CHERNENKO SUCCESSION AND BEYOND

The selection of Chernenko to succeed Andropov as general secretary came only after some debate in the leadership (four days passed after Andropov's death, as compared to two days between Brezhnev's passing and the selection of Andropov). In choosing him over Gorbachev, the Politburo elders clearly opted for an interim solution to the leadership problem, since Chernenko was 72 years old and a victim of severe attacks of emphysema. Chernenko's biography was devoid of significant line responsibility. He rose to power on Leonid Brezhnev's coattails, serving as the late leader's chief aide in Moscow since 1960. Poorly educated, Chernenko's specialty in party work has been in the realm of ideology and propaganda, where he has not been noted for original contributions or bold ideas.

Although the choice of Chernenko avoided an immediate passing of the leadership torch to a representative of a younger generation than that of Brezhnev and his associates, the actuarial tables (as well as the close-up observation of the new leader's health by Western visitors) suggest that the next Soviet succession will not be long in coming. Given the composition of the Secretariat and Politburo as of mid-1984, the odds favor the proposition that the succession to Chernenko will differ from the two previous ones in that a man considerably younger than his predecessor will finally succeed.

Both of the other CPSU secretaries who hold full Politburo membership are indeed younger men. The man who seems to act as the "second secretary" is in fact junior in age (Mikhail Gorbachev, born in 1931) and is widely believed to be the likely successor to Chernenko. Born in Stavropol, Gorbachev was educated as a lawyer and agronomist, rose through the regional leadership, becoming national party secretary for agriculture in 1978 and a Politburo member in 1980. He managed to broaden his portfolio during Andropov's rule, functioning in the realm of personnel assignment, with some duties also in the area of foreign policy.

Grigory Romanov, born in 1923, is the other feasible candidate to succeed Chernenko, offering the relative advantage (from the likely standpoint of his elderly colleagues) of somewhat greater age and longer experience in the party Politburo. First secretary of the important party machine in Leningrad since 1970, Romanov was brought to Moscow in June 1983 to assume responsibility in the Secretariat for supervision of the defense industry and other economic matters.

THE POST-STALIN GENERATION

Although eight deaths and one resignation between 1980 and mid-1984 removed several of the aging oligarchs from the Kremlin leadership, the average age of the 23 surviving and new members of the Politburo and Secretariat remained at 68 years (see Table 2). Further changes are imminent, however, and they will further diminish the remaining membership of the Brezhnev generation. Only five of the surviving top leaders were full members of the CPSU Central Committee prior to the end of the Stalin era, while fully half of the present group received their initial Central Committee–level positions during Brezhnev's tenure as general secretary. Almost half of the members of the top elite were born after the October Revolution, six of them after Lenin's death. Although the top leadership remains entirely male and overwhelmingly Slavic in its ethnic composition, the most recent appointees represent a new political generation, and at the next level of responsibility, this post-Stalin generation is even more in evidence. By the end of the decade, a majority of the members of the CPSU Central Committee will have been born after Lenin's death, will have joined the CPSU after World War II, and will have been Central Committee members only since 1970 or later.[8]

What can be said about the collective characteristics of the post-Stalin generation of political leaders in the Soviet Union? Apart from their greater youthfulness and presumed energy, they differ from their elders in several significant respects. As they launched their political careers, members of the Brezhnev generation participated in the collectivization of agriculture, forced the industrialization of the country at the expense of improvements in the average family's standard of living, and the brutal liquidation in the Great Purge of hundreds of thousands of party leaders, economic managers, and officials of the armed forces. The formative experiences of the new generation are rooted in de-Stalinization and the untidy reformism of the Khrushchev years. Better educated and materially more secure than their predecessors, the newer leaders tend to come from urban rather than

Table 2. Characteristics of the Top Soviet Leaders (23 members of Politburo and Secretariat, June 1984)

Date of Birth		Ethnic Origin		Date of CPSU Membership		Date of First Election to Full Membership in Central Committee	
Before 1917	12	Russian	17	Before 1934	5	1952	5
1918–1923	5	Ukrainian	2	1939–1945	14	1956–1961	6
After Lenin's		Belorussian	1	1946–1952	3	1966–1971	8
death	6	Azerbaidzhani	1	After 1953	1	1976–1981	4
		Georgian	1				
		Kazakh	1				

Source: Compiled by the author.

rural backgrounds and were recruited into the party at an early age rather than co-opted in the middle of their careers. They would likely be more confident in the power and accomplishment of the Soviet state, less comfortable with idle sloganeering, and yet more embarrassed by recent periods of inertia and drift. They probably share what Timothy Colton has called an "itch for improvement," and they are likely to be somewhat impatient in their desire to proceed with change.[9] And yet, while they have an obvious edge over their predecessors in education and sophistication, as victims of Brezhnev's "cadres" policy they suffer from a kind of narrowness of experience, having been denied opportunities to move across specializations or between geographical regions.

By the end of the 1980s, the post-Brezhnev succession will likely have been completed and the post-Stalin generation will be in place. While we can be sure of certain characteristic demographic and career patterns, it is difficult and dangerous to generalize beyond these objective features to infer political attitudes or values, much less preferences for particular policies. At the very least, Westerners in both official and unofficial capacities should be seeking opportunities to reverse the recent decline in contacts with leaders of the Soviet Union, so that first-hand assessments of the emerging elite can be made. More importantly, Western observers should be prepared to shed some of the prevailing stereotypes, which have hardened in the late Brezhnev years and the transition period that followed. Rather, we should for the first time in many years be prepared to perceive political change in the Soviet Union and to be ready to make the necessary adjustments in our own attitudes and policies as the post-Stalinist leaders take the helm.

NOTES

1. Alfred G. Meyer, *The Soviet Political System: An Interpretation* (New York: Random House, 1965).

2. Grey Hodnett, "The Pattern of Leadership Politics," in *The Domestic Context of Soviet Foreign Policy,* Seweryn Bialer, ed. (Boulder, CO: Westview, 1981), p. 101.

3. Edward L. Warner, III, *The Military in Contemporary Soviet Politics: An Institutional Analysis* (New York: Praeger, 1977), pp. 44–45.

4. Grey Hodnett, "Succession Contingencies in the Soviet Union," *Problems of Communism* 24, no. 2 (March–April) 1975: 16.

5. R. Judson Mitchell, "The Soviet Succession: Who, and What, Will Follow Brezhnev? *Orbis* (Spring) 1979: 15.

6. R. Judson Mitchell, "Immobilism, Depoliticization, and the Emerging Soviet Elite," *Orbis* (Fall) 1982: 595.

7. Seweryn Bialer, *Stalin's Successors: Leadership, Stability, and Change in the Soviet Union* (Cambridge: Cambridge University Press, 1980): 91.

8. For a more detailed account, see Timothy J. Colton, *The Dilemma of Reform in the Soviet Union* (New York: Council on Foreign Relations, 1984), Chapter 3.

9. Ibid., p. 50.

2
POWER AND AUTHORITY IN SOVIET ELITE POLITICS

George W. Breslauer

This chapter discusses power and authority in Soviet leadership politics since Stalin.[1] It suggests that we distinguish between elite attempts to consolidate power through patronage allocation and purges, on the one hand, and attempts to build authority by establishing confidence in one's leadership abilities, on the other. After drawing out and illustrating this distinction, the chapter discusses the interaction of power and authority considerations in influencing the behavior of Soviet party leaders. With this framework in mind, I turn to an outline of Yuri Andropov's actions as general secretary, and the relationship between power and authority in his leadership strategy. I conclude with a brief discussion of Konstantin Chernenko's leadership.

THE STRUCTURE OF POWER

Key national decisions in Soviet politics are usually taken within the Politburo, and the key actors in Soviet politics usually have positions within that body. The composition and size of the Politburo have varied considerably since Stalin's death in 1953. Nonetheless, in the 1970s and 1980s, the Politburo comprised 11 to 16 members. They have been leading officials of the major institutional pillars of the Soviet political establishment: the central party apparatus, the republic-level party apparatus, the central economic bureaucracy, the Ministry of Defense, the Ministry of Foreign Affairs, and the KGB.

The general secretary of the Central Committee of the Communist Party of the Soviet Union is the member of the Politburo who usually receives the most publicity and formal adulation. Since the victory of Stalin in the late 1920s, the party leader stands out in historical categorizations of Soviet history: Stalinism (1928–1953); Khrushchevism (1955–1964); the Brezhnev era (1964–1982); the Andropov era (1982–1984). Yet this focus on single actors can obscure a very important feature of Soviet politics: the fact that each leader has ultimately accumulated *less* power than his predecessor. The long-term trend in Soviet leadership politics has been toward an increasingly collective leadership, or at least toward increased restraints on the ability of a leader to ignore the will of the collective.

This progression has resulted from numerous factors, but the most important has surely been the renunciation of violence as an instrument of elite politics and the attendant reining in of the secret police.[2] These changes allowed the reemergence of a political atmosphere in which politicians could afford to be assertive. Other factors strengthening the trend include: the transition from a stage of "system building" under Stalin to one of "system management" since Stalin, which reduced the previous need for charismatic one-man rule to legitimize violent campaigns of transformation and control;[3] the regime's efforts, in the system management stage, to meet a multiplicity of goals, which called for more of a division of labor, respect for jurisdictions, and deference to specialized expertise within the Politburo; the memory of past examples of personalized leadership, when first Stalin, and then Khrushchev (though to incomparably different degrees) abused their colleagues.

The lack of electoral politics in Soviet leadership turnover has, paradoxically, also strengthened the trend toward collective leadership. The choice of a new leader does not include the choice, or early appointment, of a new "administration." The new party leader does not automatically have the right to appoint new members of the Politburo, to reshuffle the central party apparatus, or to bring in the functional equivalent of a new cabinet. At least initially, he must play politics with the existing team of politicians.

Within the long-term trend toward the strengthening of collective leadership, however, Soviet politics has also been marked by a powerful "monocratic" tendency.[4] Western focus on the leader has not been without justification. Khrushchev accumulated great powers, and was able to get his way most of the time on crucial policy decisions, though he never acquired the despotic powers of a Stalin, and was forced from office when he went off on his own too often, and with little to show for results. Brezhnev deferred to the will of the collective more often than did Khrushchev, but, after 1968, he was clearly "first among equals" within the Politburo, and was able to sponsor changes, or veto alternatives, with a range and decisiveness unequaled by any other member of the Politburo.[5] He was, in short, the chairman of the board, if not the boss.

The party leader accumulates power once in office by building a political machine. He is called general (or first) secretary because he is the leading figure in the Secretariat of the Central Committee of the CPSU. This organization has many functions of oversight and supervision of the economy, society, and polity. Its main function, however, is the hiring and firing of key personnel in important institutions throughout the system. Through his control within the Secretariat, the general secretary has the opportunity to remove party cadres in strategic institutions and replace them with his own people. Thus, the general secretary has the opportunity to build a political machine of supporters based primarily within the party apparatus (both central and regional), but also spanning sections of the economic, military, and police apparatuses.

Stalin, of course, made the most use of this opportunity during his quarter-century in power. Several times he built up, then destroyed, then rebuilt his political machine. Khrushchev, to a much lesser extent, also succeeded in building his machine, though when he tried to purge and recreate it, he discovered the real limits on his power in the absence of terror. Brezhnev built a machine slowly over time and never tried to purge it.

Machine building is a structural necessity in Soviet politics. Lacking a formal electoral mandate or a constitutional specification of their term of office, the scope of their role, or the extent of their powers, general secretaries must build power after they acquire the office. They usually have a "tail" of followers, supporters, or clients from previous jobs, and they can draw on these for support once in office. But that tail is rarely sufficient to meet the new goals, roles, or challenges of the office of general secretary. The Party leader speaks and acts for the nation; he may become the initiator of new policy in many areas; he bears responsibility for policy integration, implementation, and success or failure to a far greater extent than any other leading politician; and he must constantly protect himself against actual or potential challenges from within the Politburo.

This last point warrants emphasis and elaboration. The party leader works within a highly competitive political arena. Usually, two or three other members of the Politburo have substantial independent political resources of their own: prestige, due to long-standing public service in an important position (the central party apparatus; the foreign ministry; the defense sector); specialized expertise; a position within the Secretariat that allows them to wield some patronage of their own; or a preexisting tail of followers. Thus, several other members of the Politburo may have the opportunity to challenge the general secretary's control over the policy agenda or, in the extreme case, his right to stay in office. They may have the opportunity to enlarge their political machines, to frustrate the implementation of his policies (yet blame the party leader for it), to woo his clients, or to weaken these clients' support for the general secretary. Whether or not his associates in the Politburo actually seize these opportunities, the party leader must always be alert to the possibility. He must protect himself through anticipatory power accumulation. He does this by expanding his political machine, wooing the clients of others, and building a cult of his own personality as a means of reassuring his actual and potential clients that he is in control.[6]

Thus, the pressures for a "first among equals" to emerge in Soviet politics are strong. The strengthening of collective leadership since 1953, and its strong reinforcement under Brezhnev, have made it very unlikely that another Stalin or Khrushchev will be able to seize the reins. But within these limits, Soviet leadership politics are an example of non-constitutionalized machine politics, in which the Party leader has disproportionate opportunities to build a machine that will protect him against challenges.

Yet power is only part of the story. Building a political machine is a necessary condition for solidifying one's hold on office and one's control of the policy agenda; but it is far from a sufficient condition. Under Stalin, this may have been a sufficient condition, for political terror ensured that clients had little incentive to question authority, assert themselves, or defy their superiors. Patron–client relations were fundamentally asymmetrical; one is tempted to call them commander–subject relations.

Not so since Stalin. In the absence of terror, and given the growing strength of collective leadership, a much greater measure of reciprocity entered into the relationship between the boss of a political machine and his lieutenants throughout the various levels and institutions encompassed by the machine. The patron could no longer take for granted that his clients would be too intimidated to defy or desert him. Clients now came to expect more of their patrons. Patrons now came to be less certain of the support of their clients. At the same time, with the strengthening of collective leadership, clients became less certain that their patron would necessarily stay in power or maintain control of the policy agenda. In sum, a greater measure of uncertainty and ambivalence entered into the patron–client relationship.[7] Political exchange, as a result, became more reciprocal, fluid, and open-ended.

From the standpoint of the general secretary, this change meant a substantial increase in uncertainty about the powers of his office. To be sure, he was not subject to the regular discipline of a public election, parliamentary votes of no confidence, or other features of a liberal-democratic political order. There remained no regularized, authoritative means for his clients to register their satisfaction, or to enforce accountability to their demands. But the post-Stalin era gradually introduced a more contingent quality to client loyalties. Past association, past shared experience, and even shared values based on that experience usually led patrons to choose given clients for key jobs. But gratitude for present favors, and the like-mindedness resulting from past experience, have a way of wearing off as the new burdens of new jobs manifest themselves. Clients are also interested in political security, promotion, and the extra resources required to fulfill their plans, bolster their careers, and raise the image or status of their regions or departments.[8] Since clients know that their patron's power is not assured, they periodically search for assurance that their patron is retaining his grip, both on the office and on the policy agenda. For without control of the policy agenda, the patron will be in less of a position to aggrandize the material rewards of his clients.[9]

The patron knows this, and recognizes the need to provide such assurance. But his task is still broader. He must convince a broad array of Soviet bureaucrats and politicians that he is a capable, effective problem solver and politician. If he wishes to reduce uncertainty about his ability to maintain power over both office and policy, he must worry about more than just power consolidation through patronage allocation. He must also be concerned constantly with the requisites of authority building.

BUILDING AUTHORITY

I draw a fairly sharp distinction between power and authority. One's power finds expression in the ability to pull rank. One's authority finds expression in the ability to persuade others to follow your lead without having to pull rank.[10] Authority, as I use the term, is very close to the conventional meaning of the term legitimacy. A leader concerned with authority building is one who seeks to legitimize his right to remain in office and to define the direction of policy. He is concerned, then, with both personal and policy legitimation. Legitimizing both his power and his policies is a process both of building a general aura of charisma about him (a personality cult) and building confidence in his concrete abilities as a problem solver and a politician.

Stalin, Khrushchev, and Brezhnev all built up personality cults about themselves. The content of these cults, whatever their immense differences, had four things in common: close association of the leader with Lenin or Leninism; attribution to the party leader of a wide range of successes in "socialist" (or communist) construction; presentation of the writings of the party leader as filled with unusual insight and wisdom; and attribution to the party leader of unusually close and benevolent ties with the people. In sum, personality cults create the image of a charismatic leader, possessed of unusual, heroic qualities that make it uniquely possible for him to diagnose current needs and prescribe current policies in ways consistent with the central legitimizing myth of the political order—Leninism.[11]

A personality cult takes time to develop. It is rarely evident during periods of political succession, when a relatively balanced collective leadership prevents the celebration of a single leader (1922–1928; 1953–1956; 1964–1968). But once the party leader consolidates power, expands his role in the leadership, and pushes to the fore, a personality cult usually accompanies his ascendancy.

What is the intended audience of the cult? There are probably several. One is the broad masses of the population. Another is the large stratum of party members and activists among them. Each of these mass formations is intended to relate to the regime, and those who lead it, with some combination of devotion, awe, respect, deference, or intimidation. Another audience is the body of actual or potential clients of the general secretary among officials of the party and state apparatuses. For their consumption, the cult is supposed to serve as inspiration, political reassurance, or political temptation: inspiration to those who possess the need for identification with a patriarchal figure; reassurance to those whose careers are dependent on the party leader; and temptation to officials who might be inclined to hitch themselves to the party leader's wagon. A final audience of the cult would be the Politburo itself, where the purpose would more likely be the intimidation of actual or potential rivals.

Yet there is far more to authority building than just the effort to create an aura of charisma. In an era of strengthened collective restraints on the party leader, other more practical and specific considerations come into play, especially in the eyes of officials of the party and state apparatuses. These politicians and bureaucrats know that the cult has become a ritual of the regime, a form of ritualized charisma that is not necessarily an indicator of either the problem-solving success or the extent of power of the general secretary. They know that neither occupancy of the office nor fostering of a cult are guarantees of staying in power (as Khrushchev learned in 1964). As clients, allies, or nonsupporters of the general secretary, they are continuously concerned with how well he is doing. For on his success may ride their fortunes. If he falls from power, his clients and allies may fall with him, and his opponents may gain promotions. If he remains in power despite widespread policy failures (Brezhnev's situation from 1979 onward), he may lose control over the policy agenda. In that case, his clients and allies may lose access to needed material resources, which would threaten both their ability to meet plan targets and their political standing.

For these reasons, the general secretary is continuously concerned with building authority at all stages of his administration. The cult that emerges during his stage of ascendancy is more a product and symptom of his prior success. Building authority, as I use the term, refers to the efforts of the party leader, from the time he occupies office, to manipulate policy appeals and his personal image in order to demonstrate both his competence as a problem solver and his indispensability as a political leader.

Political performance is not very easy to measure, a circumstance that compounds the uncertainty of those whose political fortunes are linked to the general secretary. Hence, an important feature of his authority-building strategy will be an effort to shape the climate of opinion within the Central Committee. Leadership is not simply brokerage or mediation of existing opinions; it is also initiation of new trains of thought or commitment. The party leader tries to generate elan around the values with which he chooses to be identified. He seeks to influence the standard of comparison against which progress in realizing those values will be measured. He seeks to hoard the credit when such progress is achieved, to deflect responsibility for bottlenecks, and to alter the standards of comparison when failure has set in.

Authority-building efforts are targeted at more than just the allies and clients of party leaders. They are also targeted at the uncommitted and at ambivalent fellow oligarchs. Part of the general secretary's effort is aimed at intimidating actual and potential rivals. Another part is aimed at convincing other members of the Politburo that the policies and procedures he advocates are likely to advance the collective self-interest of the party leadership. For the Politburo as a whole is cross-pressured. On the one hand, it contains top representatives of the major institutions of the system, with each of these representatives having a clientele network of his own. This fosters competition among members of the Politburo. On the other hand, Politburo members share an interest in fashioning policies and procedures that are likely to satisfy the material and nonmaterial aspirations of a wide array of constituencies and groupings. In the absence of such policy success, Politburo members must fear challenges from within the Central Committee, or any falling out among themselves that could create an image of disunity that encourages challenges from below, be they from the Central Committee or from mass disturbances. Thus, a collective interest in a certain measure of policy effectiveness and political unity fosters cooperation among members of the Politburo.

What is the measure of policy effectiveness? On a specific level, it is difficult to generalize about this. But on a more general level, it refers to efforts to meet the priority goals of the post-Stalin era without foresaking core traditional values of the Lenin and early Stalin eras.[12] Thus, in domestic policy, Soviet leaders since about 1955 have shared a rather broad consensus on behalf of increasing consumer satisfaction and material incentives, expanding political participation by means other than severe coercion, and rationalizing public administration by overcoming the super-centralization of Stalin's days. At the same time, a broad consensus has existed on behalf of doing all this without undoing the priority status of the military–industrial complex, without foresaking the leading, mobilizing role of the Party in spurring initiative and enforcing discipline, and without creating a political or economic order based on autonomous concentrations of power. Similarly, in foreign policy since 1955, a broad consensus has existed on the desirability of breaking with the confrontational posture and continental perspective of Stalin's foreign policy in favor of striking durable deals with the United States and Western Europe. Yet, at the same time, there has been an equally strong (if not stronger) consensus to the effect that "peaceful coexistence" must not foresake competition with the United States.

Given these points of positive and negative consensus,[13] the challenge for the general secretary has been to fashion programs that synthesize new goals with traditional values. Of course, in devising a strategy for building his authority, the party leader has had to attend to the specific material and political concerns of his clients and allies. But he has also had to devise a strategy for convincing fellow oligarchs, the uncommitted, and his followers alike that he has the ability to put together packages that synthesize new values and traditional priorities in ways that are likely to work. His success at doing so may elicit envy from his rivals, but it also increases his authority in many quarters that are equally interested in seeing the country run well, to the ultimate benefit of both the broader population and the political establishment.

This form of authority building goes far beyond the propagation of a cult. It is not merely ritual; rather, it is the stuff of day-to-day politics. It is partly image building and partly demonstration of actual policy effectiveness. It is both a manipulation of audiences' perceptions, and a demonstrated responsiveness to audiences' ideal and material interests.[14] It is an effort to shape, or reshape, the climate of opinion within the political establishment, and at the same time a response to the preexisting climate of opinion. It is both an attempt to seize or maintain the political initiative, thereby keeping potential rivals off balance and cultivating an image of dynamism, and an effort to respond to the interests of a wide range of audiences. It is both an attempt to woo new clients and an effort to reinforce the loyalties of existing clients and allies.

The relative balance among these manipulative and responsive factors will vary, and is difficult to predict. It will vary by stage of administration, by personality of the leader, by the level of consolidation of the leader's power resources, and by the internal and external circumstances.

The content of different leaders' authority-building strategies will also vary greatly. Khrushchev and Brezhnev, for example, devised very different strategies for creating, expanding, and maintaining elite confidence in their ability to achieve new goals without unduly sacrificing traditional values. They also differed in the strategies adopted for creating an image of themselves as indispensable politicians. Yet both were continuously concerned with the problem of legitimizing their power in the eyes of actual and potential clients and allies. In each case, the results were different. Khrushchev's authority in the eyes of his allies and clients collapsed, and his ability to pull rank to stay in power lasted only until October 1964. Brezhnev's policy effectiveness and political indispensability also came into question as his policies began to fail in the late 1970s. But the general secretary managed to retain his grip on office to the very end of his days, even though he had to struggle to maintain control over the policy agenda.

THE INTERRELATIONSHIP OF POWER
AND AUTHORITY

Although we may analyze separately a leader's strategy for consolidating power and building authority, it is clear that the two are closely interrelated. Before I elaborate this argument, let me recapitulate several basic themes discussed above. The abandonment of terror made the loyalty of clients less certain and more contingent. The strengthening of collective restraints on the leader made the length of his term in office, and thus the security he could offer his clients, less certain. In such an environment of heightened mutual uncertainty, the need increased to build one's authority in order to consolidate one's power over the office and its policy. Thus, in addition to delivering physical security, political security, promotion prospects, and material resources to clients, the general secretary also felt a greater need than before to instill a sense of confidence in his ability to continue delivering these goods to clients, allies, and potential clients in the Politburo, Central Committee, and the broader party and state apparatuses.

The ability to continue delivering the goods depends in part on the ability to prove one's continuing effectiveness as problem solver and politician. Here the interrelationship of power and authority becomes most clear. A party leader needs eventually to forge a policy program that is likely to achieve results in advancing the goals of the post-Stalin era. Forging and securing acceptance of such a program within the Politburo requires a sufficiently broad coalition of clients and allies within that body. To the extent that a party leader lacks such a large majority, his shortage of power will probably require compromises that will undermine the coherence, strength, and ultimate effectiveness of the program. Once passed, a diluted program is not likely to achieve results commensurate with expectations. That circumstance, in turn, threatens to undermine the authority of the general secretary who initially advanced the program, and who typically had to oversell its potential benefit in order to secure passage.[15]

Beyond the stage of policy adoption, insufficient power can undermine authority at the implementation stage as well. The Soviet system can be visualized as a huge bureaucratic pyramid. Decisions made at the top of this structure are implemented by an array of more or less specialized and overlapping bureaucracies. A party leader with a vast and reliable network of clients in several of these bureaucracies has some hope that his policy program, once enacted by the Politburo, will be implemented. His clients will either implement the policies or supervise the implementation by others. In the absence of such a far-reaching power base, the program enacted by the Politburo on the urging of the general secretary is likely to be diluted or subverted in the course of implementation. Moreover, policy programs are never implemented once and for all. They require a continuing series of readjustments and elaborations, the appropriateness of which may hinge on the reliability of the information received from below by leaders at the top. Here too, the party leader will have to depend on a network of clients to ensure a reasonably accurate flow of information about what is happening on the ground. In sum, the lack of a large, far-flung power base can subvert implementation and reevaluation processes, leading to policy results far short of those promised. This threatens to undermine the authority of a general secretary who lacks the skill or luck to parry responsibility for failure.

Just as lack of power can undermine authority, so lack of authority can undermine power. This, for example, was Malenkov's problem in 1953–1954. A widespread impression existed within the Central Committee that Khrushchev was the man best suited to deal with the acute agricultural depression facing the country.[16] This impression in turn facilitated Khrushchev's efforts, first to steal the agricultural policy agenda from Malenkov, then to discredit Malenkov's image as a problem solver, and finally to force Malenkov from office. Malenkov's lack of authority as problem solver made it easier for Khrushchev to consolidate power over the office and policy at Malenkov's expense.

With the interrelationship between power and authority in mind, let us now turn to a discussion of recent trends in Soviet leadership.

AUTHORITY, POWER, AND THE
RISE OF ANDROPOV

Yuri Andropov came to power with much authority, but relatively little power. He had a mandate to try new things, but a narrow power base with which to back them up, ensure their implementation, or sustain their momentum. Before his incapacitation, he worked slowly but deliberately to build his power to a level commensurate with his mandate. But death caught up with him, and we may never know how far he might have gone.

The choice of Yuri Andropov to succeed Leonid Brezhnev reflected a mood within the Politburo and Central Committee on behalf of "getting the country moving again." The malaise, inertia, and failure that had beset many realms of policy during Brezhnev's last years had created a mood of impatience and frustration, even among officials who did not know what to do to solve the problems at a price they were willing to pay. At the same time, there existed a strong sentiment for *controlled* change that would not have an unanticipated snowball effect and threaten the privileged status of the political establishment.[17] Andropov's meteoric rise within the Politburo during the first 11 months of 1982 indicated that key individuals were looking for decisive, but trustworthy, leadership in new directions. Yuri Andropov possessed the demonstrated intelligence, leadership capacity, technocratic orientation, and decisiveness to answer the yearning for change. And he possessed the toughness and background to reassure conservatives that change would not get out of hand.

Andropov moved quickly to project the image of a leader who would fulfill the "mandate" for controlled change.[18] In his first speeches as general secretary, he dispensed with many of the empty slogans that had filled Brezhnev's speeches. He spoke frankly and unapologetically about the economic and social problems plaguing the country. And he promised to do something about them. He called for a concerted campaign against official malfeasance, against lack of discipline in the workplace (absenteeism, alcoholism, malingering, high labor turnover, and worker pilfering or theft of state property), and against those who cover up such things. He promised to reevaluate old policies: oversubsidization of prices, excessively narrow wage differentials among strata within the working and specialist classes, and an unwillingness to reform public administration to make it less centralized and bureaucratized. There were, then, two strains within Andropov's proposals for controlled change: disciplinarian and reformist.[19]

During his first six months in office, Andropov actually put muscle behind only one of these orientations: the disciplinarian. He pushed through a series of policies for cracking down on malfeasance, incompetence, and lethargy among officials and workers alike. Mobile police squads were dispatched during working hours to beer halls, public baths, stores with queues, and markets to catch workers who were carousing, bathing, or shopping when they should have been at work. Managers were punished for failing to report or discipline workers who arrived late to work, shirked their duties, came to work inebriated, and so on. A considerable number of economic executives at all levels were fired, and some were put on trial for corruption.

In summer 1983, Andropov finally acted on the long-promised reform aspect of his program, though the reforms announced were exceedingly modest in scope. Beginning January 1, 1984, he revealed, five ministries (only two of which are all-union in jurisdiction) would experiment with new operating procedures. Managers of enterprises subordinate to these ministries would be given freer rein to decide how to reward productive workers, how to introduce labor technology, and how to plow profits back into production. The government would make available additional subsidies for managers to reward the best workers and engineers with large bonuses. Before paying bonuses, however, enterprises would be required to demonstrate that they have met their contractual obligations to customer enterprises.

The crucial question for understanding the Andropov era is: Why were the reforms so very limited in scope? There are many possibilities: that Andropov's efforts were blocked by Politburo-level opposition; that neither Andropov nor his allies ever intended to go much farther when they spoke of "improving the economic mechanism"; that Andropov was poised to advocate something more far-reaching, but his health failed him at the crucial moment.[20] Any of these is possible; we will have to wait some years before evidence accumulates on which to base a judgment. At this point, however, I am inclined toward a fourth interpretation: that Andropov was a consummate bureaucratic infighter, who understood the relationship between power and authority in Soviet leadership. In the present case, he understood that reform of any scope would face overt and covert opposition. He understood also that the measures announced in July 1983 were insufficient to improve the performance of the economy over the long term. Hence, he was introducing the reform piecemeal, trying to legitimize the workability of the new approach before proceeding further. Equally important, he was working to build for himself a political machine on which he could ultimately rely to implement and defend more far-reaching changes. In the meantime, however, he had to avoid over-reaching his power base by pushing policies the implementation of which he could not ensure.

This interpretation is reinforced by events following the July announcement. In mid-August, Andropov convened a special meeting of senior Communist party officials to demand support for the faithful implementation of the reform experiments.[21] He assured them that the measures would be carried out in a thoughtful, orderly fashion, but warned that the leadership would not tolerate half measures. He then went on to imply that the experiment of 1984–1985 would be followed by the further extension of reform measures in the Twelfth Five-Year Plan (1986–1990). That Andropov's limited reform faced powerful bureaucratic opposition was suggested two days later, when senior officials of the State Planning Committee held a rare press conference. Their emphases were much different from those that had marked Andropov's earlier speech. They were much more positive about the functioning of the Soviet economy to date, and stressed that the new reform would be applied with caution. And they went on to emphasize the limits of the reform proposals.

As Andropov's authority-building strategy unfolded during his first 10 months in power, so did his strategy for consolidating and expanding his power. Andropov came to the office of general secretary with a smaller political machine than had any of his predecessors. He was never the Party leader at the provincial level, having spent 27 years in positions based in Moscow. He was never the Central Committee secretary for personnel. His opportunities for patronage allocation and machine building had been restricted largely to the KGB, a narrow base for the leader of a system in which the party apparatus and economic ministries have so much influence on policy implementation.

Before his incapacitation in August 1983 (after which he would not be seen alive in public), Andropov moved quickly to secure his control over the levers of power at the center. Doing so would make it very difficult for him to be forced out of office. Within seven months, General Secretary Andropov added the offices of chairman of the Defense Council and chairman of the Presidium of the Supreme Soviet to his possession. Acquisition of those offices had taken Leonid Brezhnev almost 13 years. In addition, Andropov moved quickly to promote several younger, energetic figures into the Central Committee Secretariat, and to add new alternate (nonvoting) members to the Politburo.[22] These skilled party executives would serve multiple functions: protection of Andropov from political challenges; steering of the economy toward more dynamic changes; and purging of corrupt, incompetent, lethargic, or resistant cadres within the party and state bureaucracies. In sum, they would be the point men for Andropov to build the political machine required to back up further policy innovations consistent with Andropov's authority-building strategy.

At the regional level, Andropov also replaced about a dozen leaders of the provincial party apparatus during his first 10 months in office. This constituted less than a far-reaching purge. But more important than numbers was a pattern that began to emerge. In many cases, regional party leaders were replaced, not by their second-in-command (as had been the case under Brezhnev), but by lower-level party officials, or party officials from other regions, or even by officials of other bureaucracies.[23] The meaning was clear. Andropov was breaking with Brezhnev's deference to the interests of local party organizations, as these interests had been defined by local party leaders. He was moving slowly but decisively to break up local party cliques, a prerequisite for building a machine that would be more responsive to central party commands.

After Andropov disappeared from public view in August 1983, a lull set in on the matter of patronage allocation. But not for long. In December 1983–January 1984, dozens of replacements of regional party leaders were announced.[24] And in many cases, the new Andropov pattern of replacement was in evidence. Since Andropov was seriously ill, it is unclear who was to benefit from this patronage. At least a part of the benefit, however, must have accrued to Mikhail Gorbachev, a bright, sophisticated secretary of the Central Committee whom Andropov was clearly grooming to be his eventual successor. Gorbachev had been one of the "point men" for Andropov in the Secretariat—young and positively inclined toward administrative experimentation. He would be a beneficiary of Andropov's recognition that an authority-building strategy of advocating both discipline *and* reform would require a dynamic new political machine for its implementation and ultimate success.

Andropov died before he could witness the fruits of his labors. His successor was Konstantin Chernenko, the very man that Andropov had beaten out in the succession to Brezhnev. The reason Chernenko was chosen remains obscure. On the surface, the choice would appear to be a reversal of the power–authority relationship that obtained in the succession to Brezhnev. In November 1982, Andropov was chosen because he was widely perceived within the Politburo and Central Committee as the man most suited to getting the country moving again without fostering uncontrollable change. He had an image of competence and reliability, but a very narrow power base, especially within the party apparatus. In February 1984, Chernenko maintained his previous image as somewhat colorless, unimaginative, and lacking in dynamic leadership skills. But he held a key position in the party's central apparatus, and may have benefited from some of the patronage allocation that took place while Andropov was incapacitated.

Although there are several possible explanations for the choice of Chernenko, they all emphasize power rather than authority. One possibility is that he was the choice of the older generation within the leadership, which was afraid that a younger leader might build his machine at the cost of their collective retirement. Faced with this blocking coalition of older but powerful leaders, the younger generation either split, deferred (recognizing that time was on their side), or struck a deal. Another possibility is that the choice of Chernenko represented the revenge of the regional party apparatus. Alienated by Andropov's machine-building strategy of breaking up entrenched local party cliques, local party leaders may have viewed Chernenko as the alternative to a younger leader's inclination to continue the Andropov pattern.[25]

Chernenko's authority-building strategy is not yet clear. He has not been in office long enough (three months as of this writing) to reveal his cards. Both his career experiences and his earlier speeches square with the image of a traditionalist—nonexperimental in matters of administrative organization, relying on exhortation, "socialist competition," mobilization of workers against managers, and infusions of consumer goods to raise productivity and mollify worker grievances. Since becoming general secretary, his rhetoric has echoed some of the themes of Andropov's speeches, warning of the need for administrative reform and warning party cadres that resistance will not be tolerated.[26] But it remains to be seen whether he acts on these words or, like Brezhnev in his last years, simply recites them. Perhaps most important to watch will be whether he continues Andropov's cadres policy.

It is possible that Chernenko came to power as a result of a deal struck between the generations in the Politburo. For Gorbachev's political status continued to rise after Andropov's death, and signs indicate that he is the number two man in the regime. If such was the case, we may be witnessing a political compromise of sorts. Andropov's appeal was that he could cultivate the image of both a reformer and a disciplinarian, while his age and career path made it possible for him to act as a liaison between the generations in the leadership. After Andropov, no such obvious liaison existed. If Chernenko represents both the older generation and the disciplinarian appeal, while Gorbachev represents both the younger generation and reformist appeal, this particular coalition may not last more than a year or two. For, on cadres policy, a compromise may not be so easy to achieve. Continuation of the Andropov pattern of breaking up local party cliques would probably benefit Gorbachev, and would be the logical complement of a reformist authority-building strategy. Reversion to the Brezhnev pattern of deference to local party cliques would surely benefit Chernenko, and would be the logical complement to an authority-building strategy of "holding the line."

Holding the line would also be a difficult policy to enforce for long. Andropov's mandate, after all, reflected widespread and deeply felt opinions within the political establishment, especially its upper levels, that new policies had to be tried. It is impossible to say whether those opinions represent a large minority or a solid majority of policy influentials. One thing is certain: they are neither a tiny minority nor an overwhelming majority. Holding the line would increase the frustrations, and perhaps the level of political polarization, within the political establishment. This too would threaten the viability of the current coalition.

NOTES

1. I have benefited greatly from discussions with Richard D. Anderson on the topic of this chapter.

2. See Grey Hodnett, "The Pattern of Leadership Politics," in *The Domestic Context of Soviet Foreign Policy,* Seweryn Bialer, ed. (Boulder, Co: Westview, 1981), pp. 87–118.

3. On the nature and causes of charismatic one-man rule during the system-building stage, see Graeme Gill, "Personal Dominance and the Collective Principle: Individual Legitimacy in Marxist–Leninist Systems," in *Political Legitimation in Communist States,* T.H. Rigby and Ferenc Feher, eds. (London: MacMillan, 1982), pp. 94–110.

4. On the continuing tension between monocratic and oligarchic tendencies, see Hodnett, "The Pattern of Leadership Politics."

5. For an examination of the range of Khrushchev's and Brezhnev's power over policy, see George W. Breslauer, *Khrushchev and Brezhnev as Leaders: Building Authority in Soviet Politics* (London: Allen & Unwin, 1982), Chapters 7 and 15.

6. See Graeme Gill, "The Soviet Leader Cult: Reflections on the Structure of Leadership in the Soviet Union," *British Journal of Political Science,* 10 (1980), pp. 167–86.

7. On the dominance of ambivalence over affection in Soviet patron–client relations, see Gyula Jozsa, "Political *Seilschaften* in the USSR," in *Leadership Selection and Patron–Client Relations in the USSR and Yugoslavia,* T.H. Rigby and Bohdan Harasymiw, eds. (London: Allen & Unwin, (1983), p. 140.

8. Gill, "The Soviet Leader Cult"; also, T.H. Rigby, "Khrushchev and the Rules of the Soviet Political Game," typescript (Canberra, Australia, 1983).

9. At the risk of monotony, I want to restate and reemphasize the distinction between power over office and power over policy. The distinction is more important since Stalin, because of the relative increase in importance of authority building. One problem with much kremlinology of the 1950s and 1960s was the as-

sumption that a leader whose control over the policy agenda was weakening was also a leader whose control over office was weakening at a commensurate rate. Of course, there is a relationship between the two, but, I would argue, that relationship is far from one to one. In any given case, one must investigate whether a leader is defending himself from questioning of his policies or questioning of his right to stay in office.

10. See Breslauer, *Khrushchev and Brezhnev as Leaders.*

11. This paragraph is based on Gill, "The Soviet Leader Cult." Gill does not include Khrushchev's cult in his study, but on the indicators cited, that cult does not differ substantially from Stalin's and Brezhnev's.

12. This is one of the themes of my *Khrushchev and Brezhnev as Leaders,* which documented the content and evolution of these two leaders' authority-building strategies.

13. I am grateful to Richard D. Anderson for this distinction between positive and negative consensus.

14. On ideal and material interests, see Kenneth T. Jowitt, *The Leninist Response to National Dependency* (Berkeley: University of California, Institute of International Studies, 1980).

15. On the need to "oversell" one's case in U.S. politics, see Theodore Lowi, *The End of Liberalism* (New York: Norton, 1969), pp. 174ff; on the comparable need in Soviet leadership politics, see Breslauer, *Khrushchev and Brezhnev as Leaders,* pp. 285–86.

16. Roy Medvedev and Zhores Medvedev, *Khrushchev: The Years in Power* (New York: Norton, 1977), pp. 5–6.

17. See the discussion in Timothy J. Colton, *The Dilemma of Reform in the Soviet Union* (New York: Council on Foreign Relations, 1984), Chapter 1.

18. Ibid., pp. 36–38.

19. Archie Brown, "Andropov: Discipline *and* Reform," *Problems of Communism* (January–February, 1983), pp. 18–31.

20. For an outline of these and other possibilities, see Jerry Hough, "Soviet Politics Under Andropov," *Current History* (October 1983), pp. 332–33.

21. *Pravda,* August 16, 1983, pp. 1–2.

22. For discussions of these personnel changes, see Brown, "Discipline *and* Reform"; and Jerry Hough, "Andropov's First Year," *Problems of Communism* (November–December 1983), pp. 49–64.

23. Interesting work on these changes is being done by Professor Martha Brill Olcott, to whom I am grateful for this information.

24. Marc D. Zlotnik, "Chernenko Succeeds," *Problems of Communism* (March–April 1984), pp. 17–31.

25. Martha Brill Olcott, "Chernenko's Old Guard," oral presentation (Berkeley, California, April 4, 1984); see also Don Van Atta, "The Reign of Indiscipline: Andropov's Failed Authority-Building Strategy," paper presented at meetings of the Western Slavic Association, Stanford University (Stanford, California,

March 29, 1984).

26. Colton, *The Dilemma of Reform,* pp. 38ff; Zlotnik, "Chernenko Succeeds," pp. 30–31.

3

POLITICAL COMMUNICATION AND THE SOVIET MEDIA SYSTEM

Ellen Mickiewicz

The media in the Soviet Union include many different channels that carry to the public the officially approved message. The Soviet term for media, "Mass Media of Information and Propaganda," is a broadly inclusive term, combining the mass media, as the West interprets the term (printed media, newspapers and magazines; and electronic media, radio and television), with a number of other "media": movies, theater, and books. In addition, the Mass Media of Information and Propaganda (SMIP is the Russian acronym) embrace a special subset, the Mass Media of Oral Propaganda (SMUP). SMUP is the aggregation of spoken, live, face-to-face messages and channels identified as political agitation, political instruction classes, and public lectures. Taken as a whole, the media system in the Soviet Union is a dense communications system, producing a high volume of messages and reaching a large population spread over a vast land mass. Since the whole area of communications is one of increasing, if not revolutionary, importance in the modern world, we would expect a correspondingly important role for the media in the Soviet political system. This chapter will investigate the organization and administration of the Soviet communications system and examine its reach and impact. As we shall see, the changes in communications technology, the intrusion of foreign information into a relatively closed information system, the development of the education and exposure of the media public, and the recent opinion probes into opinions and attitudes of that public, have created an environment for policy makers in the post-Brezhnev era that is increasingly complex and problematic.

SOVIET MEDIA THEORY

Before describing the organization and political direction of the media in the Soviet Union, it is important to provide a general understanding of information theory, as the Soviets see it. Or, to put the matter more traditionally, the guidelines and parameters of the political doctrine of Marxism–Leninism impart a specific shape and texture to the communications system. The media have distinctive functions and very clear limitations under the requirements of the political doctrine. In these functions, they differ to a considerable degree from their Western counterparts.

The primary mission of the media system in the Soviet Union is the socialization of the receiver. In a broad sense, the media are educators, just as are the schools, the law courts, the family, the many organizations for youth, women, veterans, and others. The source of this mission goes back to Lenin and to a revolution that took place before the full maturation of history had been reached, at least that maturation that Marx had envisioned. Marx's notion of the revolution puts it at a time when the ripeness of consciousness was at hand and the great masses of workers would be very near a common ethos, and common social bonds would unit them, thus virtually eliminating deviance, dissatisfaction, selfishness, and acquisitiveness—all those retrograde habits associated with the bourgeois life. However, Lenin's revolution came earlier than Marx's theory had projected, and those habits of mind were largely absent in an overwhelmingly peasant population that had yet to develop the degree of consciousness, or enlightenment, that had been predicted. As a result, as Lenin's writings and policies make very clear, changes in popular mentality had to come from external sources, and all of the instruments of socialization available to the state would be turned to this task.[1] Even the courts, institutions that are not normally associated with the function of persuasion and indoctrination, are in theory charged primarily with the task of education and only secondarily with punishment.[2] In addition to this grounding in theory, the mission of the mass media was grounded in the need to integrate a sprawling multilingual country.

The task of socialization assigned to the media has two principal dimensions. First the media must change the ethical and moral outlook of the population. The psychological orientation underlying the society of the future, when full communism has been achieved, requires cooperation and collectivism, and eschews selfishness, careerism, greed, and, in general, the development of an individualism that might supersede the societal collective. The second dimension of socialization that the media must implement is the rousing of the population to participate in such a way as to contribute to the economic goals of the leadership. Mobilizing people to meet production goals becomes, therefore, a critical role for the media. The preconditions for communism, as Marx portrayed them, would be met only when the internal value system of the vast majority had changed dramatically within a context of significantly enhanced levels of economic production. In advance of that time, as the Russian Revolution was, the state and its agencies must develop the preconditions. The media are central to this obligation.

Because the role and function of the media system in the Soviet Union are grounded in this particular theory, certain implications arise in the implementation of that mission. These give the Soviet media system, and, indeed, that of socialist systems based on the Soviet model, a distinctive cast. Recently, in Afghanistan, one of the very early moves after the Soviets invaded that country was the reform of the Afghan media system, so that with changes in personnel and operations, the media system would replicate that of the Soviet Union. As a Soviet writer put it, "A new second stage of the April Revolution was begun on December 27, 1979. In the area of the mass media of information this stage is characterized by the reorganization of the entire newspaper–magazine complex. First, certain publications were closed, the directing cadres of editorial boards were renewed, and the work of radio, television and the *Bakhtar* [news] agency was rebuilt."[3]

Perhaps the most distinctive element of the Soviet media system is the understanding of what is actually newsworthy, or appropriate for inclusion in the communications of the media system. Because the media system has the task of socializing or educating the population, as noted above, it is provided with the definition of its task and does not define the task itself. Further, that task is a single one; that is, there is a single correct method and outcome desired in the socialization of the audience. The denial of pluralism is derived from the notion that the ruling doctrine is based on science. Lenin's understanding of Marx's scientific socialism requires that a single idea be correct and that it displace any other idea that has preceded it. It is, perhaps, a primitive notion of how science operates and develops, but it is very clear that Lenin held a dichotomous view of the scientific and the nonscientific, and that coexistence of a variety of ideas was simply nonscientific. Once an advance is made, the previously held positions must be wholly cancelled. To do otherwise would be as frivolous or harmful as, say, according equal validity to the Ptolemaic and Copernican views of the universe. Marxism, as science, must, therefore, supersede all previous (and unscientific) models. It is in this sense that the newspaper *Pravda* prints what its name means: truth—the truth following what the leadership regards as the only scientifically based theory of history and human relations. As might be imagined, therefore, the charge given to the media is the presentation of the "scientific" point of view and no other.

The theory on which the media system is based also imparts a very particular notion of the proper content for the media. Many types of stories carried in Western media systems are considered inappropriate for Soviet media. For example, there is rarely mention made of domestic natural disasters, accidents, crimes, or other items tinged with sensationalism. A terse announcement might be made if the story has already broken in the Western press. The lack of coverage of these events is explained as follows: dwelling on negative events, the underside of life, as it were, would tend to encourage or suggest the wrong kind of behavior and would undermine the positive model that the paper must purvey and in terms of which it must educate the population. Similarly, the kinds of fluff that Western media carry—celebrity doings, horoscopes, advice to the lovelorn—are out of place in the educational mission of the Soviet media. Advertising is generally absent (there is a little on television). The Soviet media are not commercial enterprises, but state-owned and -operated instructional vehicles.

Since the Soviet media have the functions noted above, they evaluate the importance of fast-breaking news in a way rather different from that of the Western media. Fast-breaking news does not command attention simply because of its freshness. Only insofar as a story furthers the educational mission, does it have validity, and a fast-breaking story is not a value in itself. In fact, about 15% of a newspaper is devoted to events, domestic or foreign, that had occurred the day before.[4]

From the operation of the political doctrine, the functions of the media system may be seen, therefore, as both exceedingly restricted and excessively broad. The functions are restricted in that they must follow definite guidelines which prohibit much of the editorial initiative and investigative reporting familiar to audiences in the West. On the other hand, the charge given to the media is very broad: they are to mold and shape the audience, rather than simply to entertain or please that audience, although to be effective in this task of socialization, the message must be received and packaged in such a way as to be assimilated. I shall return later to this very difficult and often contradictory doctrine of the media and how it relates to practice.

SOVIET MEDIA OFFICIALS
AND THE ADMINISTRATION
OF THE MEDIA SYSTEM

The rules governing the content and thrust of the media are restrictive
and unidirectional, and a system of control and authority supervises the
media. The Soviet administration of the media system is both highly centralized and hierarchical. The most important figure, next to the general
secretary himself, is the secretary in charge of ideology. Until his death in
January 1982, the veteran Mikhail Suslov held this position. Suslov's influence during his long career in the Politburo went beyond the media; he
was a key participant in all important decisions and was often regarded by
Western observers as being able to swing his political weight behind contenders for the top position. During the later stages of the Brezhnev regime,
the man who is now the leader of the Soviet Union, Konstantin Chernenko,
was singled out and increasingly invested with the trappings of heir apparent to the leader. In those waning Brezhnev years, Chernenko, although he
was associated with a number of additional political initiatives, seemed to
have carved out the ideology sphere for himself. After Yuri Andropov out-
maneuvered Chernenko to secure the general secretary's position, Chernenko inherited Suslov's mantle in the ideology sphere. After Andropov
died, Chernenko came back successfully to reassert his claim to the top
position. Konstantin Chernenko, born in 1911, came from a peasant family. He graduated from a teachers' college in Kishinev, capital of the republic of Moldavia, a largely rural republic in the European part of the Soviet
Union, bordering on Rumania. He also received professional party administration training in one of the special schools run by the Central Committee. In 1929, he began his party career by directing a department of a local
branch of the youth organization. After service in various party organizations, he took over, at age 37, the department of propaganda and agitation
of the Central Committee of the Moldavian Republic. From this position,
which he held for eight years, he moved to Moscow to direct a section of the
same department of the Central Committee of the national party. After that,
he moved quickly, under the patronage of Brezhnev, into a key Central
Committee department, the Secretariat, and the Politburo. Chernenko has
been associated with important developments relating to media and their
political impact. As a protege of Brezhnev, but even more after his death,
Chernenko has been publicly associated with efforts to identify problems
affecting the efficacy of the media and their solution. As we shall see

below, these solutions have been constrained by contradictory criteria and purposes.

At the next level of authority is the Central Committee secretary responsible for the media: the propaganda secretary. This post oversees the areas of culture, education, propaganda, and science. The operations of the official censorship agency, GLAVLIT, come under its jurisdiction. The incumbent is Mikhail Zimianin, formerly editor-in-chief of *Pravda.* Zimianin, a Belorussian, went to teachers' college in Mogilev and made his career in the Belorussian Komsomol. He moved into party work and then into diplomatic work, serving as ambassador to North Vietnam and Czechoslovakia and before assuming the editorship of *Pravda,* he held the title of deputy minister of foreign affairs of the Soviet Union.

Next in line in authority over the media is the head of the Central Committee propaganda department. One of the largest departments, it is charged with mobilizing public opinion and "has extensive authority as the overall administrator of Soviet media." It has an important voice in the selection of editors, provides regular liaison with editors in the media, and generally communicates to the individual media the appropriate tone and content to follow. It also allocates budgets and defines circulation size of print media.[5] The current head of this department is B.I. Stukalin, whom Andropov promoted from his position as overseer of the publishing trade to this Central Committee post. Stukalin, a Russian, also attended teachers' college. However, for over a decade, before serving at high levels in the party, he worked for newspapers and again, between 1965 and 1970, he was deputy to the chief editor and then the first deputy chief editor of *Pravda.*

There are a number of other Central Committee departments that have some jurisdiction over portions of the media. These are the Department of Culture, the Letters Department, and the International Information Department. The new Letters Department was described at the Twenty-Sixth Congress of the Communist party, in 1981. At that time, Leonid Brezhnev expressed the need to open new channels for feedback. He proposed to do so with this new department which, with its working Group for Analyzing Public Opinion for Social Research and Development, would solicit feedback and study public opinion, self-selected, to be sure. The need to obtain more audience feedback was stated by Brezhnev as follows: "Every party worker, every director (of an economic enterprise) is obliged to examine with keen attentive consideration the letters, requests, complaints, of citizens as his duty before the people, before the party."[6] This perception on the part of Chernenko and Brezhnev of the importance of feedback and their initiative in the creation of this department is evidence of a certain policy dilemma which became exacerbated under Andropov.

The International Information Department is what the name implies, the purveyor of foreign affairs information, particularly to foreign audiences. Still, another department of the Central Committee has, as part of its function, some media oversight: the International Department, which has the responsibility of overseeing party policy toward socialist allies and supporting radical movements, sponsors publications and research in this area. In each republic, there is a counterpart of the propaganda secretary and a republic-level Central Committee department of propaganda. These two positions, in close consultation with and under orders from their superiors in Moscow, provide principal oversight for the media at the regional level.

Parallel to the party structure is the governmental structure of centralization and control. For the media, several agencies participate in policy implementation and administration. Chief among them are the Ministry of Culture and three state committees: the state committee for publishing houses, printing plants and the book trade, the state committee for cinematography, and the state committee for television and radio. In addition, the communications elite includes the director of the Telegraph Agency of the Soviet Union (TASS); the director of the news feature service, NOVOSTI; the chief of the censorship agency, GLAVLIT; and the chairman of the All-Union Agency for the Protection of Authors' Rights (VAAP).

Although the post is not, strictly speaking, a media one, it is important to note among the media elite the head of the Komsomol. As will be apparent below, the Komsomol is linked closely to the communications control and administration apparatus. The current head of the Komsomol is a young Andropov appointee. In fact, Viktor Mishin, born in 1943, is one of the youngest men in the Soviet political elite. He is a construction engineer, who from the time he was 25, has spent his entire career in the Komsomol bureaucracy. His predecessor as Komsomol chief was shifted to the state committee on publishing, and that incumbent, Boris Stukalin, during Andropov's brief tenure, was moved up to directorship of the Central Committee department of propaganda, as noted earlier. Andropov's moving of his communications officials should be seen as targeted mainly at the ouster of Stukalin's predecessor, E.M. Tiazhelnikov, an official in his late fifties, most of whose professional career had been spent in the Urals region and who, at 40, came to Moscow to head the Komsomol, before his promotion to the Central Committee. Tiazhelnikov has been identified as a protege of Andropov's predecessor, and it is likely that he was ousted for this reason.

Before analyzing in more detail the functions and characteristics of the communications elite, it is important to discuss briefly other ways in which the centralization of and control over the media is effected. Through the operation of the *nomenklatura* procedure, all appointments of key editors, journalists, and communications officials are approved by the appropriate party organization at the higher level. This process, in the communications area, as elsewhere in the Soviet political system, serves to centralize and control politically relevant appointments.

Another method of control of the media is the consolidation of journalists into the Union of Journalists, which establishes criteria for performance and authorized subject matter. Expulsion from this association closes the door to participation in all official media. The Union is administered by party officials and the majority of the journalists, in all media, belong to the party.

Finally, political control over the media is exerted by the censorship system. It is directed by the Chief Administration for the Affairs of Literature and Publishing Houses (known by its acronym GLAVLIT), founded in 1922. All publications in excess of nine copies must be approved by GLAVLIT. With the passage of time and the publicity given to sanctions, not to mention the terror of the Stalin period, the relative importance of GLAVLIT seems to have declined, replaced, as might be expected, by an informal or self-censorship system. This operates in two principal ways: First, authors understand what will be prohibited and seek to avoid difficulties with the authorities. Therefore, they tend to submit material they have censored themselves. Second, the editorial staff at the newspaper or television station checks the material for deliberate or inadvertent evasions of censors' guidelines. By the time material reaches GLAVLIT, a fine screen has generally removed objectionable items.

The officials who run the Soviet communications system, as has been noted above, staff a number of agencies and departments. If we look at them both at the national and the republic levels, we find that, as a group, they tend to share certain key characteristics. First, there is a roughly 50 percent probability that they will have had training in special schools that the party runs for those midlevel party workers who will be singled out for higher level party posts. These special ideology and management courses are given under the auspices of the Academy of Social Sciences in Moscow, and the Moscow Higher Party School as well as the Higher Party Schools in the Union republics. This training helps to integrate a geographically dispersed elite, bringing them to Moscow and sending them back to positions of regional responsibility, presumably with training and a common understanding of the sensitive line with respect to communications.

It is also apparent, from a study of the communications and ideology elites, that many have had high-level professional jobs in the Komsomol before taking on communications responsibilities. That many of the chief overseers of the media have had a long career association with the Komsomol before being moved over into communications suggests not only that patronage and personal ties are important, but also that molding the youth of the country, and preventing counterculture structures, are functions or obligations of the media.

A large number of the officials charged with directing the media are involved in international activities and in agencies with foreign counterparts. This is a surprising finding, if one considers that most of the communications jobs are defined by domestic or internal duties. The communications officials are used as spokespersons for the Soviet political system, and often travel abroad as representatives of Foreign Affairs Commissions of the parliaments of their republics or of the Supreme Soviet. A second "international" function that regional communications officials may perform is related to control. Their communications obligation is not only to produce desired communications, but also to reduce the effects of undesirable foreign communications. The Foreign Affairs Commissions of the republics, to the extent that they are involved with tourists coming to the Soviet Union from foreign countries, may have a control function. Additionally, the practice of many of the communications officials of extensive foreign travel and their international contacts do lead to obvious connections with the KGB. Finally, some studies of Soviet politics have noted a connection between Komsomol leadership positions and the security organs.

The elites who direct the media system in the Soviet Union, then, are a group who have a high probability of having had training in the professional party schools, who have advanced in bureaucracies of the party or youth organization and have then been put in charge of individual media or media oversight agencies. A minority have had actual experience working for a long time in the individual media they must now control. Their primary functions do not relate to the specificities of the media they direct nor to the efficacy (in terms of reach, exposure, and persuasiveness) of the system as a whole. Rather, their functions are international activities of a propaganda nature; security and control, especially regarding foreign communications; and youth management and control of political socialization of the next generation.[7]

THE REACH OF THE MEDIA

What is the media system over which these officials have jurisdiction? As I indicated earlier, the Soviet sense of the term media system is very broad indeed, but the main components are the media that are important in every media system: print and electronic media. The newspaper is the leading print medium and occupies a special place in the Soviet media system; newspapers are produced in massive numbers, even though there has been a paper shortage for years. They are organized in hierarchical fashion. At the apex are the central, or national, newspapers. Below them are the republic newspapers in each of the 15 Union republics. Then follow the newspapers at the province (*oblast*), city, district or precinct (*raion*), and individual factory and farm levels. In 1980, there were 8,088 newspapers of all types published in the Soviet Union. Together, they had a circulation of 176,225,000 or 660 per 1,000 population.[8] Dailies have a circulation of 400 per 1,000 population, as compared to 282 per 1,000 population in the United States. National newspapers, all of which are published in Russian, numbered 31 in 1980, and their circulation was 80,119,000. Ten of them are dailies; six come out three times a week; four, twice a week; and eleven, once a week.[9] The most well known of the national newspapers are *Pravda,* organ of the Communist party of the Soviet Union, with a circulation of over ten million; *Izvestia,* the organ of the government, with about eight million circulation; *Komsomol Pravda,* the organ of the Young Communist League, with almost ten million circulation, and *Trud,* the trade union organ, with a circulation of almost eight and a half million. However, the number of readers probably exceeds the number of subscribers by three times. Thus, *Pravda* alone, a recent survey found, has 30.5 million readers. Although, as noted above, all of the national newspapers are published in Russian, there are still some 2,851 newspapers published in other languages of the Soviet Union. Twenty-three percent of the total circulation is not in Russian, while 48.5% of the Soviet population is non-Russian.[10]

Radio production and ownership developed with phenomenal speed in the Soviet Union. By 1940, there were already 7 million radios available in the Soviet Union. By 1965, that figure had grown to roughly 74 million, and by 1970, to almost 95 million. In 1979, the figure was 144 million.[11] Between 1965 and 1970, there was a marked increase in wired sets, and their rate of growth considerably exceeded that of wave sets.[12] Thus, in 1979, there were 544 radio receivers per 1,000 population. This is still far below the comparable figure for the United States (2,009 per 1,000).

In view of the tremendous importance attached to the media and the recognition of the Soviet leaders throughout Soviet history of the role that the media system could play in the integration and socialization of the population, the very belated entrance of television on a mass scale is anomalous. It appears that the attractive powers of this new medium were only imperfectly grasped by Soviet officials, as the density figures show: In 1940, there were 400 television sets in the Soviet Union; by 1950, only 10,000. Greater growth occurred in the next decade, reaching 4.8 million in 1960. However, the real beginning of the growth of production of television sets took place during the next decade, so that by 1970, almost 35 million sets were in existence.[13] Thus the acceleration of production of television sets was great, with an average annual production of 960 between 1940 and 1950; 479,000 annually for the next decade; and three million per year between 1960 and 1970. By 1981, 75 million sets had been produced,[14] and almost 86% of the Soviet population received television programs. Color television is still relatively new, accounting for about 10% of the total number of sets owned.

Part of the tremendous lag in the availability of television is due to the difficulty of logistics across the vast land mass of the Soviet Union with its areas of virtually inaccessible terrain. The use of satellites has created opportunities and has enhanced the use of the more than 67,000 km of surface television and radio cables.[15] Television programs are both national and local. Two national channels, based in Moscow, operate across the country; others are organized at local levels. In Moscow, for example, there are two additional channels: one for instructional programs, with lessons for school children and continuing education programs for adults, and another for programs of local interest. The national channels feature delayed broadcasts to all time zones of the country.

Research on magazine consumption is relatively sparse. Production figures are large. In 1980, there were some 1,428 different magazines in circulation across the country. The total circulation divided by the number of magazines produced a figure of 157,800 copies as an average circulation per magazine. This figure excludes a number of other periodicals, such as mass political aids (for example, the agitator's notebook series) and other specialized bulletins and serial publications from research institutes.[16]

The other category, or subset, of media channels consists of oral media. The system of oral media will not be treated in detail in this chapter. Rather, the more influential mass media will be analyzed. The oral media, particularly agitation, were extremely important in the early days of the Soviet Union. Not only were rates of literacy low (therefore making newspaper reading difficult), but the mass communication system was then only developing, although at a very high speed. Person-to-person oral communication was an important innovation of Soviet policymakers. Alex Inkeles, in his pioneering study, analyzed the role of face-to-face official communication. He focused particularly on the system of political agitation, in which every member of the party is responsible for agitating, acting as advocate of party policies with his or her fellow workers at the workplace.[17] It may well be that agitation has declined in importance as the mass media, particularly the electronic media, become more highly developed and as levels of education rise. In his major speech on ideology in June 1983, Konstantin Chernenko hardly referred to the process of agitation, and when he did it came in for severe criticism for *agitpunkty* (agitation points, or offices for materials and personnel) that are mere shells, no longer functioning.[18] A major Soviet survey of public participation in the industrial city of Taganrog did not treat agitation at all, calling it "unsystematic." The implication may be that whatever role agitators played in the past, their exclusion from the study may signal, in the researchers' minds, a sharp reduction in the utility of agitation in a more highly developed communications system.[19] Increasing in scope and importance, however, is another oral medium, the public lectures given by the Znanie (Knowledge) Society. In 1979, it presented more than 26 million lectures nationwide, of which over 300,000 were broadcast on radio and television.[20] The Taganrog survey found that three-fourths of the entire population of the city attended these lectures. The reason so many of them go, they say, is because they find out from the lectures information that is unavailable from the other media. The lectures focus on a single topical concern and permit a question and answer period afterward. The lectures usually take place in the evening and are conducted by local professors, journalists, or political figures. The topics covered are often political or economic events, particularly in the international arena, but they also cover topics in philosophy, literature and art, pedagogy, psychology, agriculture, medicine, and physics and mathematics.[21]

FEEDBACK AND AUDIENCE OPINION

Until quite recently, the Soviet communications policy makers were confident that they could and did accurately assess the media audience, its preferences and exposure. They were confident because of the enormous numbers of letters sent to the media from readers, listeners, and viewers. For example, in 1980 *Pravda* received 581,700 letters. In 1974, the trade union newspaper, *Trud* (Work), received 647,439 letters. In one year alone, more than two million letters are sent to central television and radio studios.[22] To deal with these vast amounts of mail, the central newspapers maintain large staffs, some 70 people at *Pravda* and 50 at *Trud,* whose sole job is to catalogue, summarize, distribute, or respond to letters. All media, at all levels, encourage the writing of letters and have special sections for the analysis of and response to letters. Eventually, once a month or once a year, these summaries and analyses are passed to party organizations. For example, each month, *Pravda* prepares 10 to 12 summaries of its editorial mail for distribution to the Central Committee of the Communist party. With this enormous volume of letters reaching the media, it is difficult to imagine that public opinion is not being tapped. However, as we know from surveys in several countries, people who write letters to the media are not representative of the population at large. The Soviet audience surveys found that this was true in the Soviet Union as well. Letter writers are apt to be considerably older than the average reader, viewer, or listener. Older people have more time and fewer distractions. In the Soviet Union, as in the United States, they contribute letters in excess of their proportion of readership. Among the writers of letters to the editor of *Izvestia,* only 7.5 percent are 30 and under, while some 22% of the readers are in this group. The occupational spread of the letter writers does not replicate that of the readership. Engineers, technical and agricultural specialists, the single largest group in the readership of *Izvestia,* account for less than 10% of the letters to the editor.[23] In addition, as compared with the population at large, the channels of feedback are thickly clogged with party members. Since party members are more active consumers of the media, their heavy representation among writers of letters to the editor may not distort some element of readership views but do severely distort the broader picture. In the general adult population, less than 10% are party members. Several surveys have found that upwards of one-third of all letters sent to the media are from party members.[24]

Media officials, confident that this immense volume of letters reflected audience behavior, have recently had to reassess the basis for their assumptions concerning the media audience. A number of surveys of newspaper readers, television viewers, and moviegoers produced some startling contradictions. Some of the surveys incorporated "expert" predictions: i.e., editors and journalists who were asked to predict the audience response to various questions. The results of the experts' characterization of the public and the survey results of that public differed substantially. For example, the communications officials tended to overestimate the impact of the official media and to underestimate the use of word-of-mouth sources of information. Age and level of education of the public were incorrectly estimated by the experts. Audience preference as predicted by the experts does not match the survey results.[25] One striking difference, particularly at the local level of communications media, is the degree to which the audience understands the words most commonly used in stories about international events. Although illiteracy has been eradicated in the Soviet Union, the comprehension of media messages cannot be assumed. The Taganrog survey asked respondents to define a number of words commonly used in newspaper stories about international affairs. About 25% of the sample did not know what colonialism meant; about 40% did not know the word dictatorship. Almost 50% were unable to define imperialism, and almost two-thirds could not understand the meaning of leftist forces. Finally, between two-thirds and three-quarters of the respondents could not tell the survey researchers what the terms reactionary and liberal meant. Before the advent of the surveys there had not been any way for this miscalculation on the part of the journalists to have surfaced.

These surveys, which were begun in the late 1960s, revealed still another important type of misconception widely held by communications officials. The official communication theory held that the illumination of media messages would be self-evident for those who had enough cognitive skills to make sense of them. Thus, as education became more widespread, the likelihood of comprehension, and with it, persuasion, would be strengthened. Levels of education have been rising in the Soviet Union, but the surveys have found that education is inversely related to agreement and satisfaction with media messages. The surveys have found that college-educated Russians are the most avid consumers of newsprint, but most frequently disagree with the editorial point of view. They are the group most interested in television broadcasts of political and news analysis programs, but most critical of them, as well. In fact, the college-educated audience for Soviet television spends less time watching than does the average viewer (about a third less time) because of dissatisfaction with programming. Books by contemporary Soviet authors are received most critically by the college educated. In the countryside, it is the better-educated young workers who complain most about rural conditions and who are most likely to migrate to cities. Even within the network of political schools run by the party for its members and for civic activists, those with more education are more dissatisfied with the lectures and classes.[26] To a Western observer, the relationship between critical stance and education is a familiar one. If education is understood as providing an awareness of alternatives, then dissatisfaction becomes virtually the emblem of the intellectual. In the United States, it has been found that college graduates are more critical of television programs than are less well educated viewers. The college educated are more demanding; they want information. But they are not as sharply distinguished from average viewers in their behavior and in their sense of dissatisfaction as are their Soviet counterparts. It is true that television is a new medium in the Soviet Union, and it is possible that the Soviet college graduate will, in time, conform to the general pattern of viewing and attitudes about programs. But that prediction would have to be modified by the consistently more critical opinions the well educated hold about all media. Thus, the confidence expressed by the official theory that rising levels of education would be associated with rising levels of persuasive power of the media, has been challenged in a fundamental way by the survey findings.

The feedback that media policy makers had been using for over 50 years had not prepared them for the consistent and durable results they see in media audience surveys. The fundamental assumptions regarding the efficacy of the media for their distinctive mission have clearly been undermined by the new information. What is visible now is, at the same time, both a resistance to change at the higher levels of the political system and a move at lower levels toward reformulating communication theory, not only among sociologists and other survey analysts, but also among those party theoreticians who are responsible for media efficacy. At the higher levels, one recent innovation, as I noted above, has been the creation by Leonid Brezhnev of a Letters Department of the Central Committee. This would, he maintained, widen the channels of feedback. Thus the response of the highest officials is to augment the letters industry still more. The need for more information obviously is not yet seen as the need for a certain type of information—representative opinion. Similarly, when Yuri Andropov succeeded Brezhnev, his first call was for more letters from the population. He urged people to write letters exposing corruption and mismanagement in the economy. Simultaneously, at lower levels of the party hierarchy itself, there are elements of reformulation, of shifting from the archaic notion of media audiences and public opinion, to a more probabilistic and complex notion. There is also an increasing awareness among these officials that the media system is efficacious only insofar as it knows the interests and values of the audience and satisfies those demands. This theoretical development puts the audience at the center of attention and creates the dilemma for the leadership of efficacy gained at the expense of control. It is some middle ground that the party theorists are attempting now to define.[27]

Konstantin Chernenko has been at the center of these moves and continued, during Andropov's brief period of leadership, to present these issues. His major speech to the Central Committee plenum in June 1983 will be discussed later. It contains many of the dilemmas and ambiguities generated by the search for media efficacy. In the short time that Yuri Andropov held power, certain moves were made that suggested that concern with media efficacy and audience response has high priority. The media now carry a routine summary of the agenda items of the Politburo meetings. This once remote body, the political elite, is now presented as an issues-oriented committee treating a number of questions. Readers are told what issues are discussed and what general measures are ordered. Obviously there is no way of knowing how fully the report reflects the actual agenda, but the predictable and informative (if abstract) look at the workings of the hitherto obscured leadership is an important change.

The other major, indeed revolutionary, communications development under Andropov's regime was the use of a press conference conducted by the then chief of staff, Marshal Nikolai Ogarkov and the deputy foreign ministry, Georgy Kornienko, and moderated by the International Information Department director, Leonid Zamiatin. This event, lasting more than two hours, was broadcast live from the Foreign Ministry auditorium after the Soviets had shot down Korean Airlines civilian passenger flight 007. Earlier in the year, in April, Foreign Minister Gromyko had held a press conference, but this later performance was remarkable, first for its responsiveness to a major international story, second for the extended public appearance of the chief of staff, and third for the sharp and, at times, emotional questions from the audience, including those taken spontaneously from foreign correspondents. Shortly after, the pilots who were responsible for the incident were put on television and explained their story to the Soviet public. Still later, in December 1983, after the Soviets withdrew from the intermediate nuclear forces talks, Ogarkov, Kornienko, and Zamiatin once again gave a press conference. Moves of this sort, startling and unusual for the Soviet public, underline the preoccupation with international news—a preoccupation of the Soviet elite as well as of the Soviet media public.

INTERNATIONAL NEWS

In a typical national newspaper, most of the stories are about domestic events. Soviet newspapers have, usually, from four to six pages per issue (a notable exception is *Literary Gazette,* with 16 pages). About 70% of the total column inches in *Pravda* will be devoted to matters of internal interest, and about 30% to foreign news. Of this 30%, about 31% will be devoted to stories about other Soviet-type systems and about 44% to stories about the United States and its NATO allies.[28]

Television coverage of international affairs takes place in three daily programs, three weekly programs, and two monthly programs. The leading news program is the daily "Vremya" (Time). It is broadcast in a half-hour to forty minute segment in the prime-time slot (Moscow time) of 9:00 p.m. It is rebroadcast the following morning. Much of a typical broadcast will be devoted to domestic themes, which are generally concerned with the economy and developments in industrial and agricultural production. This is followed by international news, and the program concludes with about five minutes of sports and weather.

"Today in the World" was inaugurated soon after an address made by Leonid Brezhnev in which he was critical of the stultifying and ineffective use of the media. This program, broadcast twice daily, in the early and late evening, runs for a quarter-hour. It provides commentary on world events. Short news capsules, generally running anywhere from five to fifteen minutes, make up the program, "Novosti," (News), which is broadcast several times a day during the week and on the weekend.

"International Panorama" is the leading weekly program, broadcast Sunday in the early evening. It is a program of reports from foreign correspondents introduced and analyzed by leading political journalists from the print and electronic media. It runs for three-quarters of an hour and ranges broadly over issues in all parts of the world. A new entrant, dating from 1982, is "International Review," a program that was inaugurated at the same time as the second national channel. This program of news analysis is broadcast in fifteen-minute segments on Saturday afternoons. "Sodruzhestvo" (Cooperation) is a half-hour evening program devoted primarily to reports about Communist countries. It adopts a positive tone and, as the title suggests, shows the benefits of a community of nations with similar social–political systems.

The monthly program, "Studio Nine," is broadcast early in the evening on Saturdays for an hour. It is a discussion/analysis program, bringing together the leading political analysts and information officials in the country. Finally, a program of analysis by Yuri Zhukov rounds out the regularly scheduled international news and commentary broadcasts. Zhukov, political commentator for *Pravda,* is the most well known analyst of foreign affairs in the country.

Newspaper readers show a strong interest in stories about international affairs. This preference has been consistent and stable. In three readership surveys, two of national papers and one of a regional paper, it was found that readers turned first to stories of international events. This interest cuts across all age groups, all levels of education, and all occupations. Even the respondents in the survey of *Trud,* the trade union newspaper and the daily with a relatively small proportion of college-educated readers, when asked in what area they would ask for more information, cited international news first. Other areas of newspaper coverage (science, technology, culture, economics, family, youth, etc.) do exhibit the difference in readership by education, or other variables, that international stories do not.[29] In the 1973 survey of the readership of the popular national newspaper, *Literary Gazette,* it was found that fully 88 percent of the subscribers were attentive to the section on "International Life," although different areas of the "International Life" section attract a different intensity of interest. Table 3 provides a picture of the kinds of international stories that most attract the *Literary Gazette* readership.[30] It should be noted that the categories of greatest interest for readers are related to capitalist countries. For readers of regional papers, a survey found that the most important category of international affairs story was that relating to military conflicts abroad. Some 53% of the readers at the regional level were troubled by problems of war and peace and military conflicts.[31]

Television news programs attract a large proportion of the audience, although not as large as that attracted by movies and other purely entertainment features. Almost two-thirds of the Russian respondents in a major survey said that they watch the news, particularly "Vremya." However, if respondents are asked about attention to the entire category of sociopolitical broadcasts, their interest is markedly lower. The reason that this category as a whole is one that attracts relatively little interest among broad audiences is that the subcategory of news analysis program tends to pull down the percentages for the category as a whole. The news analysis program is one that is demanding for the audience and its popularity does depend on the educational level of the audience. In a Moscow survey, it was found that there is a strong association between level of education and interest in political programs.

Table 3. *Literary Gazette* Readership Survey

Story Type	Percentage of Respondents Indicating Interest
Moral system of bourgeois press, radio, and television	69
Bourgeois image of life	67
Economic and social problems of foreign countries	63
Ideology and politics of Maoism	63
Materials on bourgeois political leaders and ideologues	60
Ideology and politics of Zionism	60
Peaceful coexistence of states, including problems of European defense	54
Nationalism and its manifestations	48
Bourgeois ideology, revisionism, and anti-Marxism	47
Life of socialist countries	45
National liberation movements and neocolonialism	38

Source: Adapted from *"Literaturnaya Gazeta" i ee auditoria* (Moscow, 1978), p. 56.

In the short time that television news has competed among the media for audience attention, it has attained considerable success. It is now the chief source for informing the public about the capitalist countries. A 1977 national survey of the readership of *Pravda* found that 50.4 percent of the respondents said they learned about conditions of life in the more advanced capitalist countries from television broadcasts. Thirty-seven percent cited newspaper and magazine stories for this information, and about 30 percent cited radio.[32]

The way in which foreign news is presented in the Soviet media has also been the subject of attention in the recent surveys. What has been revealed by a number of surveys is an impatience with the single official point of view. In the *Literary Gazette* survey of 1973, some 43% of the respondents preferred stories in which there was more than one point of view; 26% wanted to read clashes of extreme positions, and only 2% approved of a single point of view in the story.[33] The later *Literary Gazette* survey of 1977 developed this dimension with more questions. It found that a majority of all the respondents argued that the newspaper's coverage of stories should acquaint the reader with "all existing points of view on the subject under discussion." They meant by this even wider exposure to points of view than simply reporting two opposing sides. As the level of education of the reader rose, so did the commitment to this view. Further, the readers indicated a clear preference for empirically based stories, for stories based on facts and actual events, rather than for stories (so typical of the Soviet press) couched in general, abstract discourse. The majority of readers, this survey found, preferred to read reprints of stories from the foreign press, accompanied only by commentary from Soviet analysts. This preference increases with level of education as well.[34] They prefer this combination of unaltered reprint-plus-commentary to the retelling of the news story by the Soviet newspaper writer. Even adding commentary to the reprint is less desirable for those who have subscribed for longer periods to *Literary Gazette*. Also, younger readers, those between the ages of 30 and 39, prefer to read stories about foreign countries in reprint without commentary, as do readers with advanced educational degrees. However, among respondents characterized by first year of subscription, or who are workers, students, and retired people, only a small proportion prefer the reprint without added editorial commentary.

Even at the level of local newspapers, the thirst for international news is manifest. For example, in a survey in the greater Perm region, it was found that 69 percent of the readers wanted to see more information about foreign countries in the local newspapers. Similar results were obtained in surveys in the greater Sverdlovsk region. However, in 1973–74, the newspapers in the greater Sverdlovsk, Perm, Kurgan, and Chelyabinsk regions devoted in a week, on the average, about 5% of their newspaper space to international stories. At the level of the local newspaper there are no international correspondents. The secretariat of the local newspaper receives information from the press services of the central newspapers. Even though the amount of space devoted to stories on international relations is small, in fact, as the Sverdlovsk regional survey of 1973 discovered, there is a relatively high proportion of that space given to stories about capitalist countries. Just as I noted earlier that almost half of the foreign news in national newspapers was related to stories about the United States and NATO, so, at the local level, it was found that a little over 41% of the stories on international themes is devoted to material on capitalism. To be sure, these stories tend to be negative, containing accusations of aggressive policies of imperialism or depictions of the crises of capitalism. Only about 30 percent of the foreign stories are related to events taking place in Communist countries. Another 13.5 percent are devoted to foreign policy initiatives of the Soviet Union, and about 11 percent to questions of the international Communist and workers movement. Interestingly, only slightly under 3 percent of the materials are related to stories about newly independent and developing countries and national liberation movements. The rest fall under the heading of "foreign kaleidoscope," or short capsules. The percentage distribution of these stories is congruent with the percentage distribution of space accorded these themes.

Even though the treatment of Western capitalist countries is negative, it occupies a very large percentage of the total foreign news coverage, indeed the single largest category. The central importance of the West for the Soviet Union is very clear, and there are those among Soviet observers who argue that this order of priorities is damaging. One such observer wrote that "the clear, deep demonstration of the strengths of the world system of socialism, of the camp of democracy and progress, should occupy the leading place among articles on international questions."[35] By focusing so intensely on the nature of the adversary, this observer seems to imply, the Soviet media might encourage interest in the West. That attention may be seen, certainly, in the prominence given to bourgeois themes in the preference scale of Soviet newspaper readers. It is interesting to compare the attention given the Soviet Union by American "elite" dailies: the New York Times, Chicago Tribune, Miami Herald, and Los Angeles Times. A 1977 study showed that news about the Soviet Union was about 4% of all foreign news, and news about Communist countries equaled 8% of all foreign news.[36] This is a dramatic asymmetry in news coverage. We should not be surprised that the Soviet population's attention to the West might be far greater than that of the West to the Soviet Union and far greater than Soviet officialdom might now appreciate. Naturally this attention to the West is designed to strengthen support by focusing on a constant and pervasive threat from the West. That another consequence as well has ensued—a virtual thirst for news of the West—is likely to be an unintended consequence.

On the other hand, it appears that this highly mobilized opinion on international issues places considerable confidence in the official sources, the central communications channels from Moscow. Soviet newspaper readers express a high degree of satisfaction with articles on international questions, although they request that more be published. In general, dissatisfaction with official coverage and the official point of view tends to increase as the story approaches issues of local life, where independent verification is possible, a relationship not unlike that found in studies of other countries' media systems, though more pronounced in the Soviet Union.[37] In fact, the local media may be said to suffer from something like a crisis of confidence. Because of the prohibition on stories about deviance and because of the mission to socialize in a single acceptable fashion, as noted earlier, the local papers present a certain view of local life that is unreal and stilted. Much that is of interest to the local populace simply goes unreported. Other events are portrayed in a way that is so didactic, the readers find them unnatural and frozen, or, as one reader put it, "It's not like in life." Only 3 percent of the readers of a district newspaper in a city said that the newspaper rarely distorts the events it describes. The pervasiveness of alienation from the local media, particularly the press, is of concern to the communications policy makers. The audience wants to know more about matters of specifically local interest: hospitals and health programs, sports, cultural events, retail trade, and shopping. It wants coverage of stories that is accurate and that they can judge for themselves because they may have received information already either at first hand or from word of mouth from participants. And, finally, the readers expect their local media to be as professional as the central media, which, after all, set the standard. It is rare, in any country's media system, that the resources available at the local level are sufficient to match the quality of communications transmitted through central channels. This has a certain depressant effect: audiences queried in Soviet surveys would rather not have more time in their television programming devoted to local questions; they would rather see more feature films on national television. They would rather see resources go to ease the critical housing shortage than to build a local television studio. They tend to be more critical of the local arts, preferring to see a first-rate performance on central television than to go to a provincial concert or recital. For these several reasons, then, the role of the local media in the Soviet Union is problematic; constrained by the very restrictive doctrine and unable to commandeer the resources available to the central media, local communications channels are caught in a web of limited initiative and reduced audience trust.

However, as I noted above, the central media are accorded much greater confidence and trust. Particularly on questions of international relations, and particularly where conflict, potential or actual, with the Western world is concerned, both interest and confidence will be high among the public. But the media system of the Soviet Union is not impenetrable to foreign communications. Some foreign sources are permitted. For example, foreign newspapers are available to the Soviet public, but they are

either newspapers imported from allied socialist countries or papers published under the auspices of Communist parties in nonsocialist systems.
Some foreign movies are shown on the regular movie circuit. Some of them
come from Western countries, having passed through the government pur-
chasing office. Many more come from socialist and Third World countries.
But some foreign films, such as *Dr. Strangelove* and *A Clockwork Orange*,
are shown to restricted audiences. For the most part, these audiences include professional film people and other elites. There is also evidence that
foreign film festivals draw their audience almost exclusively from the
upper social and economic reaches of Soviet society.

An important foreign communications source is foreign radio. Among
the foreign broadcasters, the four major Western radio stations are the
British Broadcasting Corporation, Deutsche Welle (under the Ministry of
the Interior of the Federal Republic of Germany), the Voice of America
(administered by the United States Information Agency), and Radio Liberty (administered by the Board for International Broadcasting and funded
by the United States Congress). Jamming has been a persistent problem for
these stations. Occasionally the jamming has been lifted and reimposed
when the political conditions change. For example, from 1963 until the
Soviet invasion of Czechoslovakia, large-scale jamming of Western programs was absent. In August 1968, jamming was reimposed, to be lifted
once again, in September 1973. The Polish crisis, beginning in 1980, once
again, brought jamming. Radio Liberty, which concentrates on internal
Soviet matters, has been particularly hard hit by jamming. In 1964, a
Soviet program "Mayak" (Beacon) was created to go out at the same time
that foreign broadcasts were received and interfere with the wavelengths
used by the foreign broadcasters.

Estimating the audience for Western radio broadcasts has been a difficult task, one that requires some measure of inventiveness and flexibility.
Most of the work on this question has been done by the audience research
group at Radio Liberty. By interviewing Soviet travelers to Western
Europe, in a casual setting and without a visible structure, the researchers
have been able to ask almost 20,000 Soviet citizens about their attention to
foreign radio between the years 1970 and the present. About 5,000 of these
interviews were conducted between 1977 and 1980, the years for which the
following estimates were made. First, a word about methods. It is obvious
that Soviet citizens who travel to the West differ substantially from those
who do not. The travelers might well be skewed upscale in income, and
certainly in political reliability. Further, they are disproportionately drawn
from certain geographical areas in the Soviet Union and are, naturally,

more likely to be urbanites than rural dwellers. However, the last problem, how to project onto the Soviet population the data derived from particular regional clusters, has been treated by a sophisticated statistical operation that uses data from the Soviet census to project likely estimates from the traveler figures. These estimates work best where the traveler data are most numerous, that is, among urban, well-educated, middle-aged males. The major problem is one of representativeness. How representative are the travelers of the home or parent population in the Soviet Union? This question always arises when it is impossible to sample directly the parent population and one must rely on some members of that population who are either temporarily outside the country or who have chosen to leave their home country permanently. In the case of Radio Liberty's audience research, it has been possible to apply certain validation procedures. The findings of Soviet surveys about media exposure and preferences are close to the responses on these particular issues given by the Soviet travelers abroad. Although foreign radio program preference is not among the questions asked of respondents at home in surveys conducted by Soviet sociologists, a wide range of other media activities is examined and these tend to come out very close to what the Soviet travelers say about their own exposure to and preferences in media communications. Based on the research on travelers, then, it is possible to say that between the years 1977 and 1980, about a third of the Soviet adult population "was exposed to Western radio broadcasts in the course of a year." About "one-fifth in the course of a typical week" will listen to some Western radio.[38] However, these programs may be the very popular music or other non-news broadcasts.

AUDIENCE PREFERENCES

Although the attention to foreign stories and foreign news, in particular, is high among the Soviet population, it should not be assumed that, in general, the Soviet audience, unlike media audiences elsewhere, has a taste only for unrelieved seriousness and high-minded instruction. In fact, the preferences of the television audience, the fastest-growing medium in the Soviet Union, look very much like those of audiences everywhere: entertainment is high on the list of preferred programs—feature films, musical variety shows, and sports programs. Age and level of education do not affect these preferences. Among the least popular are instructional programs, relaying information about the economy, for example, and cultural programs, such as poetry readings and symphony broadcasts. For these cultural programs, education does make a difference. Much like the audience for public television in the United States, the audience for these programs is skewed upscale: some 28 percent of the college-educated in Moscow watch opera and ballet on television, but only 1 percent of those with elementary education.[39]

Although education has a generally less powerful effect on television watching—the audience is less differentiated than that of other media, perhaps because one does not have to develop many skills in order to assimilate its messages—education does make a substantial difference in newspaper reading. The development of cognitive skills is extremely important, as we saw earlier, for the assimilation of printed, as opposed to visual, messages.

Television is still new to many in Soviet society; it has been seen as a medium for entertainment and escapism, with films, variety, and sports shows leading the program preferences. However, in a recent survey, television was not far behind the newspaper as the medium that illuminates events most objectively and reliably. The power of visual images has obviously created for television an authoritativeness and credibility remarkable for a medium that is neither of longstanding prestige nor of value primarily for its information transmission function. Whereas education is positively related to newspaper consumption, it is not nearly as important a factor in radio and television consumption; audiences for these media are for the most part, undifferentiated. For the 20 percent of the Russian population that uses a single medium of communication, that medium is likely not to be the newspaper.[40]

Age makes a difference in media consumption. Older people in Russia are less likely to be newspaper readers. In part, this relationship may be generated by health problems and the difficulty in reading that appears with advancing age. But more likely, it is related to the education variable. The older stratum in Soviet society is much less likely to have the education necessary for systematic newspaper reading. However, older people are more avid customers of television programs. Television viewing is responsive to life-cycle variables. In the Soviet Union, as in the United States, youth over 16 are the lowest consumers of television programming. It is this group that is most mobile and wishes to use its leisure time outside the home. At a later stage, marriage and family obligations keep people at home and television viewing increases. Still later, with age and infirmity, television consumption rises more. Russians over 30 are twice as likely to spend leisure time at home than are Russians under 30. Children under 16 have now become heavy television viewers, spending at least as much time in front of the set as in school.

Sex difference in media consumption may be seen with respect to newspaper reading, in that women are less likely to be systematic, regular readers of newspapers and more likely to be intermittent consumers. Their proportion of nonreaders is the same as that for males. Among television viewers, the Russian housewife is one of the heaviest consumers. But, unlike their counterparts in the United States, who are also heavy consumers, Russian housewives constitute a very small population. Since most women in the Soviet Union work, they bear the "double burden" of employment and housework. Thus, as consumers of all media, women rank below men, who have more leisure time.

Urban or rural residence makes a great difference in media consumption. First, the level of education of the average inhabitant is rather different for rural and urban residents. Thirty-six percent of the entire Soviet population is still rural, and many of them have only the most rudimentary education. It is estimated that as much as 40 percent of that rural population has not gone beyond the fourth grade. That figure for the urban areas is about 20 percent. It is true that much of this undereducated population is also fairly old. In rural areas the population is older than the population in cities; able young people have been migrating to the cities, and the population left on the farms has proportionally more females than in urban areas, and more of the older, and the less well educated. As noted earlier, education is particularly important in distinguishing the readership of the major national newspapers. For example, 39 percent of *Pravda*'s readers have had some college education; 47 percent of *Izvestia*'s, 25 percent of *Trud*'s, and, highest of all, 64 percent of *Literary Gazette*'s. This should be compared to the percentage of those with some college education in the general population, which, in 1982, was about 7½ percent. The lower levels of education in the countryside affect newspaper consumption: for example, a survey of female agricultural workers revealed that only one-third of the respondents said they read newspapers. However, the pull of television is much greater. Both radio and television may be secondary activities, while newspaper reading demands primary attention. These female farm workers spend more time watching television and listening to radio than reading newspapers. Rural wage scales are lower than those in the city, and there are many who cannot afford to buy television sets. However, even though there are 1½ times fewer sets in the countryside, the total time spent watching television is 1⅕ times greater than that spent on television in the city. In part, this attachment to television is related to the lower level of cognitive skills in the countryside and in part to the absence of alternatives for leisure time use. And, of course, with lower wage scales, the rural population has less flexibility in seeking entertainment requiring admission charges.

MEDIA POLICY DIRECTIONS

Shortly after Yuri Andropov rose to power, his defeated rival and later successor, Konstantin Chernenko, gave a speech at the June plenum (1983) of the Central Committee of the Communist Party. This speech, reprinted in full in *Pravda,* set out the tasks for the media in the period ahead. The lengthy talk is notable for some of the directions the media are now directed to take and for some principles that are reaffirmed. One theme running throughout the speech is the intimate connection between media tasks at home and the intrusion of foreign communications from abroad, against a background of an increasingly tense world scene and, in Soviet eyes, a hostile and aggressive U.S. policy. This Western, particularly American, thrust is called "unprecedented." Further, the West, he warned, was organizing a "real information–propaganda intervention" to destroy socialist regimes. For this reason, a broad program of Soviet counterpropaganda, both for external and internal use, had become necessary. This emphasis on the international aspects of communications underlines and enhances the importance of the foreign experience of the communications officials we saw earlier. The sharper accent on counterpropaganda has resulted in changes in policy.

A second major theme of Chernenko's critical speech relates to the substance of the media messages and the role of social science. Here, the message seems clear, but actually embodies some contradictions that recall the dilemma facing the communications officials examined earlier. On the one hand, Chernenko, in this speech, strongly castigates the social science research institutes for "academic," irrelevant research. In his words: "In the activity of these institutes, deficiencies have obviously been revealed, to a greater or lesser degree found also in other research institutions: being closed in one's own 'dissertation' and group interests, trivial subjects, [and] weakness of party influence."[41]

Chernenko goes on to direct the institutes and the party overseers to choose contemporary problems for research, not "idealizing what has been achieved" in the past. It is constructive analysis that is required, and methods to reach stated party goals. If such analysis is performed about contemporary problems, as opposed, for example, to the "well worked over" earlier period, then matters of change and resistance to change, of the durability of dysfunctional methods, such as "bureaucratism" and "conservatism," must be confronted and studied. Further, research institutes must be flexible, innovative, and responsive to social change. They are required "more often" than they are now doing, to do applied research and produce policy options and recommendations, and they must engage more often in forecasting and trend analysis, but it must be reliable, so that officials may use it. All this they are instructed to carry out with a Marxist–Leninist approach. No longer, states Chernenko, can problems in Soviet society be swept under the conceptual rug called "vestiges of the past," long used as a catch-all category to explain undesirable phenomena as holdovers from the pre-Revolutionary past. Rather, there are likely to be objective, real reasons for these phenomena and they must be addressed.

Chernenko then notes that letters to the editors of newspapers should be regarded as "barometers of public opinion," but later, when referring to the question of feedback, he cites three channels: letters, questions addressed to speakers at public lectures, and sociological research (understood as public opinion surveys). He concludes that "from the evaluation of the state of ideological processes, it is necessary to move on to forecasting, from uncoordinated research on public opinion to a systematic, and perhaps, even to the organization of a center for the scientific study of public opinion."[42]

Analysts of this speech have made much of the fact that it orders research to be conducted within the approved conceptual framework and disapproves of forays outside it, such as the field of sociobiology, which Chernenko regards as relying on a closed system of genetics and ignoring the influence of the social milieu. Other parts of the speech direct creative artists to be more positive and not to dwell on the nostalgic recall of past times and their disappearance. Certainly, all of these elements are contained in this important scene-setting document. But it would be unprecedented if the ideology overseer did not emphasize the decisive and generative role of the ideology and warn those he oversees not to stray from the path. What is also interesting is the coexistence of these hard-line views with a range of missions that clearly conflict with a narrow interpretation of those views. Researchers are told to stop going over "safe" issues of the past and to get into today's social and economic change. They are told to investigate that change so deeply and with such excellent methodological tools that they can produce reliable indicators for trend analysis and engage in accurate social and economic forecasting. They are told they must not sink into the rut of past practice and agenda setting, but must continually probe the social environment to discover and then to investigate new phenomena. They are told that there may be real problems "out there" that a mere allusion to the long-term effects of the pre-Revolutionary past cannot cover. Letters to the editor are called the barometer of public opinion, but it is the creation of a national survey research center that Chernenko seems to regard as the decisive move in the improvement of feedback and more effective analysis of the communications audience.

The seriousness of Chernenko's concern with media efficacy was seen very soon after Andropov's death. He presented to the media and to visitors to Moscow a new and less confrontational image, and within days after the funeral, Igor Moiseyev, the director of a famous dance company, had written an article for the *New York Times* calling for new cultural contacts on a person-to-person level. The more accommodative stance did not, however, last long. As preparations for the U.S. elections got under way and as the hostility of relations between the superpowers deepened, the Soviet leadership adopted an increasingly harsher stance, with rhetoric to match. Charges and countercharges about violations of international law, of international agreements, of Olympic regulations, and a host of other matters filled the air between the United States and the Soviet Union. Such an atmosphere leaves little room for tentative forays from either side toward improved communication. However, even within this environment of tension, Chernenko has used the media in a new way, directing a functionary of the Ministry of Foreign Affairs to conduct regular briefings of the foreign press corps and meeting himself with the *Washington Post*.

Chernenko's June speech puts forward the program for the post-Brezhnev era and is certainly a key document in an appraisal of the direction the leadership is likely to take. It mirrors the dilemmas and problems I examined earlier in this chapter: for improvement of the efficacy of the media (which is now seen to be essential, particularly in an increasingly hostile and tension-ridden world), the restrictive, methodologically unsound procedures of the past are clearly less useful than a new, reformulated conceptual framework—one that relies on scientifically sound methods and results in accurate and reliable projections. The role of Marmethods and results in accurate and reliable projections. The role of Marxism–Leninism as a true guidance system is unclear in this new orientation; ward a new understanding, but that movement is also constrained by the system of control and by hostility to foreign influences. Whether a productive and effective middle ground can be reached is clearly an unresolved problem facing Chernenko and, no doubt, his successors.

NOTES

1. See Donald D. Barry and Carol Barner-Barry, *Contemporary Soviet Politics,* 2nd ed. (New Jersey: Prentice-Hall, 1982), pp. 150–53.

2. See especially V.I. Lenin, *State and Revolution* (New York: International Publishers, 1932).

3. E.V. Kruglov, "Zashchishchaya revoliutsionnye zavoevanie," *Vestnik Moskovskogo Universiteta,* seria 10, Zhurnalistika, no. 5, 1982, p. 58.

4. Robert G. Kaiser, *Russia: The People and the Power* (New York: Pocket Books, 1976), p. 236.

5. Lilita Dzirkals, Thane Gustafson, and A. Ross Johnson, *The Media and Intra-Elite Communication in the USSR,* RAND report R-2869 (Santa Monica, September 1982), pp. 13–19.

6. L.I. Brezhnev, "Otchet tsentralnogo komiteta KPSS," *Pravda,* February 24, 1981, p. 8.

7. These observations are based on a study of the careers of some 80 communications officials, published in *Slavic Review,* Winter, Vol. 43: 4.

8. *Pechat SSSR v 1980 godu* (Moscow, 1981), p. 115; and *Narodnoe Khozyaistvo SSSR v 1980* (Moscow, 1981), p. 12. These are production figures. Actually, readership exceeds the volume of copies printed for subscription and newsstand sales.

9. *Pechat SSSR v 1980 godu,* p. 117.

10. Ibid., p. 119.

11. *Narodnoe Khozyaistvo SSSR v 1979,* Moscow, 1980, p. 352.

12. Ibid. In her discussion of radio in the Soviet Union, Gayle Durham Hollander discusses the 1967 resolution of the Central Committee of the Communist Party, "On the Acceleration of the Development of Wired Broadcasting." This policy decision called for improving the wired radio system, which "receives broadcasts from the central or local network and transmits programs by wire to speakers in homes or other buildings." This resolution called for improvements in maintaining, repairing, and extending the wired radio system. Advantages of this system were said to be improved sound quality and energy savings. Hollander suggests another attribute: wired radio is closed off from foreign radio broadcasts. Gayle Durham Hollander, *Soviet Political Indoctrination* (New York: Praeger, 1972), pp. 100–102.

13. *Narodnoe Khozyaistvo SSSR 1922–1972* (Moscow, 1972), p. 314.

14. V.S. Korobeinikov, *Redaktsia i Auditoria* (Moscow, 1983), p. 94.

15. V.I. Zadorkin and A.V. Sosnovsky, "Perspektivy kommunikativnykh vozmozhnostei televidenia kak sredstva osveshchenia kulturnogo urovnya," *Issledovanie rosta kulturnogo urovnya trudyashchikhsya* (Moscow, 1977), pp. 90–101.

16. *Pechat SSSR v 1980 godu,* pp. 103–104.

17. Alex Inkeles, *Public Opinion in Soviet Russia* (Cambridge: Harvard University Press, 1962).

18. Konstantin Chernenko, "Aktualnye voprosy ideologicheskoi, massovo-politicheskoi raboty partii," *Pravda,* June 15, 1983, pp. 1–3.

19. B.A. Grushin and L.A. Onikov, *Massovaya informatsia v sovetskom promyshlennom gorode* (Moscow, 1980).

20. *Ezhegodnik B.S.E. 1980* (Moscow, 1980), p. 25.

21. *Moskva v tsifrakh* (Moscow, 1977), p. 161.

22. Korobeinikov, *Redaktsia,* pp. 176, 233; A. Vasilenko, "Ot nashego glavnogo korrespondenta," *Gazeta, avtor, i chitatel* (Moscow, 1975), p. 30.

23. V.T. Davydchenkov, "Organizatsia sotsiologicheskogo obsledovania i vnedrenie poluchennykh rezultatov v tsentralnoi gazete," *Problemy sotsiologii pechati,* vol. 2 (Novosibirsk, 1970), p. 148.

24. See I.D. Fomicheva, *Zhurnalistika i auditoria* (Moscow, 1976).

25. See L.G. Svitich and A.A. Shiryaeva, *Zhurnalist i ego rabota* (Moscow, 1979).

26. Ellen Mickiewicz, *Media and the Russian Public* (New York: Praeger, 1981).

27. This argument is made in greater detail in Ellen Mickiewicz, "Feedback, Surveys, and Soviet Communication Theory," *Journal of Communication* (Spring 1983): 97–110.

28. These figures are based on a survey of news coverage in Hollander, *Soviet Political Indoctrination,* p. 43.

29. Mickiewicz, *Media and the Russian Public,* pp. 58–59.

30. Adapted from *"Literaturnaya Gazeta" i ee auditoria* (Moscow, 1978), p. 56.

31. *Raionnaya gazeta v sisteme zhurnalistiki* (Moscow, 1977), p. 91.

32. T.F. Yakovleva, "Obespechenie vzaimosvyazi khozyaistvennykh organizatsionnykh i vospitatelnykh zadach v perepektivnykh planakh ideologicheskoi raboty," *Voprosy teorii i metodov ideologicheskoi raboty,* vyp. 13 (Moscow, 1981), p. 60. Multiple sources were cited by respondents.

33. E.P. Prokhorov, ed., *Sotsiologia zhurnalistiki* (Moscow, 1981), p. 87.

34. *"Literaturnaya Gazeta" i ee auditoria,* p. 127.

35. V.V. Kelnik, "Bolshoi mir i malenkaya gazeta (O vystupleniyakh na mezhdunarodnye temy v raionnoi i gorodskoi pechati)," *Gazeta i zhizn* (Sverdlovsk, 1975), p. 137.

36. Mickiewicz, *Media and the Russian Public,* p. 137.

37. Ibid., Chapter 5.

38. R. Eugene Parta, John C. Klensin, and Ithiel De Sola Pool, "The Shortwave Audience in the USSR: Methods for Improving the Estimates," *Communication Research,* 9, no. 4 (October 1982): 581–606.

39. Mickiewicz, *Media and the Russian Public,* p. 26.

40. Fomicheva, *Zhurnalistika i auditoria,* pp. 53, 58.

41. Chernenko, "Aktualnye voprosy," p. 1.
42. Ibid., p. 3.

4

THE POLITICAL ROLE OF THE SOVIET MILITARY

Roman Kolkowicz

> Alternately they would call the army
> into the affairs of state and then come
> to fear it; deliver power to them and
> then quibble with them; place all their
> hopes in them and then work against
> them . . . and assert in haughty tones
> the supremacy of civil authority; little
> by little they had made a series of
> capitulations, surrendering to the
> military.
>
> —Albert Sorel, *On the Directorate
> and the Military after the French
> Revolution*

Western studies of the military establishments in Communist countries for many years were flawed by certain cognitive and political distortions. Many researchers in the field began with the premise that the Communist countries are our mortal enemies who threaten our vital interest and even survival; they therefore viewed the Communist militaries only from the perspective of this threat potential, considering them to be mere extensions of the Communist party—executants of the will of the Politburo or collective leadership, and having no specific, differentiated, or institutionalized identity or interests of their own.[1] Even attempts at the "modernization" of civil–military studies shared this unquestioned premise of total military subordination to the party's authority. Civil–military relations in Communist countries were assumed by Western analysts to be frozen in a static, bipolar (party–military structure without intervening institutions), linear (dominant party, subordinate and compliant military), and apolitical condition. The relationship between the two was postulated to be devoid of any kind of institutional interaction or political bargaining, pressures, or negotiation.

This model of Soviet party–military relations is particularly bothersome. One is asked to believe that the Communist countries have escaped sociopolitical forces ("laws") that are assumed to apply to most other political systems. It is as if some kind of immaculate conception had occurred after the October Revolution, and a wondrous, conflict-free harmonious system of institutions and bureaucracies had materialized in the Soviet Union and the other Communist countries. This notion, a deeply ingrained and rarely questioned Western belief, defies understanding, particularly when given the fact that almost everything is political or politicized in the Soviet Union; the boundary between state, society, and the individual is rather ambiguous in a country where the ruling elites of the party subscribe to a modern Hobbesian concept of *kto-kovo,* and suspicion and terror are institutionalized.

This perplexing Western image of an organic, harmonious and fully integrated political–bureaucratic party–military system without any internal tensions, disagreements, and differences remained the mainstream U.S. article of belief, despite many signals and much evidence to the contrary. The earliest signals of potential stresses and differences between civilian Communists and their military counterparts can be traced to a vitriolic comment by Engels to Marx on the military professionals who joined the Revolution of 1848: "This military pack are jealous like schoolboys of each other's smallest awards and dislike one another passionately; however, when they are confronted by civilians, they are all united."[2] Trotsky reiterated the central and indispensable role of the military in the Communist scheme of things: "The dictatorship of the proletariat would be impossible without the Red Army."[3] And Mao readily understood that "political power comes out of the barrel of a gun" and insisted that "the Party control the gun and never allow the gun to control the Party."[4]

And yet, Western analysts have only recently begun to apply a more realistic and objective approach to the study of civil–military relations in Communist societies. As the Soviet Union began to assume full superpower rank, it became increasingly clear that it was also undergoing certain internal political and bureaucratic adjustments—that the firm, vigorous, and unquestioned party leadership of Stalin, and even of Khrushchev and early Brezhnev, was giving way to a vacillating, accommodating, and unstable leadership of old, insecure, and pathetically infirm party hierarchs. And paralleling this public deterioration of the political leadership was the equally visible and increasingly self-assured presence and influence of the military.

In the face of this growing and visible body of evidence, a new Western realism about the Soviet military began to surface. This is reflected in the recent remarks by Henry Kissinger who observed that: "The irony of communist systems is that they contain the seeds of Bonapartism. For the sole organizations outside the Communist Party with autonomous command structures are the armed forces and the paramilitary units of the KGB." He added that the growth of the Soviet military power "is built into the system" and concluded that "since no one can achieve eminence, much less the top spot, without military [support]," a situation was created where "the armed forces emerged as the balance wheel in the struggles among the hierarchs of the Party."[5] These perceptions of the Soviet military are also taking hold among U.S. military analysts. A recent Pentagon publication[6] asserted that "the influence of the Soviet military within the Kremlin's power structure goes beyond the totalitarian state's intrinsic need to extend its frontiers, control its satellites and save itself from internal disintegration." Indeed, the study asserts that the "Soviet military is not averse to act in the role of kingmaker to increase its hold over the USSR's top leadership."

The Soviet military has come a long way from its earlier full submission and unquestioned subordination to Stalin, or from the need to placate Khrushchev, who selectively coopted favored marshals into the ruling elites while also selectively punishing others. Under the Brezhnev regime the party and the military seemed to have reached an institutional accommodation, established a modus vivendi, and progressively evolved into a form of institutional interdependence which continues into the current protracted succession crisis. Essentially, the military has become the benefactor of the party's decline within the system and its expansionary, ambitious imperial and superpower policies abroad. The military has benefited from the party's erosion of legitimacy, decline of authority, and failure of performance. How can one account for these developments and what are their implications?

EVOLUTION OF THE
MILITARY'S ROLE

The founding fathers of Marxism–Leninism and of the Soviet Union had only a vague notion about the role of the military in a post-revolutionary society. Although Marx, Engels, and Lenin contemplated differing roles for the revolutionary armed forces, they were in agreement on one fundamental axiom: "In a communist society no one will even think about a standing army. Why would one need it?"[7] After all, to Lenin "a standing army is an army that is divorced from the people."[8] The idea of a massive, professional standing army in a post-revolutionary society was considered an anathema, a heretical concept that violated fundamental aspects of revolutionary ideology—so much for revolutionary rhetoric and utopian visions. The erstwhile revolutionary "heresy" has become the orthodoxy of Soviet politics. Indeed, the Soviet military today is a vast and complex institution whose interests strongly influence and shape much of the country's social, economic, and even political life. The military has become a state within a state. It is a primary consumer of scarce resources, of skilled manpower and scientific and technological talent; it runs a vast educational network that parallels and often exceeds that of the civilian sector; it has become a visible and pervasive presence in society through its control of a network of mass voluntary paramilitary youth organizations and military preparedness and civil-defense training activities. The military is also strongly represented in the highest decision-making bodies of the party, the government, and economic planning bodies.

What are the implications of this steady growth of the military's role and influence in the Soviet Union? Is it likely to result in an eventual militarization of the Communist party and government and the emergence of a garrison state, or a nation-in-arms? It is important to consider these questions because our Western perceptions of Soviet politics and decision making rarely touch on the military's internal roles and influence on policy. Our perceptions of Soviet political process were first shaped by cold war antagonisms, and more recently, by the more benign perceptions and fantasies of detente. In either case, we rarely concerned ourselves with the military's internal role and policy influence. We saw the Red Army essentially as metal eaters, weapon carriers, and trigger pullers for the party. To be sure, several theories and models of party–military relations have gained some renown in the West (ranging from conflict models to cooperation models); however, the scholastic debates on this subject do not necessarily enhance our understanding.

The Soviet Union is in many ways an ideal country for the growth of military values, and for the military to play vital internal and foreign policy roles. The histories of imperial Russia and the Soviet Union alike are tales of conquest, invasion, and war, and it is understandable that Russian leaders would place a great trust in their military, and rely on it to defend the country from foreign aggression. However, while the military's role as defender of the country has been well understood, there is much less understanding in the West of the important internal and policy role of the military. The vast size and geographic, linguistic, ethnic, and racial diversity of the Soviet Union have presented perennial administrative and political problems, and have led to a strong reliance on the military for maintenance of internal stability, law and order, national cohesion, and the legitimacy of authority. The military is considered loyal to the center and therefore able to provide the necessary instrument for bureaucratic and political control. The replacement of the imperial autocracy with Bolshevik authoritarianism or totalitarianism did not significantly affect the military's role. It did, however, change the dynamics of the relationship and the rules of the game.

Under Stalin, the military's internal and external roles developed and grew, but in a suitably subterranean and tacit manner. Since Stalin's death, however, the military has proceeded to assume publicly those social and political roles commensurate with its position in the state.

Stalinist Subordination

The military was seen early on by party leaders as an excellent instrument in the systematic and rapid execution of its primary objectives. The logic and political dynamics of modern totalitarian political systems like the Soviet Union create overriding preferences for:

- *centralization* of political, institutional, economic, and military authority;
- *standardization* of rules, processes, laws, producer–consumer habits and distribution patterns;

●*neutralization* of deviances, diversities, and idiosyncracies that inhibit and constrain standardization–centralization objectives;

●*integration* of diverse political, economic, and social entities under the ruling party's banner.

Stalin and his successors considered the military an institution that could help eradicate some of the pernicious, entrenched remnants of the bourgeois–imperial past, inculcate desirable habits and patterns in generations of young people, and assist in a swift integration of the diverse Soviet society. Thus, to the evils of ethnicity, regionalism/parochialism, separatism, and traditionalism, the military by means of training, education, and discipline could counterpose the values and policies of Russification, national patriotism, communization, centralization, integration, and modernization. In other words, the army, with its national network of installations, schools and bases would serve as a school for communism and would thus in a short time create the New Soviet Man. And it would do this as a by-product of its primary mission—the defense of the country—and would do it economically and systematically. The military in the Stalinist schema was to remain a giant on a leash; they were to be a privileged elite whose spokesmen were to remain mute, whose authority was to be enjoyed at the pleasure of the party leader, and who had to accept and tolerate in their midst networks of security organs, provocateurs, party agitators, and young zealots. The military was conditioned through fear of failure to practice a form of passivism and bureaucratic inertia, thus creating a generation of officers without much independence, esprit de corps, initiative, or innovative nerve. In the purges of 1937–38, Stalin struck a further devastating blow at the military, destroying their professional elan and institutional autonomy, a blow from which they did not recover until the war years. Even then, when the generals and marshals of the Red Army were returning from their victories in Germany, Stalin once again shattered the military's self-esteem and institutional strength by lecturing them that only childish people think that the laws of the artillery are stronger than the laws of history, and by demoting and banishing the most prominent among the military leaders. In the remaining years of Stalinist dictatorship, the military had to endure the megalomania of the leader, and his various forms of chicanery, repression, and humiliation.

Khrushchevite Selective Co-optation
of Military Leaders

The death of Stalin rapidly changed the rules of the game in the system and introduced new dynamics of interaction between the party and the military. Since several party leaders entered into a struggle for succession, and since the terror machine had been eliminated from the political arena with the arrest of Beria, the military found itself for the first time in a position of potential influence. Their subsequent support of Khrushchev against Malenkov gained additional influence for the military in the affairs of the state and party. With the absence of a charismatic, dominant figure at the center, the military made inroads into the important decision-making machinery of the party.

However, as long as Marshal Zhukov appeared to be the spokesman for the military, Khrushchev and the party continued to distrust the motives and objectives of the officer corps. Zhukov's view on the military's role and place in the state were anathema to the party leaders; he was a disciplinarian, a professional who was full of contempt for the party amateurs who were meddling in the military's affairs. Moreover, Zhukov enjoyed vast support among the rank and file and the officers of the Red Army, and he was a popular war hero.

Zhukov's ouster in October 1957 laid the groundwork for a more relaxed and stable form of relationship between the party and the military. A presumably loyal group of military leaders (from the Stalingrad Group) was entrusted with the leading positions in the Ministry of Defense. After the initial purge of the Zhukovites in the military, an informal sort of co-optation of the military into party affairs and decision-making processes of the state took place. Military leaders who had been killed by Stalin in the 1937 purges were rehabilitated; the military was now given preferential treatment in the budgetary allocations and in social planning; and the political control functions in the armed forces were muted.

However, this tranquil period did not last very long. Khrushchev attempted to renege on commitments made to the military and to decrease the size and role of the armed forces, thus threatening institutional empires, careers, and traditions. The relations between Khrushchev and the military continued to deteriorate after the Cuban missile crisis until his ouster in 1964.

Brezhnevite Accommodation with the Military

The Soviet military establishment entered the 1970s amid very auspicious circumstances. Internally, the military was rather quiescent and unified, and generally satisfied with its institutional role, budgetary allocations, modern weapons and technology, and freedom to manage its internal affairs without excessive interference from the party and political organs. The military also enjoyed an unprecedented period of high morale due in various ways to the growing strength and modern technology which in effect made them equal to the military establishment in the United States. Moreover, the military expanded its reach globally, through its powerful and modern navy, military–space technology, and intensified pressures in the Third World. Having challenged and overcome Khrushchev's policies both of stringent economization and strategic–political adventurism, the military was enjoying a preferential position under the leadership of Brezhnev. Its institutional and political influence was further strengthened by the growing external commitments of the Soviet state, the mounting challenge from China, the complex situation in the Middle East and Central Asia, and the protracted arms control negotiations with the United States. The Sino–Soviet conflict became a protracted, low-level military confrontation; the tempting and risky policy opportunities in the Middle East and Central Asia were premised heavily on a military calculus; and Soviet accommodations in the SALT talks were paralleled by concessions to the military by the party leadership.

The present position of the military represents the culmination of a long trend of aggregative growth of institutional strength, corporate autonomy, professional sophistication, and political influence. What are the social and political implications of this development?

The military's dominant interests, values, and preferences include a set of conservative social and political views. They prefer a society which is stable, fairly conservative, orderly, and committed to the ideas and objectives of the party. They tend to view social deviance, "liberalism," and excessive consumerism as antithetical to their own code of values, as well as detrimental to society and state. They prefer a national planning policy in which the security and strength of the state receive first priority. To be sure, the military understands the legitimating functions of ideology and revolutionary rhetoric, as well as necessary mythologies and symbolisms associated with such rhetoric and revolutionary heritage; public military statements will therefore continue to stress the primacy of ideology, the vitality of the revolutionary heritage, and the unchallenged role of the party in affairs of the society and state. The military has become a member of the coalition of bureaucracies which presently rule the Soviet Union. The original props of party hegemony (revolutionary charisma, the terror machine, a powerful leader, a committed party apparatus) are eroding and the revolutionary dynamism in the system is abating and dwindling. The people are interested in the good life, becoming increasingly consumer oriented, tending toward embourgeoisment, and party leaders have been accommodating them while at the same time pursuing superpower and imperial policies abroad. And the military has become the beneficiary of this balance between domestic stability and external activism.

THE ORIGINS AND IMPLICATIONS
OF THE EXPANDING MILITARY ROLE

Even this brief historical account of the internal roles of the military conveys a picture of its pervasive presence, institutional interpretation and expanding social, economic, and political weight within the state. How can one account for these developments and what are their implications?

The Expanding Scope of Soviet
Foreign and Defense Policies

Starting from a rather vulnerable, defensive, and contained continental position, the Soviet Union has in the past two decades expanded into the global arena on land, sea, and in space, sharply increasing its commitments abroad. The primary motor and vehicle for this expansion has been the military establishment. Soviet arms, technology, military expertise, and advisory missions have become the most effective exports and influence-building commodities of the Kremlin in the Third World, and the Soviet military is its prime beneficiary.

By the 1970s, the Soviet leadership no longer talked about weakness or vulnerability. They asserted instead that "the historical initiative is now firmly in the hands of the socialist community,"[9] and although peaceful coexistence with the West is desirable, that must not interfere with the historical revolutionary mission of the Communist party. The military in particular vigorously rejected implications that the Soviet Union was "losing interest in the peoples' liberation movement and reducing its aid to the movement,"[10] asserting that "limitation of strategic weapons does not eliminate the danger of war" and that "it would be utopian to assume that peaceful coexistence between countries with different social systems could at once rule out armed clashes . . . that is why all this talk about an end to the 'era of wars' and the arrival of an 'era of universal peace' is premature and dangerous."[11]

In rejecting the peaceful and stabilizing "linkage" implications of detente and "peaceful coexistence" the military emphasized the expansionistic thrust of Soviet foreign and military policies. The evidence, even in the stilted party jargon of *agitprop,* is persuasive enough: the basic political, ideological, and defense interests of the party and the Soviet government depend on the might of the armed forces. Despite detente, despite arms control, the struggle against imperialism will go on and the Soviets are in the vanguard of that struggle. Translated into everyday language, that means searching for targets of opportunity, particularly in the Third World, offering military assistance, seeking some kind of foothold in the process, and then trying to expand Soviet presence and influence in these vital regions.

The Soviet military has in recent years become involved in various countries in the strategically important regions of the Middle East and Africa, from Angola to Mozambique, from Ethiopia to Yemen, and from Afghanistan to Iraq. Soviet naval ships roam the oceans of the globe, while their submarines perform deterrence functions and other missions beneath. Soviet generals train the armies and military technicians of these countries and Soviet marshals negotiate with the political leaders in the name of the Politburo.

Soviet party leaders appear to be committed to a policy of military and political penetration and expansion into the Third World, and the most effective instrument for such a new imperial policy is the military. The current party leadership and the marshals and generals are in this together.

In his analysis of the post-totalitarian trends in Soviet politics, Jerry Hough maintains that the post-Khrushchev leadership of the Communist party has modified its role in society and state from a dominant to an adjudicating, arbitrating type:

> Whereas Stalin in his last years ignored the policy suggestions of the institutional centers of power, and whereas Khrushchev challenged the

basic interests of almost every one of these centers, the present leadership has not done major battle with any important segment of the establishment and seems, on the contrary, to have acceded to the most central
desires of each.[12]

The Party leadership seems to desire an untroubled status quo, to
avoid difficult or risky decisions that might threaten the delicate balance of
the bureaucratic coalition within the party and the Politburo:

> The unwillingness or inability of the present leadership to remove mem-
> bers of the administrative elite has been matched by its abstention from
> imposing any major policy change that would seriously diminish the
> status of any important institutional group.[13]

The leadership is seen to "assume the role not of the major policy initiator
but of a broker mediating competing claims of powerful interests."[14] And
the party over which this gerontocracy presides has changed drastically in
its makeup, membership, role and vitality. In its drive to broaden the base
of the party, to make it a party of all the people, the leadership risks the
danger that "the legitimacy of the party as instrument of the proletariat will
be undermined," since it is "totally impossible for such a party to be some
kind of priesthood that stands outside of society." Rather, it must be one
where approximately "30% of all citizens with completed higher education
in 1973 were Party members, and over 50% of the men with such an education"[15] belonged to it.

Although one need not accept all of these developments as contribut-
ing factors to the decline of the party's authority and legitimacy, nevertheless in aggregate they convey the inexorable momentum of decline of the
hegemony of the party. Milovan Djilas, whose insights about the ideological decay of communist parties are both perceptive and authoritative, thus
describes the dominant new class of the *apparatchiki:*

> The heroic era of communism is past. The epoch of its great leaders has
> ended. The epoch of practical men has set in. The new class has been
> created. It is at the height of its power and wealth, but it is without new
> ideas. It has nothing more to tell the people. The only thing that remains
> is for it to justify itself.[16]

Problems of Hegemonial Authority:
Party Succession and the Military

In his study of civil–military relations in several political systems, Michael Howard observed that "in States where no orderly transition of power and obedience had yet been established . . . military force is the final and sometimes only arbiter in government."[17] In the Soviet case, problems of transition of power in the party and the state represent a key source of instability and institutional tensions that contributes to the erosion of the party's legitimacy and authority within the state.

A change of leadership in the Soviet Union is not a process governed by either tradition or established rules. No party leader has ever voluntarily relinquished his powers, and no provisions exist for the transfer of authority should the incumbent die or be removed as a result of disability or political coercion. This serves to explain why Lenin's infirmity and death, Trotsky's forced removal, and Stalin's death proved to be such critical events. A grave leadership crisis can also be expected to arise from an intra-party coup resulting from realignments of political relationships and loyalties among representatives of those institutions that carry the main political weight in the state. The former leader then finds himself with a fait accompli engineered by his opponents, to which he has no choice but to submit. This was the case, though to varying degrees, in the ousters of both Malenkov and Khrushchev.

There is, however, a basic difference in the leadership changes since the death of Stalin. Several party leaders compete for the top position thus enabling an institution outside the party apparatus to serve as an arbiter and adjudicator of the leadership competition. That institution is the military, or more specifically, the top leadership of the armed forces. This involvement of the military in the heretofore sacrosanct internal affairs of the party has fundamentally affected the relations between the party and the military. The scramble for the military's support and the subsequent need to reward the military for that support, has undoubtedly impressed the marshals and generals in the post-Stalinist state. Although the consequences of that politicized role of the military have not been fully understood, there is little doubt that party leaders will continue to pay careful attention to the military's basic interests and preferences lest they ignore them at their own peril. The Malenkov and Khrushchev episodes are instructive cases in point as we briefly review the political maturation of the Soviet military, their initially tentative and timid steps into the political arena, and the subsequent growth of their institutional strength and mounting demands on the party.

Military Demands

The military's interests and demands are threefold:

Resource Primacy. The military seeks assurance that their needs of technology, weapons, and associated capabilities will receive the highest priority in the nationally planned economy, assuring a steady flow of such resources into the military establishment. This demand is usually contained in the code words "heavy industry," which was once spelled out by Marshal Zhukov: "Above all, the major achievements of heavy industry have permitted us to rearm our army, air forces and navy with first class military materiel."[18] Thus, both in the post-Stalinist succession crisis and in the post-Khrushchev succession period the military loudly proclaimed its "heavy industry" priorities.

Mission Rationale. The military clearly prefers a set of foreign and defense policies that assign a major role to the defense sector by conveying a sense of threat expectation from outside. This need for "international tension" is again reflected in the post-Stalin power struggles with predictable results. Malenkov pushed for a relaxation of tensions, for a detente with the West, arguing that nuclear war would be suicidal since there would be no victors or survivors. Khrushchev sharply rejected this at the time, pushing hard for a tough, blustering and uncompromising strategic and political doctrine that rejected detente and peaceful coexistence proposals and spoke instead of final victory and the destruction of the bloodied capitalists.

Payoffs and Concessions. Once Khrushchev got rid of Malenkov in February 1955, the military was accorded a number of highly desired and awaited concessions: long postponed promotions to the highest ranks, rehabilitation of purged military heroes, rewriting of history so as to assign the military a heroic and vital role as defender of the country; promotion of a number of military officers to the Central Committee and other party bodies; curtailment of political organs in the military and reduction of their representation in party bodies; and the steady promotion of Marshal Zhukov, the most popular military leader and war hero, out of his Stalin-consigned obscurity until he was Minister of Defense and a full member of the sacrosanct Politburo.

Consequences of Military "Succession Management"

The three-decade period of post-Stalin party–military politics in the Soviet Union suggests that the two institutions have become thoroughly interdependent and that they interpenetrate each other to a remarkable extent. The military has come to the support of party leaders on a number of occasions, aiding in intra-party struggles and in conflicts with other Communist challengers from abroad. The military has also assumed a number of key roles and positions within the system, including those of:

- the main instrument and supporter of expanding Soviet external military and political commitments to clients and proxies in Africa, the Middle East, and Asia;
- the key stabilizing factor in the restless alliance system in Eastern Europe, where in the final analysis only the military restores order, punishes opponents, and serves as the policeman on the beat;
- the main bulwark against the pressures and demands from the former Chinese ally; and
- the educator, national integrator, and disciplined Spartan model for the restless and diverse, young and old, from the various geographic, linguistic, national, religious, and class-based sectors of society.

THE PROTRACTED BREZHNEV SUCCESSION AND THE MILITARY

The Soviet Union, which has been ruled by only three men during the preceding half century, has in the past two years seen three different leaders in the Kremlin, each old, ill, and feeble. And it is likely that still another leader will replace the current occupant in the Kremlin before too long. The stability and durability of the Stalin, Khrushchev, and Brezhnev regimes have given way to a spectacle of gerontocracy on parade. The implications of these developments to the Soviet political process and practice are profound indeed; however, our concern here is primarily with the impact of these developments on the Soviet military.

The Soviet military was the Brezhnev regime's favorite institution and enjoyed uninterrupted institutional growth and expansion through a "siphon system"[19] that could pump from the civilian sector whatever resources the Politburo decided the military needed. The three bodies comprising this military siphon system gave the defense establishment vast authority at the apex of the Soviet power structure:

- The Military Industrial Commission, chaired by the deputy chairman of the Council of Ministers, provides a central focus and management for military requirements within the state economic bureaucracy;
- The General Staff of the Armed Forces generates the military doctrines that dictate military requirements;
- The Defense Industries Section of the Central Committee Secretariat provides the Politburo with party supervision over the defense sector.

With the Defense Council providing overall leadership and direction for the entire process, the military's influence in this "iron triangle" of Soviet industrial–military–party bureaucracies became ever more powerful during the Brezhnev regime.

And yet there seems to be general agreement among specialists on the Soviet Union that the Soviet military was becoming progressively more dissatisfied with Brezhnev's policies in the late 1970s, and this motivated them to support Andropov's candidacy as Brezhnev's successor rather than Brezhnev's favorite, Konstantin Chernenko. The final years of the Brezhnev regime were generally characterized by immobility, and a pervasive reluctance to confront and deal with several important decisions in Soviet domestic and foreign policies. On the domestic front, economic entropy became the dominant trend, aggravated by widespread corruption, lax labor discipline, declining levels of productivity, a burgeoning second economy, and a persistent drain of vital resources from the civilian to the defense sectors.

The general line of Soviet foreign policy at the end of the Brezhnev era was passivity, retrenchment, a low profile, and a tendency to exploit the peace issue—that is, to use the "carrot" rather than the "stick."[20] Faced with the decline of detente, with the hardline Reagan rhetoric, a general hardening of the U.S. position vis-à-vis the Soviet Union, and an upsurge in U.S. defense programs coupled with the threat of deploying new missiles in Europe, the Brezhnev leadership chose the path of least resistance and avoided testing this new U.S. resolve and toughness, following instead a policy of vacillation. These undesirable foreign policy developments were further complicated by deteriorating situations in Poland, Afghanistan, and the Middle East.

This deterioration of Soviet foreign policy and Brezhnev's unwillingness or inability to firmly confront and deal with these challenges caused
some soul-searching and private criticism in the institutions most directly
affected by it (namely, the military, the foreign affairs establishment, and
the intelligence and security agencies) and resulted finally in a well-pub-
licized meeting in the Kremlin between the ailing Brezhnev and his military
high command. That this meeting was arranged at the demand of the military was evident from the opening lines of Brezhnev's statement in which he
noted that it was "with great satisfaction that I accepted the proposal of
Dmitri Ustinov for meeting the command personnel of the armed forces."
He went on to assure his listeners that the Soviet Union was capable and
willing to meet any challenges and threats from the capitalist world and that
he personally was on top of things: "I constantly handle matters of the army
and navy in the performance of my official duties, so to say, and know
about the state of affairs."[21] This Kremlin meeting with the military brass
(which prompted the *New York Times* to observe that "diplomats could not
recall a previous occasion when a Soviet leader felt obliged to offer such
public assurances to his military"[22]) was intended both to reassure the
military and to convey a tough policy line to the United States, China, and
other potential challengers of the Soviet Union.

The Soviet military's attitudes toward Brezhnev are strikingly similar
in many respects to those toward Khrushchev and Malenkov. Since the
death of Stalin, who had ruthlessly controlled and coerced the military
along with other institutions in the state, the military seems to have had a
love–hate relationship with each successive party leader. In each case, the
military initially sympathized with and supported the party leader until he
subsequently challenged several basic interests of the military, whereupon
the generals and marshals turned against him and transferred their support
to his challenger and successor. These fundamental institutional interests
of the military establishment are:

- the primacy of defense requirements in the planning of the national economy
- social discipline and order, labor discipline and order
- firm, coherent, and non-accommodating foreign policy that projects a
  hard image of the Soviet state in the international arena

In each case, after an initial period of military rapport and support, the party
leader found it necessary to change national priorities and in doing so challenged these basic military interests. Malenkov announced that nuclear war

was madness, and he argued for an East–West detente and for a reduction of defense spending accompanied by higher investments in non-defense sectors of the economy. He was rather quickly ousted from power. Khrushchev succeeded Malenkov and initially endeared himself to the military because he publicly championed their cause. But eventually he went the same route as his predecessor; he embarked on "harebrained" foreign policy adventures and after they failed became an ardent supporter of detente, arguing for consumer interests and more balanced defense expenditures. Khrushchev also tolerated relatively permissive social policies and corruption. This same pattern was repeated by Brezhnev, who came into power with the strong support of the military, and who became their most generous benefactor in memory. In the end, the military turned against him: most probably because of the incompetence, corruption, and passivity, and general policy drift which offended them and threatened their interests.

It is therefore not surprising that the Soviet military turned toward Andropov as a successor to Brezhnev. The former head of the KGB was known to be firmly set against the internal decay and corruption prevalent in Soviet society, and was assumed to be a strong supporter of a firm and coherent foreign policy based on credible military capabilities—a man who dealt quickly and firmly with recalcitrant allies in Eastern Europe, and finally, a party leader who eschewed the megalomania of other leaders who fostered their own personality cults at the expense of other institutions and leaders within the system.

We shall never know what kind of leadership Andropov would have provided for the Soviet Union; however, there is little doubt that at least at the outset he would have been strongly supported by the military, who saw in him at last the kind of political leader who was suitable for a nuclear superpower. It is doubtful that the party hack and Brezhnev loyalist Chernenko is likely to fit that role, and it is therefore not too precipitous to assume that the Chernenko succession is already under way, and that the Soviet generals and marshals are privately considering his likely successor.

CONCLUSION

The logic of the post-totalitarian rule and the imperial expansion of the Soviet state have endowed the military with vital tasks and roles. As the party leadership has become more dependent on the military for internal, alliance, and external policy purposes, and as the military has shown itself to be a loyal, conservative, and stable force within the state, the party has become in a sense the captive of the military. The party leadership's insistence on a protracted internal status quo and avoidance of hard choices and risky decisions has forced them to support, mollify, and rely on the military. There is no alternative institution to perform these varied tasks in a responsible and loyal way. The party and the military have become mutual captives; they need one another and they cannot let go for there are no viable alternatives. Only a systemic change or a radical regime change might break that interdependence.

NOTES

1. Among the many analysts subscribing to this view of the Soviet military I would single out General William Odom, whose various publications over the years honed this perception into an institutional dogma. William Odom, "Choice and Change in Soviet Politics," *Problems of Communism,* 32 (May–June 1983): 14.

2. Engels in a letter to Marx, cited in Reinhard Hoehn, *Sozialismus und Herr,* vol. 1 (Berlin: Gehlen Verlag, 1961), p. 44.

3. Cited in Bernard Semmel, *Marxism and the Science of War* (New York: Oxford University Press, 1981), p. 189.

4. Ibid., p. 191.

5. *Newsweek,* November 29, 1982, p. 31.

6. Edgar Ulsamer, "Will Economic Weakness Increase Soviet Militancy?" *Air Force Magazine* 66 (March 1983): 41.

7. Cited in Roman Kolkowicz, *The Soviet Military and the Communist Party,* (Princeton: Princeton University Press, 1967), p. 2.

8. Ibid.

9. V. Korionov, "The Socialist Policy of Peace," *Pravda,* July 13, 1972.

10. Ibid.

11. Ibid.

12. Jerry F. Hough, *The Soviet Union and Social Science Theory* (Cambridge: Harvard University Press, 1977), p. 28.

13. Ibid., p. 29.

14. Ibid.

15. Ibid., p. 7.

16. Milovan Djilas, "The New Class" cited in *Essential Works of Marxism,* A.P. Mendel, ed. (New York: Bantam Books, Matrix edition, 1965), p. 332.

17. Michael Howard, *Soldiers and Governments: Nine Studies in Civil–Military Relations* (London: Eyre and Spottiswoode, 1957), Introduction.

18. *Pravda,* February 23, 1955.

19. Odom, "Choice and Change," p. 11.

20. Seweryn Bialer, "The Soviet Union and the West in the 1980s: Detente, Containment, or Confrontation?" *ORBIS* 27 (Spring 1983): 43.

21. *New York Times,* October 28, 1982.

22. Ibid.

5

SOVIET LEGAL POLICY UNDER ANDROPOV: LAW AND DISCIPLINE

Robert Sharlet

The Western discussion of Andropov's legacy has begun and will no doubt continue for some time. Early entries in the emerging debate suggest a failed leader unable to launch needed economic reform due to lack of time, a resistant bureaucracy, the "shooting down" of the reform coalition by the Korean plane incident, or all of the above. A less ambitious line holds that reform was never the issue, that merely "perfecting" the economic mechanism was the limited undertaking which was cut short by Andropov's failing health.[1] Yet another view argues that on the eve of his death in early 1984, his men were in place in the higher party apparatus, poised to push through a major turnover of the regional Brezhnev–Chernenko old guard while a new, younger, more competent governmental team was waiting in the wings for its cue to move economic reform centerstage.[2]

Ancillary to his efforts on the economic front, whether they be deemed failed, limited, or forthcoming, it is generally conceded that Andropov did launch a "discipline" campaign. However, there appears to be no consensus as to its results. Was it "cosmetic" and doomed to fail in the face of entrenched corruption in the system and society,[3] or was it responsive to a popular yearning for "order" and hence responsible for the gains in labor productivity in 1983?[4] Even the duration of the discipline campaign is in dispute; did it wane in the spring of 1983,[5] or was it under way throughout Andropov's brief incumbency?[6] All of these perspectives neglect to pay adequate attention to the scope of Andropov's concept of discipline, the breadth and intensity of his campaign, and, especially, the extraordinary task of reconstructing and revitalizing the legal infrastructure of the Soviet system carried out under his aegis.

85

THE USSR AT THE END OF THE BREZHNEV
ERA: DIAGNOSING THE PROBLEMS

What domestic problems would have caught the eye of General Secretary Andropov at the end of the Brezhnev era in late 1982? Surely, as a former KGB chief and self-styled disciplinarian, he no doubt realized he had inherited a pre-modern, even feudal society in which

> Local political elites tithe collective and state farms and all other producers and vendors of consumables within their fiefs. The sale of offices and pardons is not unheard of, reminiscent of the medieval Church, and the most significant economic relations are frequently at the level of barter. The population is stratified along nearly rigid caste lines based on one's proximity to power or access to ever scarce consumer goods. This is a world of perpetual shortage in which almost everyone's energies are focused on the quest for the essentials of everyday life.[7]

From his vantage point, he surely knew that everything was for sale, even academic grades and university admissions, including admission to law schools. Large parts of the higher educational system were just another branch of the vast, largely illegal "second economy" whose leading indicators included the high volume of pilferage of consumer goods from the national rail freight system and the wholesale "diversion" of foodstuffs from public catering establishments and retail food stores.

Undoubtedly, as a Politburo member, Andropov had been privy to confidential surveys which showed a surprising degree of public tolerance and even support for "second economic" behavior officially regarded as crimes, including a most "conciliatory attitude" toward petty theft of public property.[8] Less surprising to a person with Andropov's regular access to classified information but equally dismaying would have been the secret tabulations of crime statistics which reflected these negative public attitudes in action, in such data as convictions for theft of public property and certain "economic crimes" constituting 21–22% of all crime.[9]

In the interstices of the crime data one could detect a burgeoning rate of vandalism of, say, public pay phones and a still minor but troubling trend of burglary and armed robbery for the purpose of obtaining narcotics.[10] Both of these crimes testify to the rampant juvenile delinquency problem throughout the Union, of which the average fearful and angry Soviet adult was well aware and frequently complained of in thousands of letters to the press, rarely noted publicly in Brezhnev's day.

Andropov, however, would have known that teenagers and young adults were not the sole source of concern. He and his colleagues were probably appalled at the incidence of train crashes and boat accidents caused by drunken engineers and helmsmen, not to mention the mounting and costly accident rate among private car owners as a result of mixing drinking with driving. There would be the troubling reports marked for official eyes only on the level of violence by criminal convicts in the prisons and camps, and their comrades, the career criminals and recidivists back on the streets of the cities and towns. Compounding these already difficult problems, Andropov, as a former KGB man, would most assuredly be cognizant of the real state of affairs in the Ministry of Internal Affairs, the courts, and the Procuracy in Brezhnev's last years. At best he would know that routine law enforcement work had fallen to a low level in many local agencies, with indifference, apathy, and even incompetence increasingly becoming the norm among militia workers or ordinary policemen. At worst he probably felt indignation toward those legal officials for whom the administration of justice had become yet another branch of the ubiquitous second economy, and justice a cash commodity.[11]

Last but not least, in his survey of the country he was to lead into the 1980s, the new general secretary's eye would most assuredly come to rest on the most prevalent and perhaps the potentially most subversive problem of all—chronic indiscipline at work, in particular absenteeism, tardiness, and leaving work early. Just one of the available surveys of the Moscow region alone where goods and services are in greater supply and more readily available than elsewhere, would have revealed to him that in some factories and offices "no more than 10% of the workers were at their places during the final hour of the shift," and that throughout the region 73% of the work force take time off during working hours to take care of personal business.[12] As a reportedly intelligent leader, Andropov recognized the linkage between work indiscipline, inefficiency, low productivity, poor quality control, a declining economic growth rate, and back once again to the beginning of the cycle "a world of perpetual shortage."[13]

INTERIM REMEDIES: 1980–1982

During his two last years in power, Brezhnev and his associates (including Andropov) attempted to cope with some of the myriad internal problems, but his age and failing health prevented him from providing the personal leadership and sense of urgency needed for success. Although individually the proposed remedies were sound and probably to some extent even bore the imprint of Politburo member Andropov's disciplinarian bent, they tended to fragment into isolated, ad hoc reactions to specific situations. Lacking any programmatic coherence and direction, the Brezhnevist remedies proved at best to be interim holding actions.

Ironically, the Brezhnev leadership's drive against corruption was stimulated by events in Poland. The Polish crisis of 1980 was naturally a major source of concern to the Soviet Union, but that story is well known. What is less well known was the influence of the independent trade union Solidarity's success on the concern for corruption in the USSR. On August 31, 1980, Lech Walesa representing Solidarity, and a Polish deputy prime minister signed the Gdansk Agreement, signaling Solidarity's victory after a summer of strikes and negotiations. Two of the 21 demands agreed to by the government were intended to eliminate certain material privileges by the party elite and police personnel.

The principal cause for the Soviet reaction to their own corruption problem, however, was probably the case of Maciej Szczepanski, a member of the Polish Central Committee and chairman of the State Radio and Television Committee. Dismissed from his government post on August 24, Szczepanski became the object of a special high-level investigation on September 4. What followed was the disclosure of the most extraordinary case of official corruption ever made public in a Communist country. Using public funds, Szczepanski had acquired seven cars, a helicopter, two executive aircraft, a luxury yacht equipped with a stable, a mountain villa, a large collection of x-rated movies, and a 16-room palace complete with resident prostitutes. Gierek fell from power, the Polish party opened a campaign against corruption in its ranks, and Szczepanski was, predictably, arrested, tried, and convicted after a long trial.[14]

The Szczepanski case must have caused consternation among the Soviet elite, because in September 1980 the Central Committee quickly passed a resolution on how to deal with official corruption. However, it was distributed to lower party organizations in the form of a secret party circular and never made public, indicating the party's reluctance to deal with such a sensitive issue openly, and by means of legal action. For the most part then, the anti-corruption campaign aimed at officials was treated as an internal party matter, except for a few cases that achieved national notoriety, such as the "Great Caviar Scandal."[15]

In spite of the party's concern over corruption in its ranks, the only significant legislative response during the interim period was addressed to rank-and-file personnel in the retail trade and service organizations such as clerks in stores selling consumer items, food service employees, and others who would extort under-the-counter payments for scarce goods or services,[16] or sell or conceal for personal gain goods under their control.[17] Both of these new rules were added to the criminal law in 1981. The former rule under the unwieldy title "Receipt of Illegal Remuneration from Citizens for Fulfillment of Work Connected with Servicing the Populace" was aimed at those employees who demand an advance "tip" for selling a scarce consumer item or performing a service, and imposes punishment from "correctional work" for up to a year (usually a pay reduction of 10% or more for the duration of the sentence, served at one's place of work) or a fine, to three years imprisonment. The latter rule, "Violation of Trade Rules," was intended for those warehouse or restaurant employees who sell goods or foodstuffs entrusted to them "out the back door" so to speak and pocket the money, and related offenses, and entails punishment from up to a year of correctional work with or without deprivation of the right to work in that particular job, to three years imprisonment.

Up to 1981, only officials were liable under the law for taking bribes and subject to harsh punishments, including even the death penalty under especially aggravating circumstances,[18] while illegal diversion of goods for personal gain was considered "abuse of authority or official position."[19] Under the new rules, subordinates as well were now liable, although with commensurately milder penalties. In this way, and by amending the law on petty theft of public property to include the stealing of parts of automobiles by dismantling them while in transit as freight or in storage,[20] the Brezhnev regime attempted to close several loopholes through which commodities flowed into the underground second economy. A number of cases brought under the new and amended rules, were publicized in the press in 1981–82 to deter others. However, the party's secret circular and legal maneuvers were disjointed and without focus, and at best were stop-gap measures as the problem of pervasive corruption continued to plague Brezhnev's final years.

A year later during the summer of 1982, the all-Union fundamental principles for legislation on criminal law and corrective-labor law, or penitentiary law, were amended. The changes and additions were long overdue. After the ratification of the new USSR constitution in 1977, a five-year legislative plan was formulated and published by the Presidium of the Supreme Soviet for implementing the provisions of the constitution through recodification, revision by amendment, and altogether new legislation. Most of this work was scheduled for completion by 1978–79, with only six of the 34 projects projected for 1980–82.[21] By the end of 1979 many of the projects were not completed, the plan was well behind schedule, and the Presidium found it necessary to publicly admonish the USSR minister of justice, V.I. Terebilov, who was responsible for coordinating the plan.[22] A year later, in early 1981, the Presidium found it again necessary to address Terebilov on the delays, and on the need to improve the quality of the drafting work already done. The minister was ordered to report back to the Presidium on January 1, 1982.[23]

The revision of the criminal and corrective-labor legislative principles had been two of the projects originally scheduled for completion no later than the end of 1979, but like so much else during Brezhnev's latter years, things did not go as planned. Two and a half years later, in July 1982, these amendments (except for one liberalizing change) meant that convicted persons serving sentences other than imprisonment, parolees, and recidivists were to be brought under the much tighter control of the authorities while serving their sentences or probation.[24]

The single change involved extending the use of deferred or "stayed" sentences for juvenile first offenders to adult first offenders sentenced to no more than three years imprisonment.[25] Generally, the Russian Republic Ministry of Justice reported that the past five years' experience with deferring or staying execution of sentences of juveniles had been highly encouraging in that no further crimes were committed by the great majority of minors.[26]

The rest of the amendments involved increasing the maximum corrective work sentence to two years, and substantially raising the ceilings on the maximum fines imposable for all crimes that incur corrective work or fines as punishment. New provisions were also added for dealing with convicted persons who either shirk serving their corrective work sentence or fail to pay fines.[27]

In addition, the rules governing conditional (suspended) sentences and conditional release (parole) were strengthened to avoid and punish for abuses of these procedures. In the latter case, parole was denied altogether to two new categories of prisoners: double recidivists and persons committing offenses while on previous parole.[28] Finally, related changes were made in the corrective labor legislation concerning individuals serving suspended sentences or on parole with the obligation to work under specified conditions. The effect was to increase police control over such individuals and enlarge the range of penalties for infractions.[29]

One last edict on criminal justice legislation bearing Brezhnev's signature as chairman of the Presidium was published in the official law gazette on October 15, 1982, just weeks before his death. This final edict on the subject testifies eloquently to the belated, ad hoc, and fragmented approach to legislation on the criminal justice process during the last two years of his administration. The edict, which was probably rushed through to appear before the November anniversary of the Bolshevik Revolution, shows signs of haste and carelessness in legislative draftsmanship.

The main purpose of the October edict was to bring the 10 USSR edicts on criminal and administrative liability for various crimes and administrative violations (which provide for corrective work or fines) issued over the previous two decades 1961–81, into conformity with the summer amendments raising the ceilings on those two penalties. These criminal edicts cover such diverse offenses as report padding, unwarranted train stopping, hooliganism, and assault on a policeman or police auxiliary. The same realignment of penalties was accomplished for the several relevant articles of the USSR Statute on Criminal Liability for State Crimes of 1958.[30] This updating was to be expected since the summer amendments were to go into effect on January 1, 1983.

However, the fall edict was also used as a vehicle to insert omissions in the summer edict. For instance, four more articles of the all-Union criminal legislative principles were slightly revised by semantic changes such as "new crime" instead of "new intentional crime" that had already been made in related articles by the summer edict. The parole provision of the corrective-labor legislation principles, which had been amended in three different parts by the summer edict, was additionally amended in yet another part.[31] The earlier official concern about quality control in the legislative drafting process still seemed warranted in late 1982. This manner of incremental amendment as an afterthought suggested the absence of a clear policy as well as a consistent and systematic approach to the possible remedies for many of the problems besetting the Soviet Union under Brezhnev.

The general malaise afflicting the Soviet system was probably best epitomized by the slogans for the 65th anniversary of the Bolshevik revolution, echoing the familiar themes of a tired administration devoid of ideas and energy, and facing a troubled future with little left to offer the public other than ideological rhetoric.[32]

ANDROPOV TAKES CHARGE: CAMPAIGNING FOR DISCIPLINE

Almost immediately following Brezhnev's death on November 10, 1982, Andropov took charge, sounding the clarion call of "discipline" as the *leitmotiv* for his administration. Not since Khrushchev's campaign for de-Stalinization had a Soviet leader so clearly enunciated a "metalegal" policy for his stewardship of the Soviet system. By this, I am referring to Andropov's general political theme of discipline, a policy of systemwide scope which significantly impacted the process of regulating Soviet society as well as the system itself.[33]

While emphasizing continuity and legitimating his program with references to Marx, the 26th Party Congress, and current Central Committee resolutions, Andropov set a course for change.[34] His goals were ambitious—to regenerate the immobilist system, reawaken a dormant society, and reinfuse the "old" Soviet Man with a new sense of discipline. Key to all his goals, his systemic concept of discipline embraced executive, planning, labor, and diverse aspects of social discipline, including even the observance of traffic safety rules.[35] In his brief remarks at a Moscow factory in December 1982, he made it clear that the drive to reinstall discipline would include ministers as well as workers.[36] As the campaign unfolded during 1983, it came to include party secretaries, government officials, prosecutors, policemen, and, of course, the man in the street.

Andropov did not see his prescription of discipline as the panacea for all of the Soviet Union's ills. It was merely a first essential step which he hoped would stimulate higher labor productivity, better quality control, a faster economic growth rate, and ultimately, a rise in the standard of living and a more efficient political and economic system.[37] This was a tall order which he realized could not be accomplished "by slogans alone."[38] To set in motion these broad social changes, Andropov turned to Soviet law; "implacable" law would be his instrument for social engineering.[39]

In relying on law to translate his vision of a "disciplined" developed socialist society into reality, Andropov was in the mainstream of the post-Stalin period. With the abandonment of terror, Stalin's successors increasingly relied on law to govern an ever more complex and differentiated Soviet society. Khrushchev and Brezhnev each made major contributions to this post-Stalin tradition, as they progressively built the Soviet-type *Rechtsstaat*, or legal state, through which the party rules today. Andropov continued this tradition, but with some notable differences. Khrushchev had refurbished the tarnished concept of "socialist legality," giving it a connotation of anti-arbitrariness. Brezhnev shifted to a more pragmatic anti-deviance emphasis.[40] Both had built their legal structures gradually over time, and both had reasonable expectations as to what the law could accomplish after years of Stalinism on the one hand, and the persistence of an urban industrial crime problem on the other.

By contrast, Andropov refashioned socialist legality into a pro-discipline instrument, reflecting greater confidence in the efficacy of law in general, and, in the short space of 15 months, carried out more legal changes than had been seen since the onset of the post-Stalin legal reforms in the late 1950s and early 1960s. Andropov's prolific legislative output and process of institutional revitalization encompassed criminal, labor, and administrative law as well as the police, the Procuracy, and even the law schools.

To be sure, the party-state under Andropov did not legislate in a vacuum. Some legislation flowing from the still unfulfilled legislative plan of 1977 had been in the "pipeline" when Andropov took charge. This was certainly true of many of the extensive revisions in the criminal codes of the Union republics. However, a number of significant changes in these codes, not foreshadowed by the 1982 summer and fall amendments to the fundamental principles of criminal legislation, tend to suggest that Andropov had a hand in the criminal law revisions even though he took office at a late hour in the drafting process.

In fact, the long delays in fulfilling parts of Brezhnev's 1977 legislative plan may have been beneficial to Andropov, affording him the opportunity of putting his imprimatur on the drafting process. Such was the case with the USSR Statute on Labor Collectives, mandated by the new constitution of 1977 and scheduled in the follow-up legislative plan for early 1980.[41] When it was finally passed nearly three and a half years late in mid-1983, the statute bore the imprint of Andropov's discipline campaign, especially in Article 9.[42]

Even in instances where legislative revision had occurred under Brezhnev, such as in the USSR Statute on Criminal Liability for State Crimes, further substantial revisions were carried out under Andropov not long after.[43]

As final testimony to Andropov's penchant for social engineering through law, a good deal of the legislation for implementing his discipline policy had not been provided for in Brezhnev's 1982 legislative plan for the years 1983–85, and hence was conceived during Andropov's tenure as party leader.[44]

LEGISLATING FOR DISCIPLINE: THE ANDROPOV RECORD

Andropov's first order of business in the campaign for discipline was to place trusted and tested men, disciplinarians like himself, in key positions. His major cadre changes in December 1982 were clear indications of the direction he would take. Shchelokov, the long-time USSR minister for internal affairs and a Brezhnev crony, was sacked, subsequently dropped from the Central Committee, and expelled from the party on the basis of his poor management of the police ministry and rumored allegations that he was personally involved in corruption as well. Fedorchuk, Andropov's successor as KGB chairman in the spring of 1982, was named Shchelokov's replacement as head of the uniformed police. The appointment of Fedorchuk, a career KGB professional, immediately signaled a tough new attitude toward ordinary crime. Subsequently, Fedorchuk installed his own men, former KGB associates, as his deputies.[45] Chebrikov, another seasoned KGB official, became the new chief of the secret police. In another dramatic move, Aliyev, also formerly a senior KGB official (whose reputation of managerial prowess as a party leader in the Caucasus preceded him to Moscow), was elevated from a candidate to a full voting member of the Politburo. Not long after, Aliyev was appointed first deputy prime minister behind the aging Tikhonov, a Brezhnev man. Aliyev's successful assault on corruption in the Azerbaidzhan economy during the last months of the Brezhnev era in the fall of 1982 would prove to be a precursor for Andropov's nationwide drive for discipline.[46] The team of Andropov, Aliyev, Fedorchuk, and Chebrikov meant that the "new puritans" were in command in Moscow, ready to wage war against crime, corruption, and indiscipline.

The general staff of the discipline campaign very quickly had in hand new weapons with which to conduct the struggle. Effective January 1, 1983, the most extensive revisions of the post-Stalin criminal codes since their inception in 1960 went into effect. In the Special Part (which defines the specific crimes) of the Russian Republic code, the model for all other Union republic codes, 133 of the 246 articles had been amended in December 1982. The most heavily amended chapters covered the crimes against public and "personal" or private property.

In response to widespread public concern and anger over the crime problem expressed in thousands of letters to the Politburo and the press,[47] Andropov added a half dozen new crimes and increased the punishments for dozens of other crimes. The new crimes of theft, stealing, and robbery of public or private property, accompanied by "forcible entry" into a residence, office building, or warehouse, were introduced, with penalties ranging from two to eight years imprisonment plus the confiscation of the offender's personal property.[48]

While penalties were reduced for less than a dozen offenses including performing an illegal abortion, violations of authors' and inventors' rights, and moonshining,[49] the penalties for scores of other crimes were increased. Wherever the sanction of corrective work was provided for, the maximum was raised to two years, consistent with antecedent legislation. Where fines were indicated as an alternate punishment, the amounts were doubled and tripled, probably in acknowledgement to some extent of hidden inflation in the Soviet economy. In some of the articles of the code where the judge could use his or her discretion on supplementary punishments such as confiscation of property, the option was deleted and the penalty made mandatory. Generally most "Official Crimes," "Economic Crimes," and crimes against persons were assigned heavier penalties.

Special problem areas for the new law and order drive (such as petty theft of public property and social parasitism) received separate legislative attention, also effective with the new year 1983. A person committing petty theft (for example, at his factory, where it is most common) could now be deprived of certain fringe benefits such as bonuses and vacation time in addition to facing criminal charges.[50] In regard to the offense of parasitism, certain key qualifying criteria for a *corpus delicti* were deleted, greatly increasing the potential applicability of this vague violation of the work ethic in Soviet society.[51]

Juvenile delinquency, a persistent problem, also came in for increased attention during 1983, with the press drawing thousands of letters from irate citizens in response to published accounts of especially heinous crimes by minors. The general theme has been a call for tougher sanctions against juvenile lawbreakers. The public perception reported in the press has been that they are treated too leniently by the authorities, which by midyear was sounding like a party-contrived prologue to a possible forthcoming legislative revision of the use of suspended sentences and other nonconfinement measures against juveniles.[52]

In the same vein, discussions in the press have called for sterner measures in the reform schools, where internal order apparently leaves much to be desired. Nostalgic references are heard to the methods of Anton Makarenko, a strict but effective pedagogue of discipline for delinquents during the 1920s and 1930s.[53] The Politburo also warmly praised the *druzhinny* or volunteer police auxiliaries on the eve of their 25th anniversary in early 1984.[54] This may have been intended to presage a strengthening of this organization for future redeployment in the struggle against criminals and delinquents.

As the year 1983 wore on, Andropov's legislative prescriptions for social ills became harsher. The effort to instill greater discipline was extended to the corrective labor camps, to arrangements for parole, to practicing or would-be dissidents, and to those who might pass "official secrets" to foreigners.

Beginning October 1, 1983, imprisoned convicts, who had previously been punished by being sent to a corrective labor camp's internal prison, ran the risk of courting an additional sentence of up to three years if they were tried in the camps for the new crime of "malicious disobedience" or "any other opposition" to the lawful demands of the camp administration.[55] Similarly, after release from imprisonment the convict found the rules of administrative supervision over released convicts completely revamped and much stricter.[56]

As for the small dissident community in the Soviet Union, their activities have been at a low ebb during the past few years with stern taskmasters such as Andropov, Fedorchuk, and Chebrikov consecutively at the helm of the KGB. Their position has appreciably worsened since the United States imposed economic sanctions over Afghanistan and Poland, leaving the Soviet authorities with little to lose for cracking down on the human rights movement.[57] The extensive revision of criminal law, in force since the beginning of 1983, also encompassed the political crime articles under which dissidents have been most frequently "sentenced and tried."[58] Prosecution for defamation of the Soviet system now can cost more. The three-year maximum term of imprisonment remained, but consistent with previous legislation, the maximum for corrective work or a fine was respectively increased from one to two years and from 100 to 300 rubles. As a matter of course, these milder alternatives are rarely applied to dissidents (who are invariably sentenced to imprisonment), so that this change presents no serious threat to the already beleaguered dissident community. The same would be true of the related article, also amended, on organizing group disorder, say outside a courthouse where a political trial is taking place.[59] The same increases in corrective work penalties applied to the two articles of the code under which religious dissidents are most frequently brought to trial. Here the raising of the penalty is more consequential because local authorities have frequently used repeated fines in a confiscatory manner as an alternative in many cases to imprisonment.[60]

The infamous Article 70 ("Anti-Soviet Agitation and Propaganda"), or the crime of subversion, was also amended as part of an edict decreed in January 1984, just a few weeks before Andropov's death. In a perverse way, one could say revision was overdue for this much-used weapon against dissidents, since it had remained unaltered since 1961, well before the emergence of the contemporary Soviet human rights movement in the mid to late 1960s. The thrust of the amendment has been to outline more precisely the definition of what constitutes subversion. The general term "literature" as one of the media for subverting the republic has now been replaced by the more differentiated phrase "written, printed" or other forms of work of similar subversive content. Presumably, this was meant to reflect the realities of the 1980s when dissent may rear its head in the form of a written letter to the leadership, to the Italian Communist party, or even to the president of the United States, or, possibly, in the form of a printed leaflet stuffed surreptitiously in mailboxes or deliberately left on park benches. The already heavy penalties remain unchanged.[61]

The dissidents, however, have expressed the most concern over the new code provision on resentencing of convicts. In the past few years the news that a prominent dissident just on the eve of completing his term for a political offense found himself falsely accused of an ordinary crime and reconvicted, has become all too common. The new code article on resentencing would now appear to institutionalize the scandalous tendency not to release political prisoners, since most of these people have served time in the camp "cooler" and hence could be set up for retrial for the slightest infraction of the camp rules.[62]

Finally, a January 1984 edict further amending the USSR Statute on Criminal Liability for State Crimes has defined as a new crime the transmission of an "official secret" in the form of economic, scientific or technical, or "other" information entrusted to a person at his place of work. The penalties range from up to two years of corrective work to eight years imprisonment. Although it is too early to see the full implication of this recent addition to the criminal law, it would be reasonable to assume Andropov was seeking to impose discipline and restraint on contacts between Soviet businessmen and their Western counterparts, and between dissidents (especially Jewish "refuseniks" fired from their jobs for applying to emigrate to Israel) and the foreign press corps in Moscow.[63]

Upon taking charge in late 1982, Andropov also launched a simultaneous attack on the endemic lack of labor discipline. His early speeches, accompanied by much fanfare in the press, laid out the line of advance on the labor "front" against such foes as absenteeism, tardiness, drunkenness on the job, as well as against managerial incompetence in forcefully dealing with these enervating problems in the production process, throughout the service sector, and at the administrative level.

Andropov's dramatic, unannounced visit to a Moscow machine tool factory in January 1983 keynoted the labor phase of the discipline campaign. In talking to the workers, he expressly reminded them of the essential linkage between good work discipline and yearned for improvements in the Soviet citizen's well-being and general standard of living.[64]

Andropov's factory visit was coordinated with "Operation Trawl," a spectacular countrywide dragnet to round up absentees from work during regular hours. Police were sent into the grocery stores, beauty shops, and even Turkish baths at midday to check documents and identify "work shirkers," people who were away from their desks and workbenches on personal errands during working hours. In one of many dramatic raids

> police burst into a crowded theater in a provincial city near the Black Sea. Suddenly . . . the lights went on, and everyone in the 12th row was ordered outside.
> Each was asked why he was at the movies rather than at work. If he didn't have a convincing explanation, the police called his boss. "We have your employee," the standard conversation went, "Why is he with us instead of with you?"[65]

Scenes such as this sent shock waves through the population, punctuating Andropov's insistent message that discipline was the order of the day. In fairness to the public's shopping problems in a society of scarcity, the leadership ordered shops and consumer services to remain open in the evening, to afford people the opportunity to do their chores on their own time.[66] By late spring 1983 "Operation Trawl" began to wind down, leading some Western observers to mistakenly assume that Andropov's discipline campaign was meeting bureaucratic resistance and foundering.[67] More likely, Andropov never intended "Trawl" as a continuing operation, merely as a dramatic device to get people's attention for more institutionalized responses to the problem, such as the draft version of the new all-Union statute on labor collectives which was published for public discussion as the dragnet was being phased out.[68]

Andropov's legislative program for tightening labor discipline consisted of the draft bill on labor collectives (published in April 1983 to elicit public comment during April and May); the amended statute passed in June; a joint implementing resolution of the party's Central Committee, the USSR Council of Ministers, and the centralized trade union system issued in early August; enabling legislation enacted a week later to amend existing labor law; and explanatory interviews in the press on the changes introduced, with the whole package taking effect September 1, 1983.

Soviet and Eastern European sociologists have defined the labor collective as "a group of people organizationally united for common socially useful activity on the basis of public ownership of the means of production."[69] Although the concept was introduced into Soviet jurisprudence in the constitution of 1977, the statute, as it slowly evolved through the Brezhnevist legislative process after 1980, was probably intended at least partially as a reaction to the labor and political unrest in Poland during 1980–81. However, by the time Andropov came to power a year later with the legislation still unfinished, General Jaruzelski had imposed martial law in Poland, abating the crisis from the Soviet perspective and giving Andropov more space to deploy the new concept in his struggle for discipline. Although the bill included 23 articles, the majority on different aspects of carefully limited worker participation in economic affairs, most of the ensuing public discussions (as filtered through the controlled press) seemed to concentrate on Article 9, the section on discipline. A number of letter writers offered suggestions to further strengthen this section, and when it appeared in the published law, it had indeed been considerably amended.[70]

The essence of Article 9 was that the state and management were no longer alone in the effort to maintain labor discipline. The individual's "collective" had now been formally enlisted into the struggle, equipped with the authority to recommend significant material deprivations for truant and slothful workers or employees from temporary demotion to reduction of bonus and ultimately dismissal. In addition to this method of social peer pressure, the summer also brought changes in the work brigade system to the effect that bonuses would now be paid on the basis of collective rather than individual performance. Thus, for example, if "one member of the brigade is absent from work, the others will suffer economically."[71]

During the summer the party, the government, and the trade union system jointly spelled out specifically the correlations between various violations of labor discipline and material penalties. For instance, in the past absence from work without a valid reason for most but not all of a day was classified as tardiness. Under the joint proposals absence for three or more hours would now be regarded as absenteeism, which now entails reduction of vacation time on a day-for-day basis down to a minimum vacation leave.[72] Several days after the joint resolution in mid-August, Andropov, in his role as chairman of the Presidium, signed an edict legally codifying the resolution's provisions. The edict decreed a series of amendments to the relevant articles of the all-Union principles of labor legislation. Under the new rules, a worker must give longer notice (from one to two months) before leaving a job, shirking as a violation received a precise definition (more than three hours of unjustified absence), a worker's financial liability for damage caused on the job (usually while intoxicated) was increased, and the penalties of transfer to a lower-paying job and demotion for set terms were strengthened.[73] When asked what those changes would mean for the Soviet labor force, a government spokesman described the new regime for work as "greater differentiation between rewards for good work and penalties for violating labor obligations."[74]

Finally, Andropov did not expect to get the country moving again by means of law alone. Recognizing the distinction between "law in the books" and "law in action," Andropov sought to mobilize the public, began a purge of corrupt or incompetent government and lower party officials, and set in motion the revitalization of law enforcement agencies. On an experimental basis in a few cities, citizens were invited to send the police anonymous pre-printed postcards if they wished to report social infractions, labor violations, or criminal offenses.[75] Throughout his short term in office, Andropov also presided over an extensive purge of officials in the trade, transportation, and service networks, where corruption was most rife, as well as some lower party cadres who had tolerated these situations. Thousands of government officials were dismissed, demoted, subjected to disciplinary procedures, or charged with crimes. At least three prominent officials were sentenced to death in the most egregious cases. Even corruption in the military was targeted in Andropov's broad sweep.[76]

Last but hardly least, he came down hard on those whom he was ultimately counting on to carry out his new law—the police, prosecutors, the courts, and even the law schools. Corruption in the law school admissions process was exposed and corrected.[77] Very early in the Andropov incumbency, the Procuracy was subjected to a withering critique. A. Rekunkov, the USSR procurator-general, was obliged to make a public self-criticism, acknowledging corruption in his ranks and promising to root it out.[78] The courts, in turn, were scored for long delays, low sentences, lenient treatment of recidivists, and a host of other shortcomings.[79] Finally, the ranks of the internal affairs agencies, the police themselves came in for the harshest criticism. The press was unleashed and extraordinary accounts of police abuses, mistakes, and venality were aired in public. The Politburo assigned political commissars to their stationhouses to oversee their ideological training. Fedorchuk relentlessly purged the ranks at all levels. Many landed in jail, and many others were bound over for trial as Fedorchuk strove to rebuild "the professional authority of the Soviet police."[80] At the time of his death Andropov's revitalization of the administration of justice was in full swing, but far from complete. The question is, will it continue?

ANDROPOV'S LEGACY

It is perhaps ironic to speak of a Soviet leader's legacy after so short a time in power, but as Romanov remarked in what may be a fitting epitaph, Andropov's brief term in office was marked by "a closer unity of words and deeds."[81] By means of the "power of persuasion and the force of law,"[82] Andropov sought to bring about a sea change in attitudes and behavior of both rulers and ruled in the USSR. To accomplish his mission with its neo-Calvinist overtones of secular salvation through honest work, Andropov presided over one of the most prolific periods of legislative activity in recent Soviet history. In the space of 15 months he constructed and reconstructed a legal infrastructure designed to re-energize the Soviet system and remould the Soviet people into law-abiding, hard-working, punctual citizens. In so doing, he continued the work of his post-Stalin predecessors in leaving behind the ways of arbitrary fiat in favor of the further "juridicization" of system and society into a stable, predictable, and efficient legal order.[83] Although some of his methods may have been too jarring for his hapless subordinates and too harsh for many of his constituents, there is some evidence (circumstantial, to be sure, at this point in time) to suggest that his campaign for discipline may have struck a responsive chord in the popular mind. Whether his successor Chernenko, who in 1983 described "discipline and order" as "inalienable aspects of socialist democracy," will match deeds with words remains to be seen.[84]

NOTES

1. Kevin Devlin, "Andropov's First Year: Italian Communist's Judgment," *Radio Free Europe Research,* Vol. 8, no. 48, Background Report/267 (November 23, 1983), p. 2.

2. "Zhores Medvedev Assesses Andropov's Power and Priorities," *Labour Focus on Eastern Europe,* 7, 1 (Winter 1984): 2–3.

3. Konstantin Simis, "Andropov's Anticorruption Campaign," *Washington Quarterly,* 6, 3 (Summer 1983): 121.

4. Marshall I. Goldman, "Chernenko's Inheritance: A Low-Tech Economy

at Home . . .," *New York Times,* Sunday ed., (February 19, 1984), Section F, p. 2.

5. John F. Burns, "Andropov's Changes: Early Pace Bogs Down," *New York Times,* May 5, 1984, p. A-14.

6. Serge Schmemann, "Policy After Andropov: No Drastic Changes Expected in Moscow," *New York Times,* February 11, 1984, pp. 1, 8.

7. Robert Sharlet, reviewing *USSR: The Corrupt Society* by Konstantin Simis, *Worldview* 26 (January 1983): 25.

8. "Poll Finds People Don't Care About Petty Thefts of Public Property," *Current Digest of the Soviet Press,* 35, 26 (1983): 3.

9. This statistic is drawn from Soviet crime data on the late 1960s in Peter H. Juviler, *Revolutionary Law and Order* (New York: Free Press, 1977), pp. 138, 238; and crime data on the late 1970s in Fridrikh Neznansky, "New Information on Soviet Criminal Statistics: An Inside Report," *Soviet Union,* 6, Part 2 (1979): 208–11.

10. On phone vandalism in Latvia, see *Soviet Nationality Survey,* 1, 1 (January 1984): 3.

11. Simis, *USSR: The Corrupt Society* (New York: Simon & Schuster, 1982), Chapters 4, 7.

12. "Campaign for Labor Discipline Continues," *Current Digest of the Soviet Press,* 34, 52 (1983): 6.

13. Requoted from *Sharlet Review.* See note 7, above.

14. "Maciej Szczepanski and Associates Sentenced by Warsaw Court," *Radio Free Europe Research,* vol. 9, no. 5, Poland Situation Report, January 23, 1984, pp. 8–12. On the Polish crisis in 1980, see Radio Free Europe, *August 1980: Strikes in Poland* (Munich: Radio Free Europe, October 1980), and on the corruption campaign in particular, pp. 209–12.

15. Zhores Medvedev, *Andropov* (New York: Norton, 1983), Chapter 14.

16. See Article 156-2 of the RSFSR Criminal Code in *Basic Documents on the Soviet Legal System,* W.E. Butler, ed. (Dobbs Ferry, NY: Oceana, 1983), p. 354. The new rule was introduced first in the all-Union legislation and then in the RSFSR and other union republic criminal codes.

17. See Article 156-3, ibid.

18. See Article 173, ibid., pp. 359–60.

19. See Article 170, ibid., p. 359.

20. See Article 96, paragraph 2, ibid., p. 338.

21. "Ob organizatsii raboty po privedeniiu zakonodatel'stva Soiuza SSR v sootvetstvie s Konstitutsiei SSSR," *Vedomosti verkhovnogo soveta SSSR,* no. 51, December 21, 1977, item 764, pp. 849–54.

22. "O khode podgotovki zakonoproektov, predusmotrennykh Planom organizatsii raboty po privedeniiu zakonodatel'stva Soiuza SSR v sootvetstvie s Konstitutsiei SSSR," *Vedomosti verkhovnogo soveta SSSR,* no. 1, January 2, 1980, item 3, pp. 20–21.

23. "O khode vypolneniia Plana organizatsii raboty po privedeniiu zakonodatel'stva Soiuza SSR v sootvetstvie s Konstitutsiei SSSR i o podgotovke Svoda zakonov SSSR," *Vedomosti verkhovnogo soveta SSSR,* no. 2, January 14, 1981, item 49, pp. 37–39.

24. "O dal'neishem sovershenstvovanii ugolovnogo i ispravitel'no-trudovogo zakonodatel'stva," *Vedomosti verkhovnogo soveta SSSR,* no. 30 July 28, 1982, item 572, pp. 505–508. The edict was scheduled to go into effect January 1, 1983 (hereafter cited as the July Edict).

25. See Article 39-1 of the Basic Principles of Criminal Legislation of the USSR and the Union Republic, in *Legislative Acts of the USSR* (Moscow: Progress, Book Three, 1983), pp. 202–204.

26. "Tougher Penalties for Criminals Set," *Current Digest of the Soviet Press,* 35, 5 (1983): 8.

27. See the July Edict, parts I-2 and I-3, p. 507, and the corresponding Article 25 and 27 of the Basic Principles of Criminal Legislation . . ., in *Legislative Acts of the USSR* (Book Three), pp. 194–96.

28. See the July Edict, parts I-4 and I-6, pp. 506–508, and the corresponding Article 38, 44-1, and 44-2 of the Basic Principles of Criminal Legislation . . ., ibid., pp. 200–202, 209–11.

29. See the July Edict, part II, p. 508, and the corresponding Article 39-2 of Basic Principles of Corrective Labor Legislation of the USSR and the Union Republics, ibid., pp. 268–70.

30. "O vnesenii izmenenii i dopolnenii v nekotorye zakonodatel'nye akty SSSR," *Vedomosti verkhovnogo soveta SSSR,* no. 42, October 20, 1982, item 793, parts III-4, III-5, and V, pp. 714–15. The edict was scheduled to go into effect January 1, 1983, hereafter cited as the October Edict.

31. Ibid., parts I and II, pp. 712–13.

32. "Slogans of the Revolutionary Anniversary," *Current Digest of the Soviet Press,* 34, 42 (1982): 17–18. The 1982 slogans were published on October 17, two days after the October Edict. See especially slogan nos. 23–26, 42, 43, 46, and 47.

33. For a typology of legal policy, see Robert Sharlet, "Soviet Legal Policy Making," in *Social System and Legal Process,* Harry M. Johnson, ed. (San Francisco: Jossey-Bass, 1978), pp. 209–29.

34. "Andropov on Marx and the Soviet Economy," *Current Digest of the Soviet Press,* 35, 10 (1983): 1–3, 23.

35. "Andropov Speaks to Party Veterans," *Current Digest of the Soviet Press,* 35, 33 (1983): 3; and "Stiffer Penalties for Breaking Traffic Rules," *Current Digest of the Soviet Press,* 35, 18 (1983): 12–14.

36. Serge Schmemann, "Andropov, on Plant Tour, Tells Workers to Produce," *New York Times,* February 1, 1983, p. A-4.

37. See USSR minister of justice Terebilov's formulation of this linkage in "New Laws on Labor, Management Scanned," *Current Digest of the Soviet Press,*

35, 33 (1983): 6.

38. Quoted in the *New York Times* from Andropov's first major speech as leader on November 22, 1982. See Serge Schmemann, "Andropov Lights Fire Under a Slumbering Nation," *New York Times*, February 7, 1983, p. A-14.

39. "Andropov Outlines Party Program Changes," *Current Digest of the Soviet Press*, 35, 25 (1983): 6.

40. See Robert Sharlet, "Legal Policy Under Khrushchev and Brezhnev: Continuity and Change," in *Soviet Law After Stalin*, vol. 2: *Social Engineering Through Law*, D.D. Barry, G. Ginsburgs, and P.B. Maggs, eds. (Alphen aan den Rijn, Holland: Sijthoff & Noordhoff, 1978), pp. 319–30.

41. *Vedomosti verkhovnogo soveta SSSR*, no. 51, December 21, 1977, item 764, part I-15, p. 852. On the constitution, see Robert Sharlet, *The New Soviet Constitution of 1977* (Brunswick, OH: King's Court, 1978).

42. "The Law on Labor Collectives," *Current Digest of the Soviet Press*, 35, 28 (1983): 9–10.

43. Revised under Brezhnev in the October Edict of 1982, and again, more extensively, under Andropov in early 1984. See "O vnesenii izmenii i dopolnenii v nekotorye zakonodatel'nye akty SSSR ob ugolovnoi otvetstvennosti i ugolovnom sudoproizvodstve," *Vedomosti verkhovnogo soveta SSSR*, no. 3, January 18, 1984, item 58, pp. 91–93.

44. "O proekte plana podgotovki zakonodatel'nykh aktov SSSR i postanov-lenii Pravitel'stva SSSR na 1983-1985 gody," *Vedomosti verkhovnogo soveta SSSR*, no. 39, September 29, 1982, item 743, pp. 667–71.

45. "2 Ex-KGB Officials Given New Soviet Posts," *New York Times*, September 14, 1983, p. A-9.

46. "Aliyev on Azerbaidzhan's Economy, Crime," *Current Digest of the Soviet Press*, 34, 47 (1982): 19–23.

47. See the Politburo's concern for "law and order in cities and rural communities, bearing in mind that these questions seriously disturb working people and are urgently raised in their letters." "First Reports on Politburo Meetings Appear," *Current Digest of the Soviet Press*, 34, 50 (1983): 13.

48. See Articles 89–91 and 144–146 of the RSFSR Criminal Code in Butler, *Basic Documents on the Soviet Legal System* (1983), pp. 335–36 & 144–146. In a related move, for the first time in the last four major amnesties, Article 162, the economic crime of "Engaging in Prohibited Trade," was excluded from the amnesty on the occasion of the 60th anniversary of the formation of the USSR. See "Amnesty Decree Frees Some Criminals, Cuts Terms," *Current Digest of the Soviet Press*, 34, 52 (1983): 8–9.

49. The reductions were from possible imprisonment for up to a year to corrective work for up to two years.

50. "Penalties for Petty Theft Stiffened," *Current Digest of the Soviet Press*, 35, 14 (1983): 14.

51. "A Crackdown on Parasites Begins," *Current Digest of the Soviet Press*,

35, 2 (1983): 5–6. The new legislation went into effect on January 1, 1983. The previous criteria that parasitism had to be practiced systematically and over a protracted period of time were dropped.

52. "Leniency for Young Criminals Protested," *Current Digest of the Soviet Press*, 35, 22 (1983): 11–12.

53. "Life in a Juvenile Delinquent's Colony," *Current Digest of the Soviet Press*, 35, 34 (1983): 8–10.

54. "Communist Party: In the Politburo of the CPSU Central Committee," *Current Digest of the Soviet Press*, 36, no. 2 (1984): 20.

55. "Disobedient Convicts' Terms Can Be Extended," *Current Digest of the Soviet Press*, 35, no. 47 (1983): 9. The new law became Article 188-3 of the RSFSR Criminal Code.

56. "More Surveillance for Released Convicts," *Current Digest of the Soviet Press*, 35, no. 50 (1984): 12, 23.

57. See Peter Reddaway, "Dissent in the Soviet Union," *Problems of Communism*, 32, no. 6 (November–December 1983): 1–15.

58. The phrase suggests the actual order in which political prosecutions proceed. It is taken from a book by Eugene Loebl, *Sentenced & Tried* (London: Elek, 1969).

59. See Articles 190-1 and 190-3 of the RSFSR Criminal Code in Butler, *Basic Documents*, p. 365.

60. See Articles 227 and 142, *ibid.*, pp. 382, 348–49.

61. *Vedomosti verkhovnogo soveta SSSR*, no. 3, January 18, 1984, item 58, part I-3, pp. 91–92. Article 7 of the USSR Statute on Criminal Liability for State Crimes is the antecedent legislation for Article 70 of the RSFSR Criminal Code and its equivalent in other Union republic codes.

62. See *Help & Action Newsletter*, 6, no. 28 (November–December 1983): A, A-1.

63. *Vedomosti verkhovnogo soveta SSSR*, no. 3, January 18, 1984, item 58, part I-4, p. 92. The new Article 13-1 of the statute was reflected in code law and went into effect on February 1, 1984.

64. Schmemann, "Andropov, on Plant Tour, Tells Workers to Produce," *New York Times*, February 1, 1983, pp. A-1, A-4.

65. Karen Elliott House and David Satter, "In the Andropov Era, Soviet System Reverts Quickly to Old Ways," *Wall Street Journal*, July 21, 1983, p. 1.

66. "Politburo Discusses Store Hours . . .," *Current Digest of the Soviet Press*, 35, no. 2 (1983): 18.

67. John F. Burns, "Andropov's Changes: Early Pace Bogs Down," *New York Times*, May 5, 1983, p. A-1.

68. "The Draft Law on Labor Collectives," *Current Digest of the Soviet Press*, 35, no. 15 (1983): 14–18.

69. A.S. Pashkov, "Pravovoi status trudovogo kollektiva," *Pravovedenie*, no. 6 (1983): 13.

70. "Debating the Draft Law on Labor Collectives," *Current Digest of the Soviet Press*, 35, no. 18 (1983): 10–11.

71. *Labour Focus on Eastern Europe*, 7, no. 1 (Winter 1984): 5.

72. "Steps Taken to Tighten Labor Discipline," *Current Digest of the Soviet Press*, 35, no. 32 (1983): 4–7.

73. *Vedomosti verkhovnogo soveta SSSR*, no. 33 August 17, 1983, item 507, pp. 555–58.

74. "Explaining the Changes in Labor Laws," *Current Digest of the Soviet Press*, 35, no. 33 (1983): 7.

75. "Soviets Introduce System of Denunciation by Mail," *Samizdat Bulletin*, no. 127 (November 1983): 1–5.

76. See *New York Times*, November 25, 1983, p. A-16; and January 14, 1984, p. 4 on the death sentences. On military corruption, see Konstantin Simis, "An Officer and a Crook: Ripping Off the Red Army," *Washington Post* (January 8, 1984), pp. C-1, C-2.

77. "Legal System Under Fire for Abuses," *Current Digest of the Soviet Press*, 35, no. 44 (1983): 1–3.

78. For the criticism and self-criticism, see *Sotsialisticheskaia zakonnost'*, no. 3 (March 1983): 3–4, 5–10.

79. V. Terebilov, "Immediate Tasks before the Organs of Justice and the Courts in Light of the Decisions of the November 1982 Plenum of the CPSU Central Committee," translated from *Sotsialisticheskaia zakonnost'*, 22, no. 1 (Summer 1983): 27–38.

80. "Fedorchuk Reviews Law Enforcement," *Current Digest of the Soviet Press*, 35, no. 32 (1983): 4.

81. "Romanov Keynotes Nov. 7 Celebration," *Current Digest of the Soviet Press*, 35, no. 45 (1983): 2. Romanov stood in for Andropov, who by that time could no longer appear in public because of his health.

82. Paraphrased from *Pravda*, December 27, 1982, in *Labour Focus on Eastern Europe*, 6, nos. 1–2 (Summer 1983): 45.

83. See Robert Sharlet, "Constitutional Implementation and Juridicization of the Soviet System," in *Soviet Politics in the Brezhnev Era*, Donald R. Kelley, ed. (New York: Praeger, 1980), pp. 200–34.

84. See "Chernenko Keynotes CC Session," *Current Digest of the Soviet Press*, 35, no. 24 (1983): 5. However, for Chernenko's previous, pre-Andropov views on the "discipline" approach to the USSR's problems, see Archie Brown, "Andropov: Discipline *and* Reform," *Problems of Communism* 32 (January–February 1983): 19.

6

ASSESSING THE IDEOLOGICAL COMMITMENT OF A REGIME

Alfred G. Meyer

"When *I* use a word," Humpty Dumpty said in rather a scornful tone, "it means just what I choose it to mean—neither more nor less."

"The question is," said Alice, "whether you *can* make words mean so many different things.

"The question is," said Humpty Dumpty, "which is to be master— that's all."

—Lewis Carroll,
Alice's Adventures in Wonderland

Ideology in the Soviet Union is one of its most conservative elements. It does not change very perceptably, but appears rather frozen in its present form. When leadership changes occur, the new chairman may introduce slightly new formulas or indicate moderate shifts in national priorities, but they appear more cosmetic than substantial. Hence this chapter will not deal so much with changes in Soviet ideology since the death of Brezhnev, but with ideology from a much broader perspective.

When we inquire about the ideological commitment of a regime, we are ipso facto trying to assess how realistic or unrealistic the views of its rulers are, and how their political rhetoric is related to what in fact they do, that is, how seriously they take their own ideology. Let me point out at once that the first question is itself ideological, because "realism" is a subjective, not an objective concept, one person's realism being another person's delusion or ideology.

Let us assume for a moment that "realism" could be defined in a way we all could accept. We would then have to recognize that in all governmental systems there are obstacles to realism. Whether they are constitutional heads of governments or communist dictators, all leaders receive inadequate and distorted information about the world around them. Since they do not have time to learn everything, the information going to them must be filtered and screened; and since this is done by people whom they have appointed, presumably because they share some fundamental views, government leaders listen predominantly to people echoing and reinforcing their own views.

How much of this self-reinforcement deserves to be called ideological in the case of the Soviet leadership? My own answer would be not that much. To be sure, there is an official ideology in the Soviet Union, functioning as the language in which all political communication is transmitted. It is a formal doctrine which in its broad outlines has not changed much since the revolution or at least since the establishment of Stalin's dictatorship in the mid-1930s. It has things to say about the nature of the entire universe and how one studies it, but is primarily a theory about politics, which includes vague notions about the goal of human history—the Communist utopia—as well as models of capitalism and imperialism, defined as the evil forces in the contemporary world.

The extent to which members of the Soviet elite take this doctrine seriously and actually think in its terms cannot be determined with certainty; we will come back to that problem. Yet there is considerable evidence that even while its rigid vocabulary and its frozen models of reality do serve as a medium of communication, this formal ideology permits a great deal of the kind of thinking and analyzing that we like to call rational or realistic. Indeed, among Western students of Soviet politics there is a growing number of scholars who view the Soviet elite neither as dreamy utopians nor as deluded paranoiacs but, rather, as experienced servants of the state, reasonably capable administrators, who may indeed share certain national anxieties and a great deal of national pride, but yet make honest attempts to manage their society as effectively as possible. In this attempt they face mounting obstacles and difficulties, but ideological blindness, excessive devotion to the holy writ of Marxism–Leninism, may not be a very important one. I would go so far as to say that in foreign policy matters Soviet leaders today are more pragmatic, more realistic, and less guided by ideological preconceptions than those who have guided the foreign policy of the United States since World War I.

At the same time it is obvious that the people governing the Soviet Union are also careerists and members of a privileged elite who jealously guard their personal positions and that of their class. To the outside observer, notwithstanding their competence and achievements, this elite of bureaucrats may appear obsolete or dysfunctional, at least as it is now constituted. But one must assume that those who wield power are unable to recognize their own obsolescence and dysfunctionality, and that their thoughts, their ideas, the language of their political discourse, the way they define problems and the kinds of solutions they propose, that all this inevitably is affected by their blindness. However determined an entrenched elite may be in its attempt to gain an objective view of the world and of the possible alternatives for coping with its problems, their realism sooner or later must encounter limitations due to systematic self-deception.

With this notion of systematic self-deception I have now reintroduced ideology, though it may now be quite different from the formal dogma taught in Soviet ideological textbooks. The subject of ideology and its role in politics is controversial. The terms we must use in discussing it are poorly defined; nor is there agreement on the contents and meaning of the official Soviet doctrine. Ultimately, in discussing the relationship between ideology and political action, we are seeking to comprehend human understanding and motivation; but that is a quest which in the final analysis must be deemed unattainable. The best we can do is to talk around the subject.

Let me begin by talking about the official ideology. How much, and in what way, are the people of the Soviet Union and/or their leaders committed to Marxism–Leninism? Does it function as the screen through which they perceive and interpret reality? Does it serve them as a set of moral or political guidelines for their interaction with others? Does it define the ultimate goal of politics for them, and does it determine the manner in which the leadership administers the state and the economy? Does it define government programs and shape public institutions? All these questions have some bearing on the overall commitment of party leaders as well as the general citizenry to the officially sanctioned doctrine.

Several standard answers have been given to this question; each of them comes in various forms; and any one of them may be in conflict with all or most of the others.

One standard answer, which I like to call ideological determinism, argues that Marxism has always been and still is a guide to action for the Soviet leadership, that it functions as the program and defines the goals of Soviet politics. In this view, the Communist party is consistently Marxist, and Soviet history is a direct application of the doctrine, either in its original form or as amended by Lenin and Stalin. In its crudest form, this view was held by such people as John Foster Dulles, who carefully read Soviet ideological texts because he regarded them as a predicter of policy. In a more sophisticated fashion, ideological determinism is expressed by Hannah Arendt and Leszek Kołakowski, among many others, who suggest that the history of the Soviet regime is an acting out of dangerous utopian ideas.

In its weakest form, ideological determinism suggests that the official dogma acts as a limitation on elite decision making, and thus as the political conscience of the system; because they must stay within the bounds of the ideologically permissible, there are certain possible policies that the Soviet leadership dare not adopt.

I have tried to think of policies that the ideology would debar the Soviet leadership from adopting, but cannot think of any. In the 1920s they temporarily reintroduced free enterprise in agriculture, trade, and light manufacture; and the example of Hungary suggests that they might do so again. Obviously they will never give their large industry to private owner- ship, but then why should they? One of the unthinkable policies would seem to be the removal of the Communist party from its vanguard position; but then one might argue that Stalin did precisely that. As early as 1918 it became clear that the ideology would not prevent the Soviet leaders from dealing with capitalist or imperialist powers; and history since World War II has shown that neither does it compel them to ally themselves with self- proclaimed Marxist–Leninist regimes.

The one act, short of actual counterrevolution, that the Soviet Union seems unwilling to condone in any of its client states and therefore presum- ably in the Soviet Union as well is the abolition of censorship; that was the act that became the immediate pretext for armed intervention in Czechos- lovakia; and censorship seems to be one of the first institutions established in any area that comes under Soviet control. What this suggests to me is that the principal command of the ideology is to maintain the monopoly of the ideology: I am the word, and ye shall have none other beside me. To this we must add that the only other act that the regime would consider impermissi- ble is to have any autonomous organization or association formed within Soviet society, autonomy being considered identical with subversion. Thus the one unbreachable law of Soviet ideology is the maintenance of full con- trol over the minds and the activities of all citizens. That hardly deserves to be called ideology.

The matter gets a bit more confusing when we realize that the prag- matism we must attribute to the Soviet leadership is demanded by the ideol- ogy itself. Because of Lenin's often expressed impatience with theoretical disputations, because of his repeated emphasis that all party policy be goal specific (*tselesoobrazno*), Soviet ideology demands of its hierarchs a great deal of flexibility and asks them to be attuned to the political constraints and opportunities of the moment. Of course, it also predisposes them toward certain standard solutions. Yet in reviewing the standard solutions preferred by the Soviet leadership, I cannot think of an example that could not be explained by other than ideological factors: Russian tradition, accumulated experience, or bureaucratic inertia.

Some scholars therefore believe that the top Soviet leadership is in no wise committed to Marxism–Leninism. Instead, they suggest, the top leaders are abject cynics without any ideology except a firm resolve to perpetuate their own power and privileges. While mouthing Communist slogans, it is asserted, these leaders have utter contempt for the masses, especially peasants, workers, and ethnic minorities, and for the rhetoric that declares the masses to be sovereign. There are, in fact, hints of evidence that in the privacy of the innermost circle of power, the Soviet leaders abandon the language of Marxism–Leninism and converse in a much cruder language of naked power, hatred, and aggressiveness—just as in the privacy of the Oval Office Richard Nixon dropped the language of constitutional democracy.

Cynical contempt for the official doctrine has more often been attributed to the masses of the Soviet population at the grass roots of society, the popular U.S. image of the Soviet Union being that of a system in which a powerful group of true believers at the top has been trying desperately, and not all that successfully, to indoctrinate its citizens in the Marxist–Leninist faith. But the opposite may very well be true: cynicism at the top and general acceptance of the ideology at the grass roots. That does not, of course, mean the formal ideology in all its details. Anyone probing deeply into the minds of ordinary Soviet citizens—to the extent that is possible for Western visitors—is likely to find that they are not likely to have detailed knowledge of Marxist–Leninist philosophy or any other aspect of the official doctrine. In this they are comparable to the average citizen of the United States, who is likely to know very little about the workings of his own political system, and nothing at all about the theories of democracy, constitutionalism, and free enterprise, to which it is, in some fashion, committed.

Even recent graduates from Soviet institutions of higher learning, who have been compelled to take college-level courses in Marxism–Leninism, when asked to explain this doctrine or the policies outlined at party congresses, will give answers that show their knowledge of the official ideology to be no more than skin deep. Western visitors who have studied Soviet scripture usually have an easy time demonstrating their own superior knowledge of these matters to Soviet citizens. Yet even though these citizens would fail an examination in this subject, in a deeper sense many of them have taken in the basic assumptions of Soviet ideology and made them their own, just as the average American, without understanding U.S. political theory or institutions, nonetheless is likely to accept the American way of life, take it for granted, defend it when challenged, and denounce the ideology and the system of the rival superpower.

This often is true even in the case of people who regard themselves as critical of the Soviet system. Many people who have dealt with recent refugees from the Soviet Union have remarked about the extent to which even these people have internalized Soviet attitudes and assumptions. It is likely to be true also for people who manifest their alienation from the system by varieties of deviant behavior—worship of American imports, alcoholism, work avoidance, and the like. One might compare some of these alienated strata of the Soviet population with Native Americans who, even though they have received most shabby treatment from the United States, nonetheless often display super-patriotic feelings.

In short, at the bottom of Soviet society just as in the top elite, mouthing the regime's orthodoxies, and doing it sincerely, may be quite compatible with violating its norms of behavior. Ideological commitment and cynicism, it seems, can coexist within the same person. Perhaps they even support and reinforce each other.

Between the top elite and the working masses one can identify a professional elite of specialists in a wide variety of fields—administrative, military, scientific, educational, and others. Members of this elite receive far more intensive and long-lasting indoctrination than the average citizen, and many of them are members of the party. They acquire considerable skill in the use of Marxist–Leninist terms; indeed, in all professional dealings they can be expected to be careful to use the accepted terms of the official ideology. That does not mean that they will all be saying the same things; instead, they argue with each other. Marxist–Leninist language can be used quite effectively to express divergent interpretations of any given information and conflicting policy proposals. Indeed, Soviet professional journals are the place where the middle-level elite carries out lively discussions of conflicting views. Such discourse is carried out with degrees of freedom that vary from one period to another and from one professional elite to another. The boundaries to stretching or amending the official language are sometimes drawn tightly, at other times more loosely. One might argue that virtually all such discourse in the Soviet Union involves the continual testing of these boundaries.

Disagreements within the specialized professions of the Soviet Union are often about quite technical matters. But observers of Soviet society have in recent years begun to identify (however tentatively) specifically ideological currents within the Soviet establishment, a left and a right, and a center. Within the Soviet elite there seem to be influential people who believe in the need for trenchant reform. If they have some managerial responsibility, they may believe in greater reliance on sociological research, in the increased application of computers, in intensified technological or commodity exchange with the West, which in turn depends on a lessening of international tensions. Against such reform-minded people are pitted the conservatives who may wish to return to various policies or institutions of classical Stalinism; and in between these "left" and "right" orientations may be a middle that wishes to stay clear of both reform and a reversion to old methods. We know that in addition to these ideological currents Soviet society harbors a liberational underground that constitutes the far left; and there also is a far right, with sympathizers in high places, that preaches a romantic Russian nationalism, harsh disdain of the West, and other views that echo Slavophile populism and the nativist ideology of the prerevolutionary Black Hundred.

Now, when editorials in *Molodaia Gvardia* begin to sound like the reactionary journalism of Fedor Dostoevski in praising the traditions of Old Rus' and in denouncing the West for modernism, individualism, and the trend toward the mechanization of life, how much is there left of Marxism, of Leninism, or even of Stalinism?

It is no longer controversial to assert that Marxism–Leninism in the Soviet Union has been drained of its contents and has become an empty shell of words and phrases into which any meaning can be poured. In the period of Khrushchev's chairmanship it was still possible to argue that the regime was making an effort to keep alive the utopian aspirations of Marxism, i.e., the ultimate goal of a communist society without classes and without inequalities of wealth, status, opportunity, authority, and power. Even then, a close look at the way in which the prospects for full communism by the 1980s was spelled out would have revealed that Khrushchev's image of this dream society was a bureaucrat's dream in that it spelled the perpetuation of the stratified and authoritarian system over which he was ruling. At the time I referred to his program as the withering away of utopia; and his successors were careful to scrap even this caricature of the communist goal.

Marxism originally aimed to restore freedom and spontaneity to human beings; Lenin and his successors have always regarded spontaneity and freedom as threats. Marxism in its original form was based on a charitable view toward human failings because it saw them as symptoms of evil social systems. Soviet ideology today can no longer acknowledge any fundamental evil in the system and cannot show understanding for so-called deviants. It must therefore explain them on the basis of personal moral defects and control them through punitive measures.

One could go through dozens of assumptions made by Marxism, dozens of attitudes and positions we can associate with it, and show how under Lenin or Stalin and their successors the ideology was turned into its opposite, and how policies and strategies developed by the Marxist movement in its formative years were reversed. It is thus reasonable to say that Marxism in the Soviet Union is dead. Where echoes of it survive, they serve as a source of embarrassment. For instance, the dream society predicted in Lenin's *The State and Revolution* is so different from the Soviet system that developed out of the revolution that the work can only be read as an indictment. At a recent international conference on labor history that took place in Moscow, a left-wing labor historian from the United States read a paper that obviously discomfited his Soviet colleagues. After hemming and hawing for a while, they finally came out with the gist of their criticisms: Your paper, they told the American historian, is too Marxist.

The ideological determinism to which Mr. Dulles subscribed, and which still has adherents in the Western world, thus is demonstrably nonsense. The Soviet Union is no more a Marxist state than Spain under the dictatorship of General Franco was a Christian state. At the same time, if Kołakowski, Arendt, and others regard the Soviet Union as the result of ideology, because the system was created by people genuinely committed to a political faith and allowed this faith to guide them in shaping its institutions, they are correct. All revolutionary regimes are results of historical processes in which spontaneous or organized action by broad masses of unhappy and impatient people is channeled with the help of a revolutionary ideology. That is true of Puritan Massachusetts and Fascist Italy, of the French Revolution and the Weimar Republic. In every case, however, the utopian dreams give way to something that today is called "realism", and so in ideological matters we observe the turn from Puritanism to Congregationalism, from the Declaration of Independence to the Federalist papers, from Robespierre to Guizot, from Jacksonian democracy to the elitist theories of contemporary pluralist theory, and from Marx to Stalin and his successors.

The effective emasculation of Marxism in the Soviet Union does not mean, however, that it is a country without an ideology. The shell of orthodox Marxism may have been drained of its old contents, but it is not empty. New contents have been poured in. Can we describe those contents? Is there an identifiable body of beliefs and assumptions about the nature and purpose of the Soviet state that can be attributed to the Soviet elite and is accepted by those who live and work within the system? It seems to me that there is; and as long as we do not deceive ourselves by calling this Marxism, we can talk about a Soviet ideology, just as we can identify a current U.S. ideology as long as we do not deceive ourselves into identifying it with Jefferson's ideas.

Soviet ideology is one of the principal denominations in the global religion of the nineteenth and twentieth centuries—the religion of progress. It is, in other words, an ideology of modernization. *Modern,* in this context, implies a commitment to up-to-date technology and therefore, to the education of a literate and technologically competent citizenry. It implies a belief in the economy of scale, hence a faith that bigger is better. More generally, it includes a preoccupation with efficiency and a consequent resolve to eliminate all obstacles to full efficiency; among the obstacles to full efficiency the ideology identifies are peasant culture, religious beliefs, and other traditions.

The cult of efficiency is supported by a profound faith in science and rationality. The Soviet elite appears convinced that it is possible to gain realistic understanding of the world and, through scientific management, shape this world to specifications and impose rationality on human affairs. This is an ideology of bureaucratic management similar to that taught in our own schools of business and public administration. An application of engineering principles to societal problems, this managerial theory tends to regard human beings as merely another resource and seeks to replace all traditional relations and habits by the artificial culture of bureaucratic rules and bureaucratic organization. This is the essence of what contemporary scholars and politicians like to call "realism," and it should be remembered that Lenin was one of the pioneers of this kind of thinking.

I am deliberately stressing the affinities of this Soviet faith in rational management with similar beliefs prevalent in our society. In many significant respects, indeed, Soviet ideology is a carbon copy of Americanism. The guardians of Soviet ideology have always been aware of this. Stalin defined the task of the Soviet Union as that of catching up with the United States and overtaking it. From the earliest days of the Soviet state, Lenin preached that those governing the Soviet Union must learn from the Western bourgeoisie, and particularly from that of the United States. The Taylor system of intensified worker exploitation caught his fancy, just as later Soviet administrators were fascinated by the assembly line and started a Henry Ford cult which is still very much alive in the Soviet Union. There is nothing that pleases Soviet visitors to the University of Michigan more keenly than a VIP tour through the Ford Motor Company. But the Soviet Union wishes to catch up with the United States not merely economically, but also militarily, culturally, and in every other endeavor, from sports and chess to its general standing as a superpower.

Having brought out the affinities of Soviet ideology with Americanism, let me lay equal stress on the differences. They are in part a function of the fact that Soviet ideology is *substitute* Americanism: The aim of the Soviet leadership is to make a deliberate, organized effort to copy achievements that in the New World were made spontaneously, in an unplanned fashion, through uncoordinated individual enterprise, though often subsidized and encouraged by the state. What capitalism achieved with seeming spontaneity the Soviet leadership hopes to attain through concerted effort and with coercive means, through an absolute state that seeks to eliminate all traces of heterodoxy and heterogeneity. Politically, this appears as a throwback to the very pattern of sovereignty against which the American political ideology rebelled. Soviet ideology thus is the ideology of substitute capitalism; it is a species of entrepreneurship in which the *state* is designated as the one and only entrepreneur. If American entrepreneurship conformed to the ideas of Ricardo, the Soviet mode of capital accumulation has much more affinity with mercantilist ideas.

Note here, too, the inversion of Marxism. According to Engels and Marx, the political system is superstructural to the economy. That means that it is regarded as no more than a system maintenance device generated in any society that is rent by class conflict. The economic system thus creates the political system. Yet, according to Stalinist and neo-Stalinist theory, it is the socialist state that is primary. The state is the active historical force that creates its own economic base. The original Marxist assumption about the relationship between base and superstructure here is reversed; philosophically, Soviet ideology has returned to Hegel.

Thus while the state, according to Soviet ideology, functions as the substitute for the Western business corporation, the individual is defined by his or her obligations to this sole employer. Soviet ethics therefore resembles Western corporate ethics. It demands respect for rank and authority, obedience to rules and regulations, and strict self-confinement to the well-defined channels of official communication. It incorporates not only a work ethic but also the expectation that individuals will participate as much as possible in public life near and away from the place of work. Further, it encourages competition for advancement and for material goods; careerism as well as consumerism are accepted parts of current Soviet ideology.

If we trace these various elements of Soviet ideology to their historic roots, we might make the somewhat startling discovery that those ideas that

Soviet ideology most obviously shares with current American beliefs tend to come from Marxism: the worship of science, technology, rationality, and bigness; the resolve to ride roughshod over traditional cultures to bring modernization to backward countries; the work ethic; and the emphasis on the accumulation of material wealth. Marxism shares these preoccupations with Western liberalism to such an extent that I have been tempted to call it the last of the great bourgeois ideologies. Yet the spirit in which this ideology of modernization is applied in the USSR, the organizational forms and managerial habits, and most of all the sharply competitive, not to say combative, spirit of this entrepreneurship seem to me to express attitudes about their own country and its relations with the rest of the world that are familiar to any student of nineteenth-century Russian intellectual history. Soviet communism converted Marxism into a theory of development; but the form this theory assumed is indebted primarily to ancient Russian themes going back to at least the sixteenth century.

Among the specifically Russian attitudes that have been incorporated in the Soviet theory of state entrepreneurship is, first, a marked sensitivity to boundaries, to impending invasion, and to cultural domination, which ultimately may be the consequence of the openness of Russia's land frontiers in the West. It makes all Russian rulers anxious to protect their subjects, their institutions, their territory, and their culture from foreign contact and alien encroachment. Paradoxically, it is linked to a fear of being bottled up or sealed in, which presumably has been generated by Russia's lack of access to warm-water ports.

Russian intellectuals in the nineteenth century were intensely preoccupied with the relationship between their own country and its Western neighbors. Self-conscious about Russia's backwardness, they developed a nagging feeling of national inferiority, but often compensated for it by declaring Russian culture to be superior to that of the West. The whole conflict between Westernizers and Slavophiles revolved around this ambivalence. One of its manifestations today is the preoccupation of the Soviet leadership with questions regarding their country's prestige and image, with its standing in the world community. But in a broad sense the total of Leninist strategy and revolutionary theory can be seen as an expression of this ancient Russian brooding about Russia's relations with the West.

The general label we attach to this syndrome of attitudes is nationalism. Soviet ideology is intensely nationalistic, so much so that to the outsider it often looks like paranoia. But Russia has grounds for fearing her neighbors. Mongols conquered the country in the thirteenth century, and Tatars harassed it for hundreds of years afterwards. Poles invaded it in the seventeenth, Swedes in the eighteenth, the French in the nineteenth, and the Germans twice in the twentieth; and to these deep incursions we must add the intervention by practically the whole world during the civil war of 1918–1923. Like Tsarist Russia, the Soviet Union is still anxiously keeping the world at bay; and, like Peter the Great, the rulers of the Soviet Union do so by arming to the teeth and by trying to catch up with Western science and industry.

Soviet ideology thus is an ideology of international competition. It expresses the aims and nature of its own system and those of its rivals in the esoteric terminology of Marxism–Leninism which it adopted as its own in the revolution of 1917. But the meaning of the ideology can be summarized by the two words entrepreneurship and nationalism. Material accumulation and national defense are the chief preoccupations expressed by the ideology; and since these are also important aspects of our own U.S. ideology, what looks like a clash of ideologies is in many respects nothing else than competition between similar and in many respects identical ideologies. One is reminded of the religious wars of the seventeenth century, in which Protestant states and Catholic states in the name of their denominations sought to destroy each other; yet as systems of government they appeared like carbon copies of each other.

But this raises the puzzling question why, given this similarity in contents, any leadership would be so insistent in clinging to the frozen language of Marxism–Leninism. What is it that causes seemingly rational, pragmatic administrators with lots of very modern ideas to cling to empty phrases with religious fervor, and what does this say about the relationship of their faith to the political activities in which they engage?

The comparison of Communist leaders with militant religious believers and of the Communist movement with a church is by no means far-fetched, and has been made often. After all, communism maintains an elaborate set of dogmas ultimately derived from scriptural exegesis, the holy writ in this case being the works of Engels, Marx, and Lenin. While claiming to explain the entire cosmos, the ideology is, in the final analysis, a theory of salvation and damnation, and because it asserts the certainty of a happy outcome, it is also a song of praise to the ultimate wisdom of its god, history. The party is organized very much like a church. While Jerry Hough has compared the provincial party secretary to a French préfet, it might be just as apt to compare him with a bishop. The Central Committee functions as the Curia, and the general secretary is analogous to the pope. Like the Bishop of Rome, he is generally assumed to be infallible, even though this is expressed in somewhat different words.

What this suggests to me is that the commitment of Soviet leaders to their faith may be analogous to that of, say, Gustavus Adolphus to

Lutheranism. Undoubtedly the Swedish king was a devout and militant Protestant. But did this make him behave differently from any contemporary Catholic ruler?

Or consider the infamous Torquemada, the Stalin of the Spanish Inquisition. (Shlomo Avineri at a recent conference, when asked to define the relationship between Marx and Stalin, suggested that Stalin was to Marx as Torquemada was to Jesus.) Torquemada committed mass murder in the name of Christ. The church that gave him his authority had long before changed from a small band of simple fishermen ready to turn the other cheek into a giant authoritarian bureaucracy and an *ecclesia militans*. Was Torquemada a true believer deluding himself that he was carrying out the founder's mission? Was he a cunning machiavellian cynically using his grim office to secure his own power? Or should we accept Dostoevski's suggestion that he may have been a genuine idealist who recognized the falseness of the formal dogma but confessed it nonetheless for the purpose of governing his people wisely?

Our inability to answer these questions suggests a similar inability to be sure about the commitment of the Soviet leadership to its own ideology. At the same time, the similarities of contemporary ideologies shared with religious beliefs and the analogies between the "religious" wars of the seventeenth century and the conflicts of the twentieth suggest that the analogy might be worth pursuing.

I am using religion in its loose, but conventional, sense as that experience and knowledge that is not empirically verifiable in any commonly accepted manner but rather goes beyond conventional experience and may in fact be in conflict with strict scientific evidence. What is of interest here is precisely the distinction between religious knowledge and that kind of knowledge which we regard as scientific and realistic. What I will suggest is that ideologies fulfill a useful function precisely because they seem unrelated to real life, precisely *because* they are not in tune with the realism and pragmatism of those who confess them, and are not in fact being practiced. Moreover, they are of importance to those political elites that think of themselves as pragmatic and realistic.

This is most obvious (and, I might add, most trivial) when we realize that all political ideology in the age of mass communications serves a public relations function. Like TV commercials and presidential press conferences, it must be able to conceal rather than reveal, to obscure reality in a fog of circumlocutions.

The term "public relations," however, suggests that ideology is primarily a web of lies, half-truths, or myths deliberately and cynically used to manipulate mass opinion. I believe this to be false. Some years ago

I argued in an article that the people most in need of ideological convictions are the elites, not the masses, and I pointed to the fact that in all political systems indoctrination becomes more intensive, the higher up one moves in the hierarchy. I explained this as serving the function of self-legitimation.

People with political authority always feel compelled to violate the norms of personal morality. From Plato to the church fathers, from Machiavelli and Hobbes to Lincoln and Lenin, political philosophers and practitioners have distinguished between private ethics and political necessity, and have taken it for granted that success in politics depends on the practitioner's ability to disregard individual morality. People in politics therefore need an ideology that assuages whatever conscience they may have by telling them that even though they are violating ethical norms they are doing the right thing.

This need for self-legitimation is low in periods when the political leaders are successful in what they seek to achieve. Good performance, the ability to make the state into a stable and prosperous system, legitimizes the rulers. Their need for self-assurance increases when in their political action they are not as successful as they would like to be. If the failures are minor, political elites may want to conceal them from the public. But when they become systemic, they must conceal them from themselves. When a political system begins to defy common sense by perpetuating policies or institutions that are obviously ineffective and self-defeating, when it does not manage to fulfill its own stated performance goals, then its leaders will not only attempt to anticipate and parry criticism from those whom they rule but must also reassure themselves that they are doing well.

Politics is a contradictory pursuit. It can be defined as problem solving, but also as a struggle for power and privilege. Those two pursuits tend to get in each other's way. Revolutions occur because problems are not being solved. New ruling elites come to the fore, determined to do the job, but they will inevitably seek to perpetuate their newly won power and privilege and will therefore sooner or later avoid solving societal problems if that requires methods that would endanger their rule. But, by thus avoiding system-threatening methods of problem solving, the ruling elites hasten their own obsolescence.

Indoctrination and self-indoctrination then are means for shoring up a faltering political system in the minds of its ruling elite; and the greater the need, the more fanciful the ideology. Life has become beautiful, Stalin proclaimed at the height of the blood purges.

We began with the question of how to assess the strength of a regime's commitment to its confessed ideology. The answer that now suggests itself is that the more the ideology is violated in practice, the more loudly will it be proclaimed and confessed. Political religion is paid the most fervent lip service wherever the system does not live up to its demands and to its definitions of reality. Except in times of catastrophic change (revolution), when political religions do in fact inspire political action, the strength and cohesion of an official ideology tend to indicate the degree of its nonrelatedness to action; and even though in every society there are people who take the commands of the ideology seriously, such people do not generally understand its actual function. Real Marxists therefore cannot be tolerated in the Soviet Union, just as in our own society people who propose to practice in fact what Jesus, or Jefferson, or Thomas Paine taught, can survive only at the margins of society.

Thus, even though ideology is indirectly a function of certain inadequacies of the political system, its nonrelatedness to social action is essential to its definition. This seems true whether the ideology is codified in carefully formulated dogmas, as in the Soviet Union, or whether it is a set of vague but commonly acknowledged assumptions, as in Western societies. Hence the distinction between "ideologies" and "belief systems" suggested by Huntington and Brzezinski becomes irrelevant to our discussion.

In the beginning of this essay I referred to the two polar hypotheses about the relationship between ideology and practice in the Soviet Union: an ideological commitment that I called ideological determinism as against cynical contempt for the ideology. What I am suggesting in conclusion is that these two attitudes may be compatible and may indeed be mutually reinforcing. When Humpty Dumpty says that word definitions are a consequence of power, we must understand that power is also a function of word defining.

7

RUSSIAN NATIONALISM AND SOVIET POLITICS

Darrell P. Hammer

The resurgence of Russian nationalism in the contemporary Soviet Union has attracted considerable attention. It has been the subject of journalists' reporting[1] as well as scholarly analysis.[2] It is hardly disputed that Russian nationalism has grown into a factor of some importance in Soviet life. There is considerable argument, however, both over the causes of the phenomenon, and its possible consequences.

Two explanations have been offered for the new nationalism. The first, which might be called the theory of the "substitute ideology," goes something like this. The Russian nation has experienced a crisis of faith, because of the erosion of ideology that has taken place since the death of Stalin. In seeking a new faith, the people have turned to their historical traditions, and have found what they sought in the new nationalism. While I do not discount this theory entirely, it does overstate the case, and more important, it glosses over the real problems in Soviet life that have led to the nationalist revival.

The second explanation, which is developed in the writings of Mikhail Agursky, treats nationalism as a response to the real cultural and social dislocations that the country has experienced since the 1917 Revolution.[3] Nationalism is interpreted as a reaction against urbanization, modernization, and the cult of technology, and not merely an idea that has filled an ideological void. Nationalism is an ideology of opposition. Aleksandr Solzhenitsyn, for example, describes the "progress" that the country made after the Revolution as "a furious dash into a blind alley." "We must renounce . . . the gigantic scale of modern technology in industry, agriculture and urban technology."[4]

The transformation of Soviet society since the Revolution has indeed had a profound effect: it destroyed many traditional values, without always creating new values to take their place. The industrialization and urbanization of the country brought other dislocations—an increase in divorce and the loss of traditional family values, juvenile delinquency, and urban violence. These social problems should not be exaggerated, because (except for the problem of alcoholism) the Soviet Union is probably no worse off than other urbanized societies. Nonetheless, the contrast between the official ideology and the reality of Soviet life has caused a certain nostalgia for traditional values, and this nostalgia is easy to translate into nationalism. Furthermore, the transformation of society has shifted the population around so that large minority groups have settled in areas where once only ethnic Russians lived. One of the familiar complaints of the nationalists is that "Moscow is no longer a Russian city," because so many non-Russians now live there. Russians complain that they are strangers in their own country.

It is not easy for Americans to understand the discontent of the Russians, because we are so accustomed to identifying Russia with the Soviet Union. However, we cannot understand the resurgence of Russian nationalism until we realize that it is a response to real problems. Even Roy Medvedev, a dissident historian who is not friendly to the new nationalism, notes that the Russians have genuine complaints. Medvedev has pointed out that certain nationalities (he mentions the Georgians, Armenians, and Uzbeks) have fared better under Soviet rule than the Russians have.[5]

Some Western analysts suggest that the Russian nationalist revival portends the eventual demise of the Soviet regime in its present form. A nationalist ideology could replace the official Marxist–Leninist doctrine, and this would lead to the emergence of a conservative, and even fascist regime. Yanov, for example, warns that a regime motivated by "military–imperialist" nationalism could be even more dangerous to the West than the Soviet system. Other writers have suggested that such a regime is not just a remote possibility. It is said that there exists a secret "Russian party" which could be a combination of right-wing nationalists and Soviet generals, and that this "Russian party" could conceivably come to power.[6]

THE MULTINATIONAL STATE: AN OVERVIEW

The fact that the Soviet Union is a multinational state is never far from the surface of Soviet politics. Nationalities policy—dealing with the problems of the almost 100 nationalities that make up the Soviet Union—is one of the main concerns of the regime. Indeed, Hough has pointed out that in previous leadership successions, the man who was chosen as the national leader has always been the candidate who had the most experience dealing with the non-Russian nationalities.[7] This factor, experience in the management of a non-Russian region, may have been one of the considerations in the election of Yuri Andropov and Konstantin Chernenko. At an important stage in his career, between 1940 and 1951, Andropov served in various positions in the Karelian Republic, rising eventually to be the second secretary of the Karelian party organization. Karelia was then a Union republic on the border with Finland, and its population was mainly Finnish. Chernenko, who was an ideological specialist, served for eight years (1948–1956) in the propaganda apparatus in Moldavia, another small Union republic with a Rumanian-speaking population. Of the other ethnic Russians who were considered contenders for the office of general secretary in 1982 and 1984 (Romanov, Gorbachev, Grishin, Ustinov), none had had comparable experience outside the Russian republic.

The Russians are the largest nationality, but they make up only about 52 percent of the total Soviet population. The Russian Republic, although only one of the 15 Union republics that make up the USSR, occupies about 75 percent of the Soviet land mass. There is clearly a potential for trouble in the relationship between the Russian and the minority nationalities. The objective of Soviet nationalities policy is to satisfy the conflicting interests of these diverse ethnic groups, while at the same time suppressing any movement towards separatism. The policy has been to give the nationalities some autonomy in managing their own affairs (especially in the related fields of culture and education) while retaining centralized political control in Moscow. The Soviet socialist economy, too, is managed by a centralized authority, without significant concessions to the national minorities. In Soviet terms, the goal of nationalities policy has been to find a middle ground between the two extremes of bourgeois nationalism (a code word for separatism among the national minorities) and great-power chauvinism (which refers to Russian nationalism). As we shall see in the discussion that follows, the policy seems to have worked. This is quite clear if we look at the Soviet record in historical perspective. The other multinational empires that existed prior to World War I disappeared as a consequence of that war. The Austro-Hungarian empire and the Turkish empire both broke up into a number of small (and often quarreling) nation-states. Only the Russian empire, though in a radically altered form, managed to survive.

The Soviet Union, however, is much less "Russian" than the empire that it replaced, and the Russians as a national group are less dominant

today than they were in the empire. Some Russian intellectuals in fact feel a
genuine sense of threat from the regime's nationalities policy. They are
fearful that Russian culture could be overwhelmed by a new, supra-national Soviet culture, and the Russian nation within the USSR could be absorbed into a new community called the Soviet people. Indeed it is possible
that Chernenko's principal problem in the nationalities sphere will not be
nationalist agitation among the minorities, but dealing with the new Russian nationalism.

There is not a single, organized Russian nationalist movement in the
Soviet Union. There are two main tendencies among Russian nationalists,
and a number of lesser forms of nationalism. On the one hand, there is a
group of writers who emerged in the 1960s with a plea for greater respect
for Russian culture, and especially for the tradition represented by the Russian Orthodox church. They can be called the Russophile group, although
other names have been suggested.[8] A second group can be called, following a suggestion of Aleksandr Solzhenitsyn, the National Bolsheviks. Before we examine the ideas of these two groups, we need to review the history of the nationalities problem in the Soviet Union.

LENIN AND THE RUSSIAN FUTURE

As a Marxist, Lenin believed that the divisive forces in modern society were the result of economic exploitation. Marxism taught that after the
socialist revolution, exploitation would disappear. When this happened,
social conflict would also disappear. On the other hand, Lenin had a somewhat more sophisticated view of social conflict than Marx. In the *Communist Manifesto* Marx had written that all preceding history was the history of class conflict. Lenin, too, believed that the division into social
classes was in some sense the fundamental division within society. But as a
revolutionary politician, Lenin could not ignore the existence of other
forms of conflict and social cleavage. Society, he recognized, may also be
divided along national or religious lines, and these cleavages were also a
potential source of social conflict. As a revolutionary politician, Lenin
wanted to appeal not only to those who were oppressed economically, but
also to those who felt themselves oppressed because they belonged to religious or national minorities.

Lenin expected that his Bolshevik party would be the vanguard of the
working class. But the vanguard party had to appeal beyond the working
class alone. The party had to formulate an agrarian policy, which would ap-

peal to the peasants, and it had to have a nationalities policy that could enlist the support of the minorities in the empire.

Lenin's proposals for a Bolshevik nationalities policy were set down in a short pamphlet written in 1916 under the title, *The Socialist Revolution and the Right of Nations to Self-Determination*. Here he began with the argument that the aim of the revolution was "complete democracy," and therefore the revolution would give to all nationalities the right to determine their own future. This meant, in particular, that small nationalities had the right to demand their independence from great empires such as Russia or Austria-Hungary. Lenin here seemed to support the traditional demand of nationalists: political independence and the creation of a sovereign nation-state.

On the other hand, allowing small nationalities to demand their independence is not the same as actually granting it. Lenin confidently expected that as a country approaches the socialist revolution, there would be less demand for independence on the part of the smaller nationalities. This would come about in part because men would recognize that there are definite advantages to living in a large state, as compared with a small state organized around a single nationality. But the interest in national independence would also recede, according to Lenin, because with the coming of the revolution, national differences would begin to disappear. Men would no longer think of themselves as Czechs, or Poles, or Ukrainians, but as citizens of the new socialist commonwealth.

Although he was a practicing politician, Lenin was also a visionary. He had a rather utopian view of the future society, which he described as a society without classes, without a state, and without nationalities. In the long run, the aim of the revolution was not merely to draw nations together, but to bring about their "merger." This distinction that Lenin made between the "drawing together" (*sblizhenie*) of nations, and their "merger" (*sliianie*), is of great importance in understanding the later course of Soviet nationality policy.[9]

NATIONAL BOLSHEVISM

The Revolution of 1917 nearly caused the complete disintegration of the empire. Independent governments were created in the borderlands where the non-Russian nationalities lived. From Finland, in the northwest, to Georgia, in the Trans-Caucasus region, some new "republics" proclaimed themselves to be independent both of the tsar and of the Bolsheviks. Under conditions of the civil war and the Allied intervention (which lasted through 1920), the Bolshevik regime was powerless to hold on to these borderland regions. But after the defeat of the white (anti-Bolshevik) forces, Lenin's government was able to establish its authority in some of these borderland republics, which were brought into a new federation called the Union of Soviet Socialist Republics in 1922.[10] The territory of the USSR, with some exceptions, corresponded to the territory of the empire. The Baltic states (Latvia, Lithuania, Estonia) managed to maintain their independence until World War II, and Finland, of course, remains independent to the present day. Poland, too, became independent, although after World War II the country was brought under Soviet political control.

This absorption of the borderlands into the new Soviet state would appear to violate Lenin's earlier ideas about self-determination. But as noted above, Lenin had said only that a nationality had the right to demand independence, and not the right to acquire it. Moreover, it could now be argued that even the right to demand independence had become outdated as a result of the revolution. To demand independence from the tsarist empire was "progressive" but to demand the same thing from the Bolshevik regime could be called "counterrevolutionary." Using that argument, separatist movements in the borderlands could be suppressed.

The centralizing and antiseparatist policies of the Soviet regime helped to attract support from elements of Russian society that did not accept the Marxist–Leninist ideology. An alternative set of ideas, under the misleading name of National Bolshevism, appeared shortly after the Bolsheviks came to power. The leader of this movement was Nikolai Ustrialov, and its basic ideas were laid down in an article he wrote in 1920. Ustrialov was a Russian who had fled from the country after the revolution. But he soon became reconciled to the existence of the Bolshevik regime, and he decided that no Russian could escape the consequences of the revolution. The basic idea of National Bolshevism was the belief that Bolshevism, however repulsive it might seem, was somehow a true expression of the "Russian spirit." Ustrialov called on all Russians, of whatever political persuasion, to support the Soviet regime because it was the successor of the Russian empire.

National Bolshevism took a fatalistic view of the revolution of 1917, which it regarded as the inevitable outcome of previous Russian history. The revolution may have been a catastrophe for the country, but it was an event that was national in character. Because it was a purely Russian revolution, it was not likely to be repeated in the West. The Bolshevik regime hoped to see its own brand of revolutionary socialism spread to Western

Europe. But in the view of the National Bolsheviks, that hope was bound to be disappointed. Eventually the regime would face up to this fact and would abandon the expectation of a world revolution. Thereafter the Bolshevik regime would evolve into a more or less normal state.

Ustrialov wanted to see the Russian nation, and Russian culture, saved from extinction. But the past, he warned, could not be brought back. Russian culture would have to be "renewed from within." The revolution, strange as that may seem, had made this national renewal possible.

> However, for this to happen—and here we return again to "politics"—Russia must remain a great power and a great state. Otherwise there is no solution to her current spiritual crisis. And because the government of the revolution—and at the present time only that government—has the power to restore Russia as a great power, to restore the international prestige of Russia—it is our duty, in the name of Russian culture, to recognize the political authority of that government.

Although National Bolshevism has long been used to describe this philosophy, the term is misleading. Ustrialov and his followers were not Bolsheviks, and they were not nationalists in the usual sense of this word. Ustrialov voiced some anxiety about the survival of Russian national culture, but his real concern was the survival of the imperial state. Ustrialov openly anticipated the restoration of the Russian empire under Soviet leadership, and he was certain that the "small states" that had broken away from the empire would sooner or later return to Moscow's control.

> The Soviet regime will strive with all its power to reunite the borderlands with the center—in the name of world revolution. Russian patriots will fight for this too—in the name of a great and united Russia. Even with the endless difference in ideology, the practical road is the same. . . .[11]

The ideology of National Bolshevism had an obvious appeal to Russians who wanted to serve the country, but could not bring themselves to accept the new Marxist–Leninist ideology. Such Russians were to be found in particular among army officers and industrial managers who were ready to put their technical know-how in the service of the Soviet state. The National Bolshevik idea was reflected in the career of A.A. Brusilov, who had been a general in the tsarist army. After the revolution, General

Brusilov not only served in the Red Army, but he appealed to other former tsarist officers to join with him.

STALIN AND RUSSIAN NATIONALISM

The task of implementing Lenin's program for the future of Russia fell to Joseph Stalin, an ethnic Georgian who was the Bolshevik party's expert on the nationalities question and became minister for nationalities in the government Lenin established in 1917. After Lenin died in 1924, it was Stalin who succeeded to the leadership of the party. Stalin's nationalities policy clearly aimed at steering a middle course between the dangers of "great-power chauvinism" and "bourgeois nationalism." Even more than Lenin, Stalin was determined to hold intact the multinational state which the Bolsheviks had inherited from the empire. In order to accomplish this overriding objective, Stalin was prepared to make some concessions to the national minorities. In fact, he admitted that one of his objectives was to avoid the mistakes of the Austro-Hungarian "experiment" in trying to create a multinational state.[12]

Like Lenin, Stalin said that the eventual goal of the revolution was that national differences should disappear, and that the nationalities should merge. Unlike Lenin, Stalin was willing to postpone this process almost indefinitely. Stalin insisted that the merger of nations would come, not with the victory of "socialism in one country," but only with the final victory of socialism on a world scale.[13] Furthermore, Stalin drew a distinction between the merger (*sliianie*) of nations and assimilation (*assimilatsiia*). Assimilation, in Stalin's definition, was a policy carried out by force, and Stalin asserted that he was opposed to the use of force to solve the country's nationalities problem. He said that the merger of nations would come voluntarily. Stalin's own policy, which he called "socialism in one country," was to concentrate the resources of the country on the internal development of the Soviet Union. This policy had the effect of postponing the "final victory" of socialism, and therefore the merger of nations, to the indefinite future. What was happening under socialism in the Soviet Union, as Stalin described it, was a rebirth of nations and a new flourishing of national cultures among people that had been oppressed in the empire. The nationalities not only were not merging, but the cultural differences among the nations were growing. But Stalin defended the nationalities policy of the regime, which allowed the development of schools and cultural institutions that used the national language in each republic, and in general encouraged the development of each republic's own culture.

On the other hand, Stalin was not willing to grant political independence to the Soviet nationalities. In fact, he argued that the creation of a sovereign nation state, as a goal for an oppressed nationality, was now out of date, and the nationalities were better off within a multinational state. All the nationalities could find full scope for the development and "flowering" of their own national culture in the federal structure of the Soviet state. This culture, Stalin said, was to be "national in form and socialist in content."[14]

In the 1920s, Soviet nationalities policy concentrated on the political organization of the minorities. One by one republics were created that represented the interests of the minorities—the Ukraine, Belorussia, Georgia, Armenia, and Uzbekistan, for example. The goal of the regime was to raise the cultural and economic level of these minorities, and in so doing it raised the national consciousness of these peoples. The sense of national identity varied considerably among the republics. In some cases (as in Georgia or Armenia) Moscow was dealing with a proud nation with a long history. In other republics, Moscow was to force the development of a backward society where the Muslim tradition was firmly entrenched and the people literally had to be brought out of the Middle Ages. In Uzbekistan, for example, Moscow had to start from the beginning and create a new alphabet, because before 1917 the Uzbeks had no written language of their own.

As a result of this policy a new sense of national identity began to grow in all the republics. No concessions were made to Russian nationalism. The Russian "imperialism" of the tsars was blamed for the backward and impoverished state of the smaller nationalities. Russian history was rewritten, under the supervision of the leading Communist historian of the period, M.N. Pokrovskii. In accordance with Marx's teaching, Pokrovskii's interpretation of history emphasized the class struggle and played down the importance of nationalism. Little attention was given to the heroes of the Russian past, such as Peter the Great. But worst of all, from Stalin's point of view, Pokrovskii regarded the extension of Russian rule to other peoples as colonial exploitation, and he drew no distinction between Russian imperialism and the imperialism of the Western powers.

In the 1930s there was a significant change in nationalities policy, and the change was reflected in a reinterpretation of Russian history. Pokrovskii was denounced and his books were removed from the library shelves. A more traditional view of history now became the official interpretation, and Peter the Great reappeared in the history books. The history of the expansion of the empire into non-Russian regions was also revised. The conquests of the Russian tsars were now viewed as a "positive" development in the life of the national minorities; their absorption into the Russian empire was said to be "progressive" compared with their fate if they had remained outside. Russian patriotism now became acceptable.

However, throughout this period of change in nationalities policy, one aspect of Stalin's plans remained constant. In his 1929 statement he had put off the idea of the merger of nations, and he never changed his mind on this point.

It is sometimes said of Stalin that although he was born a Georgian, he became a Russian nationalist. It is true that Stalin restored some of the institutions of the former empire, and encouraged a positive view of Russian history. This is not the same thing, however, as encouraging Russian nationalism. The Russian empire had never been a national state, and the policy of the tsars was imperialist rather than nationalist. Like the National Bolsheviks, Stalin gave priority to the state rather than the nation.

NATIONALITIES POLICY AFTER STALIN

After Stalin died in 1953, nationalities policy began to tilt once again toward the minorities. The change was most evident in the party organization. With the encouragement of Nikita Khrushchev the party began an active program to recruit new members from the minority nationalities that had been underrepresented in the past. In the republic party organizations, non-Russians were promoted to positions of leadership. In 1957 the Uzbek party leader, N.A. Mukhitdinov, was transferred to Moscow and made a member of the national party secretariat as well as of the Politburo. He was the first party official of Muslim background to reach the top level of the political system. In 1961, however, Mukhitdinov was removed from the party leadership.

Like Stalin, Khrushchev avoided calling for the merger of nations. In fact he said that it would be "premature" to talk about the merger. For the time being he was content to encourage only the "drawing together" (*sblizhenie*) of nationalities. Khrushchev did introduce one new concept into the theory that underlay nationalities policy. He described the Soviet people as a "new historical community of people of various nationalities." This concept was a convenient device for papering over the nationalities problem. In effect Khrushchev was saying that the merger was not taking place, but that the merger was now irrelevant. National differences continued to exist, but the Soviet people can rise above them. Note, however, that Khrushchev was careful not to describe the Soviet people as a "nation." It was something else, different from a nation: a "new historical community."

Khrushchev's views were reflected in the new program of the Communist party, which was adopted in 1961.[15] The party officials who put together this program carefully avoided the very term "merger." They settled on "drawing together" as their objective. Like Khrushchev, they warned that wiping out national differences was a prolonged process, and they offered no timetable for reaching this objective.

Leonid Brezhnev, too, shied away from the idea of "merger." Khrushchev's idea of the supra-national "community" of the Soviet people became the formal basis for nationalities theory.[16] This concept was enshrined in the new Soviet constitution of 1977, although Khrushchev, needless to say, was not given credit for the idea.

RUSSIAN ORTHODOXY AND
RUSSIAN NATIONALISM

Bolshevik theory taught that religion, like nationalism, would eventually disappear after the revolution, as part of a natural historical process. For this reason in the early years after the revolution the Bolshevik regime did not wage a serious antireligious campaign. In the course of the 1920s and the 1930s, however, it became evident that religion was not going to disappear very quickly, and the regime gradually stepped up its efforts to destroy it. Theological schools and large numbers of churches were forcibly closed down, many clergymen were imprisoned, and it appeared for a time as if the regime might succeed in eradicating religion from Soviet life. The Russian Orthodox church, through its acting head, the Metropolitan Sergii, frantically sought some compromise with the regime which would allow the church to function on a limited basis. Sergii argued that a Soviet citizen could be an Orthodox Christian and still be loyal to the state. But the regime ignored Sergii's appeals and the antireligious campaign continued even through the 1930s, when Stalin promoted a revival of Russian traditions. Later, Sergianism was a term used for this policy of seeking a compromise with the Soviet regime.[17] Until the war came, Stalin rejected any idea of compromise with the church. The reasons are not hard to see. Stalin could tolerate the rediscovery of Russian history and Russian literature, because these measures could be kept under political control. The church, on the other hand, was an organization that propagated an ideology that was clearly antithetical to Marxism. If allowed to function freely, the church might prove hard to control.

Sergianism, however, triumphed during the war, when the church proved itself to be "loyal" to the Soviet state. Immediately after the German attack in June 1941, Sergii issued an appeal for Orthodox believers to support the war effort. The Soviet government, which literally had its back to the wall in the first year of the war, accepted support wherever it could be found, even from the church. The result was that toward the end of the war the state and the Orthodox church entered into a kind of concordat: the church agreed to support the regime and refrain from political activity, while the state allowed the church to function in the purely religious sphere. This agreement led to a virtual rebirth of the Russian Orthodox church. Sergii was elected patriarch (the office had been vacant for almost 20 years) and enthroned in a great ceremony in Moscow. Many churches were reopened and the church was allowed to open seminaries for the training of priests, and to publish a limited amount of religious literature. A large number of priests were released—some from service in the Red Army and some from incarceration in the labor camps—to serve in the newly opened churches.

This compromise lasted through the end of the Stalin era, but policy toward the church changed after Khrushchev came to power. Khrushchev's goal was to restore "true" Leninism to the country, and for him Leninism meant (among other things) rooting out religious belief. So beginning in 1959, the regime mounted a new antireligious campaign; once again churches were forcibly closed and some of the seminaries were also shut down. This time the Orthodox church managed to survive as an institution, because it did not actively oppose Khrushchev's religious policy. In fact some Orthodox bishops have been accused of cooperating with the regime in closing down churches. Furthermore, under pressure from the government, the Orthodox church changed its own rules to transfer authority over church affairs from the parish priest to a council of laymen. Obviously, the regime thought it would be easier to subject laymen to political pressure.

But while the patriarchal church was quiescent in the face of this new threat to its existence, some laymen and a few members of the clergy were willing to speak out against the antireligious campaign. In 1965 two parish priests, Gleb Iakunin and Nikolai Eshliman, published an open letter condemning the failure of the church to protect its own interests.

The antireligious campaign subsided after the resignation of Khrushchev, but the churches and seminaries that had been closed were not reopened. The campaign seemed to demonstrate that the survival of the Orthodox church, at least as an organized religion, depended entirely on the tolerance of the state. The result was that the official church hierarchy seemed even more submissive than it had been before.

THE NEW RUSSIAN NATIONALISM

But in one respect, the antireligious campaign had the opposite effect from what was intended. The next decade saw a remarkable resurgence of Russian nationalism and many Russian intellectuals tried to defend the church from continued oppression. Khrushchev's campaign against the church thus must be counted as one of the reasons for the nationalist revival. In addition, Khrushchev's call for de-Stalinization (beginning with his "secret speech" in 1956) created the crisis of faith among many Russian intellectuals referred to at the beginning of this chapter. They had been taught to believe that Stalin was the source of all wisdom. Now, when they were told that Stalin had made tragic mistakes, they began not only to question the Stalin myth, but to entertain doubts about the whole Soviet system. For some, faith in Russia did indeed become a substitute ideology.

Vladimir Osipov was one of the young Russians who experienced this crisis of belief, and he has given us an account of his own transformation from a sincere Marxist to a Russian nationalist. As a student he was a rebel, and in 1962 he was sentenced to a corrective labor camp for engaging in "anti-Soviet agitation and propaganda." His change in belief came in the camps. As Osipov described it:

> It is not for nothing that the concentration camp is called a "corrective-labor" camp. People go in as atheists and leave as Christians. . . .
>   I was certainly reformed by the corrective-labor camp. In the past I had been a materialist, socialist, and atheist. The camp made me a believer in God and a believer in Russia. . . .[18]

Osipov, as we shall see, was to be one of the main nationalist activists in the 1970s.

The new nationalism found expression in many ways. The nationalists ranged from subversives who conspired to overthrow the regime to writers who were in good standing with the Soviet establishment, and managed to get their thoughts past the rigorous censorship.

One of the first expressions of this new movement was the appearance of a secret, conspiratorial organization which called itself the All-Russian Social Christian Union for the Liberation of the People (VSKhSON). VSKhSON has also been called the Berdiaev circle because it took some of its basic ideas from the Russian religious philosopher Nikolai Berdiaev (1874–1948). VSKhSON was dedicated to the overthrow of the Soviet regime, and the establishment of a conservative and nationalist government. The organization came into existence in 1964, or earlier, but it was broken up by the KGB in 1967 and its leaders were imprisoned. The VSKhSON program, which has been published in the West, called for the creation of a theocratic state in which the bishops of the Orthodox church would have a veto over acts of the government. But the program also called for establishing political freedom, including freedom to oppose the government.[19]

At the opposite end of the spectrum was a group of nationalists around the journal *Molodaia gvardiia* (Young Guard). This journal is the official organ of the Communist Youth League, and during most of its existence it has slavishly followed the party line. Begining in 1966, however, *Molodaia gvardiia* began to publish articles pleading the case of Russian nationalism.[20] The pro-nationalist line of *Molodaia gvardiia* was tolerated for several years. But in 1972 a high-ranking official of the Communist party's ideological apparatus, Aleksandr Iakovlev, published an article attacking the nationalist line. The publication of this article was a clear indication that the party was concerned about the new nationalism, for it appeared to be an authoritative statement approved by the top party leadership. Shortly after the article appeared, however, Iakovlev was removed from his post and appointed Soviet ambassador to Canada—in effect, sent off to exile. The regime was sending out mixed signals on the question of Russian nationalism, and that seemed to indicate a conflict over the issue within the leadership.

THE RUSSOPHILE IDEA

The crackdown on *Molodaia gvardiia,* however, did not stop the revival of nationalism among Russian intellectuals. In 1971 Osipov, who had now been released from imprisonment, began to publish a *samizdat* journal devoted to the nationalist cause.[21] The journal, called *Veche,* promised to follow the teaching of the Slavophiles and Dostoevski. Its goal was the revival of Russian national culture. Osipov meant to restore a sense of pride in being Russian: he wanted not only to restore the cultural heritage of the past, but to solve the social problems of alcoholism, the breakup of the family, corruption, and the vulgarization of the language. The journal was produced under difficult circumstances; every issue had to be typed and retyped because it existed only in manuscript form. Furthermore, Osipov himself, as a former political prisoner, was closely watched by the authorities. Nonetheless he managed to put out nine issues of the journal over a period of two years.[22]

Another manifestation of the new nationalism is the "village" writers (*derevenshchiki*) who have been extraordinarily popular with the Russian reading public. Among them are Valentin Rasputin, Vladimir Soloukhin, and the late Fedor Abramov. The views of these writers remind one of Aleksandr Solzhenitsyn, although Solzhenitsyn is not usually included in this group. The village writers find the roots of Russian culture in the village, and they look on the peasant as the best representative of the Russian tradition. They clearly would like to preserve the village and the culture that it represents. Thus the village writers, at least implicitly, are criticizing 60 years of Soviet history. For if there is any one constant aim of Soviet policy, it is the rapid industrialization of the country, which has meant urbanization and the destruction of traditional village life. The village writers are critics of the cult of technology and the new social order brought about by the revolution.

A third variant of Russophilism was the group of Orthodox believers who became active in the mid-1970s. Their spiritual leader was a dissident priest, Dimitrii Dudko. So great was Dudko's influence that Dunlop has described him as a "shadow patriarch" whose courageous opposition to the regime, and in particular his defense of the church, was a sharp contrast to the tradition of "Sergianism."[23] When Dudko's preaching in his Moscow parish attracted large crowds, especially of youth, the patriarchal authorities (probably under pressure from the government) transferred him to a rural church. His followers could travel to the countryside to hear him, but foreign journalists could no longer attend his services. (Dudko's new parish was in a "closed" zone where foreigners were forbidden to travel.)

In 1974, some of Dudko's younger followers organized a "religious–philosophical seminar," possibly the largest opposition organization to appear in the post-Stalin era.[24]

In a sense, the seminar was not an organization at all. It had no formal leadership, no unified organizational structure, and apparently kept no list of members. The seminar consisted of several study groups, which met informally to discuss philosophy, religion, and other concerns of the participants. No news of these activities reached the West until 1976. However, the seminar was not a conspiratorial organization. The organizers made no attempt to conceal their activities once they became known to the security police.

If the VSKhSON was a "Berdiaev circle" then the religious–philosophical seminar might well be called a "Solzhenitsyn circle." The seminar did not even come into existence until several months after Solzhenitsyn's forced exile from the Soviet Union, so it functioned at a time when Solzhenitsyn's works, and even his name, were under ban. Yet the members of the seminar display an easy familiarity both with his ideas and with his style. However, the seminar had no "program." It was devoted to the study of philosophy, and to propagating the Orthodox faith, but it had no political aims. In its "Declaration of Principles" the seminar said that it was open to people of different political convictions, although Communist party members were to be excluded from participation.

"To understand Russia, one must love her. And to love the real Russia means to take up her cross. It is our hope that Russia's protracted crisis will be a way of discovering, through suffering, a new historical path."[25] This statement, from the seminar's "Declaration of Principles," which was widely disseminated in samizdat, sums up their beliefs. The seminar was indisputably nationalist as well as Orthodox in its outlook, but in the declaration it promised that it would not overlook the problems of the national minorities, or fail to respect their rights.

In 1976, the dissident priest Gleb Iakunin organized the Christian Committee for the Defense of Believers' Rights. This was an important step in the history of the movement for human rights (*pravozashchitnoe dvizhenie*) for two reasons. First, it was an organization specifically concerned with religious rights; second, it brought into the human rights movement people with a Russophile and Orthodox orientation. The creation of the committee was thus a significant political achievement. Although composed of Orthodox believers, the committee professed to speak for the interests of all religions. (In fact it was concerned mostly with the rights of Christians, but Christians of all denominations.) The committee succeeded not only in cooperating with other human rights organizations (such as the Helsinki Watch group), but with other Christian churches as well. The committee also accumulated a large file of data about Soviet policy toward the churches. These documents reveal an appalling pattern of religious discrimination.

In its programmatic statement, the Christian Committee insisted that it pursued "no political goals," and that it was "loyal" (*loial'ny*) to Soviet laws. This appears to be a carefully worded formula. The committee was not professing loyalty to the regime (as in Sergii's proclamation), but *loyalty to the regime's laws,* a much narrower formulation.

Iakunin's own writings, which were widely circulated in samizdat, show that he had typically Russophile concerns. He describes Russia as a "martyred" nation, but he looks forward to the rebirth of the nation in a kind of religious renaissance.

The regime was slow to respond to Russophilism and for a time treated it with a benign tolerance. For example, it permitted the creation of the All-Russian Society for the Preservation of Historical and Cultural Monuments in the 1960s. This organization, generally regarded as a hotbed of Russian nationalism, campaigned to save old churches from destruction, and to restore old religious art. Eventually the party leadership came to recognize the Russophile idea as a threat to the official Marxist–Leninist ideology, and it responded accordingly. In 1974 Aleksandr Solzhenitsyn was forcibly expelled from the Soviet Union, and a few months later Osipov was arrested and put on trial for "anti-Soviet propaganda." But in keeping with its general policy on coping with political dissent, the regime moved cautiously. It was not until 1979–1980 that the police arrested the leaders of the Christian Seminar, Poresh and Ogorodnikov, as well as Iakunin and Dudko. After languishing in a KGB jail for several months, Dudko recanted his views; he made a rather strange appearance on Moscow television in which he acknowledged past errors and confessed to "anti-Soviet activity." The others were put on trial, convicted of political crimes, and given long sentences.

THE NATIONAL BOLSHEVIK IDEA: REPRISE

"Governments come and go, but Russia remains, and we must all serve her." This statement, which has been attributed to General Brusilov, summarizes the philosophy of National Bolshevism.[26] The National Bolsheviks of the present day, like their predecessors in the 1920s, seek a reconciliation with the regime. Possibly they share Ustrialov's belief that the Soviet Union must eventually evolve into a more traditional type of authoritarian state.

Like the Russophiles, the National Bolsheviks are Russian nationalists, but there is a vast difference between them. The great hero of the Russophiles is Solzhenitsyn. The National Bolsheviks, in contrast, despise him; one of the leading members of this school, the historian Nikolai Iakovlev, has lent his services to the regime in the effort to discredit Solzhenitsyn.[27] For the National Bolsheviks, the most admired men are probably General Brusilov and the writer Mikhail Sholokhov.

Solzhenitsyn feels no differently about the National Bolshevik idea. He describes it as an ideology that is unable to distinguish between the good and bad in Russian history, and unable to distinguish between tsarism and Bolshevism. Thus Communism is identified with patriotism and Russia with the USSR.[28] Unfortunately many Western writers, in commenting on Solzhenitsyn, have overlooked his criticism of the form of Russian nationalism represented by National Bolshevism.

As Dunlop points out, there is an affinity between National Bolshevism and fascism.[29] Without being overt militarists, they are fawning in their praise of the armed forces. No previous society, according to Sergei Semanov, has seen such an "organic unity" between the army and the nation.[30] He comes close to saying that the officer corps is the best representative of the people; even before the revolution the Russian officer corps was not a closed caste (as in Western states), but came from different sections of the population. And unlike the Russophiles, who are willing to respect the rights of the minority nationalities, the National Bolsheviks insist that the annexation of the borderlands was progressive, and in the best interests of the peoples who lived there.[31]

Another important difference between the two variants of nationalism is that some of the leading Russophiles have been dissidents. Although this means that they were hounded by the regime and ultimately silenced, the Russophile writers did for a time exercise the peculiar freedom of speech that samizdat provided. This made it possible for them to put forth a concrete political program.[32] By contrast the National Bolshevik writers are very much members of the Soviet establishment, and thus are not completely free to speak their minds. For this reason, the National Bolshevik program can only be inferred indirectly from their writings.

Some of the leading National Bolsheviks are historical writers, and much of their work is concentrated on World War II or World War I. One of the most popular books in this genre is Iakovlev's *August 1, 1914.*[33] The work was clearly written and published to counter Solzhenitsyn's *August 1914,* but it provides a useful statement of the National Bolsheviks' interpretation of the fall of the tsarist regime.

The National Bolsheviks are not monarchists; their view of the monarchy is summed up in a curious formulation of Iakovlev: "Tsarism . . . kept Russia from taking her proper place in the world."[34] Iakovlev does, however, present a picture of the last tsar, Nicholas II, which is somewhat unusual for a Soviet work. He defends the tsar against the charge that he was dominated by the "holy man" Rasputin, and he defends the empress Aleksandra against the charge that she was pro-German during the war.

The regime finds the National Bolshevik writers useful (especially for propaganda work), and at the same time potentially dangerous. In the 1920s, in the formative years of the regime, Ustrialov's ideas provided a useful tool in the regime's efforts to win mass support and consolidate its power. Today, however, the National Bolshevik ideology, if clearly articulated, could be a serious challenge to the internationalist ideology of the regime. Although the regime has been more tolerant of National Bolshevism than of the Russophile idea, it has shown that there are limits to this tolerance. In 1982 Sergei Semanov was more or less publicly disgraced.[35] The treatment of Semanov was undoubtedly intended to be a message to others.

THE ANDROPOV INTERLUDE

During Yuri Andropov's brief tenure as general secretary, it was clear that he was opposed to Russian nationalism.[36] Andropov made no sweeping pronouncements on the question, but his views and his intentions can be inferred from some specific steps that were taken in 1982 and 1983.

The first major appointment of the new general secretary was to summon Geidar Aliev to Moscow. Aliev, who is an ethnic Azeri (and thus of Muslim and Turkic background) was then the first secretary of the Azerbaidzhan party organization, and he had spent his entire career in the republic. As first secretary, he had been made a candidate (or nonvoting member) of the Politburo under Brezhnev. But at that point he seemed to have risen as high in the system as he could. Now Andropov promoted him to full membership in the Politburo, and appointed him USSR vice-premier. In the vice-premier's job, Aliev became the most logical candidate to succeed the premiership when N.A. Tikhonov (who was then 77) finally vacated the post. Furthermore, as an experienced party official and full member of the Politburo, Aliev (despite his non-Russian background) cannot be ruled out entirely as a possible contender for the office of general secretary. Like Mukhitdinov 20 years ago, Aliev is a living symbol of the internationalist ideology of the Soviet regime.

Two weeks later Andropov removed the director of the Communist party's propaganda department, E.M. Tiazhelnikov, and replaced him with Boris Stukalin. The director of this department is the operating manager of the party's ideological apparatus. Tiazhelnikov had once been head of the Communist Youth League and thus had some responsibility for *Molodaia gvardiia*. (The Russophile line of *Molodaia gvardiia* was at its height during Tiazhelnikov's tenure.) Stukalin had been the chief executive of the Soviet publishing industry, and his attitude toward the Russophiles is not known. There is some evidence, however, that he was not friendly to the village writers and the ideas that they represented.[37]

Another appointment was also significant. Aleksandr Iakovlev was brought back from his exile in Canada to become director of the Institute for World Economy and International Relations (IMEMO), a think tank for specialists in foreign policy. These personnel changes offer somewhat obscure hints about Andropov's thinking on the Russophiles, but this is typical of the evidence that Kremlinologists must sometimes pursue in their study of Soviet policy making.

Andropov's first direct pronouncement in nationalities policy came a little more than a month after his accession to office. On December 21 he spoke in the Kremlin at a ceremonial meeting held in observance of the 60th anniversary of the Soviet Union. Much of his speech reviewed the policy line that had developed over the preceding two decades. He spoke of the "new historical community" of the Soviet people, and of the "flowering" and "bringing together" of all the nationalities. But then he unexpectedly revived the half-forgotten concept of merger: "Our final goal is clear. It is, using the words of V.I. Lenin, 'not only a bringing together of nations, but their merger.' "[38] Andropov did not raise the question of *sliianie* again. He did, however, call for better representation of the minority nationalities in both party and government bodies.

Another clear signal about Andropov's attitude toward the nationalists came with the trial of Leonid Borodin, which took place in May 1983. Borodin was a former member of VSKhSON who had already served a term for this activity, and in 1974 was briefly involved in Osipov's *Veche*. As far as we know, during the intervening years Borodin had not been politically active. Nonetheless he was put on trial for "anti-Soviet propaganda" and as a repeat offender he received the maximum sentence of 10 years incarceration followed by five years of internal exile. Georgii Vladimov, a Soviet writer who emigrated to the West after the sentencing, has suggested that the trial of Borodin was deliberately staged as a warning to other Russian nationalists.[39]

Andropov seems to have become critically ill in August or September 1983, and no longer had an active role in policy making. We can presume that had he lived longer, he would have continued to follow a hostile line toward manifestations of Russian nationalism.

CHERNENKO AND RUSSIAN NATIONALISM

The election of Chernenko, as already noted, brought to the office of general secretary an ethnic Russian with significant experience outside the Russian republic. His views on the national question, as far as they are known, do not appear to differ significantly from those of Andropov. Chernenko has followed the party line in support for the "flowering" of national cultures, and at the same time has spoken out against Russian nationalism.[40]

In June 1983 the party's Central Committee, for the first time in 20 years, held a plenary meeting devoted to questions of ideology, and Chernenko delivered the principal address. With its implicit criticism of the village writers and its explicit criticism of the Central Committee's department of culture, this address can also be interpreted as a direct attack on Russian nationalism. The main theme of the speech was the need for a revival of Marxism–Leninism. The address was filled with ideological cliches (references to the "class enemy," for example) that had been heard rarely in recent years. Chernenko was especially critical of the social sciences, insisting that they should be guided by "revolutionary theory." And in a particularly chilling passage, he reminded his audience: "there are truths that are not subject to reexamination. . . . We must not, in the guise of science, 'forget' about the basic principles of materialist dialectics."[41]

Later in the address, Chernenko criticized certain "errors" that had appeared in literature, such as "God-seeking" or the "idealization of patriarchal society."[42] Finally, in a somewhat surprising statement, Chernenko mentioned the large number of believers that still were to be found in Soviet society.

THE DEMOGRAPHIC PROBLEM

One of the policy problems that Chernenko will have to deal with is the changing ethnic structure of the Soviet population. In this chapter we have referred to the non-Russian nationalities as the "minorities." However, if present population trends continue, the Russians themselves could become a minority by the year 2000. The recent demographic development of the Soviet Union has been described as a race between the Slavs and the

Figure 1. Total Fertility Rate for the USSR, Russian Republic (RSFSR), and the Uzbek Republic

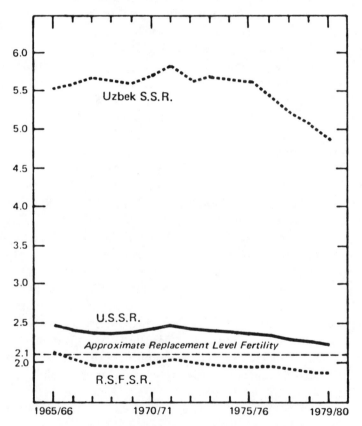

Note: The "total fertility rate" is the average number of children that would be born to each woman if she were to live through her childbearing years.

Source: Rosemarie Crisostomo, *The Demographic Dilemma of the Soviet Union* (Washington, D.C.: U.S. Bureau of the Census, Center for International Research, International Research Document no. 10, August 1983), p. 5. Reprinted with permission of the author.

Muslims, with the Slavs losing out.[43] This threat to the Russian majority is the result of the high rate of birth in families living in the Central Asian republics, compared with the much lower birth rate among Russians. The peoples of Soviet Central Asia are Muslim by tradition, and most of them speak a Turkic language. As Fig. 1 shows, the Muslim population is growing at about three times the rate of the Russian population. At the present time, Islamic peoples constitute about 17 percent of the total population. Given present trends, by the year 2000 their proportion will grow to about 25 percent.[44]

The demographic problem is one that Soviet population specialists do not discuss openly. Russian nationalists whose writings appear in samizdat, however, have expressed genuine concern about the possibility—indeed the likelihood—that Russians will eventually become a minority in the Soviet Union.[45] This increase in the Muslim population has confronted the regime with some difficult policy choices, both with regard to manpower and in nationality policy. First, a crucial decision will have to be made about the Soviet armed forces. In the past, draftees with a Muslim background have been segregated from soldiers of Slavic nationality. The Slavs have gone into regular military formations, but Muslims have been assigned to construction units where they were put to work both for the military and sometimes for the civilian economy. Some Muslims have gone to military units of the Ministry of Internal Affairs (MVD) where they have such assignments as camp guards. In the future, if the armed forces are to maintain their present strength, the regime will have to consider assigning more Muslim soldiers to regular military units. The consequences of such a change in the ethnic composition of the army are hard to predict.

The demographic problem also will affect the civilian labor force. In the past, the Soviet economy has been able to draw on a seemingly endless supply of labor. That era is now past, at least in the Slavic part of the Soviet Union. But there is a large pool of manpower in the Muslim republics. The regime must decide how to tap this manpower. It has two choices. It can either: (a) encourage the migration of Muslims from their own republics into the more industrialized areas of the country, or (b) it can move industry to where the labor is, and concentrate future industrial development in the Muslim republics. Chernenko dealt with the problem with unusual frankness in his June 1982 address, and declared that his preference was to send the manpower to the area where it was needed.[46]

CONCLUSION

The demographic problem is only one of the challenges that the new general secretary faces. The nationalities question covers a host of social and political problems that the Soviet leadership will have to address sooner or later. It was suggested above that Russian nationalism is more than just a substitute ideology; it is an attempt to deal with real issues as perceived by thoughtful Russians. But insofar as we can understand Chernenko's thinking, he appears to be approaching nationalism as if it were basically an ideological problem. Even before the death of Andropov, Chernenko had become the chief ideologist of the Politburo, and seemed determined to force through a revival of Marxism–Leninism.

Solzhenitsyn's great challenge to the Soviet leadership was his demand that the official ideology be abandoned.[47] Other Russian nationalists would argue that even if the regime refuses to abandon it (and there is no sign that they want to follow Solzhenitsyn's advice), the official ideology is, for all practical purposes, dead. Restoring Marxism–Leninism, if that is Chernenko's intent, means simply wasting resources to support a useless bureaucracy, that is, the ideological apparatus of the party. Chernenko could achieve the appearance of success. But he will find (so the Russian nationalists argue) that he faces an increasingly apathetic and disillusioned population for which the old slogans have no meaning, that he can no longer use the doctrine to mobilize support for the regime and its program.

At that point the regime will face the temptation to exploit Russian nationalism, as Stalin did during the war. But the problems that the regime faces now are more complicated and more long-range than the problem of winning a war. For the regime to appeal openly for support on a platform of Russian nationalism would not only undermine the official doctrine which is its major source of legitimacy. It would certainly alienate the national minorities and could conceivably threaten the breakup of the multinational state.

NOTES

1. David K. Shipler, *Russia: Broken Idols, Solemn Dreams* (New York: Times Books, 1983).

2. John B. Dunlop, *The Faces of Contemporary Russian Nationalism* (Princeton: Princeton University Press, 1983).

3. Mikhail Agursky, *The New Russian Literature* (Hebrew University of Jerusalem, Soviet and East European Research Centre, research paper no. 40, July 1980); Mikhail Agurskii, "Natsionalsnyi vopros v SSSR," *Kontinent*, 10 (1976): 149–72.

4. Aleksandr Solzhenitsyn, *Letter to the Soviet Leaders*, Hilary Sternberg, trans. (New York: Harper & Row, 1974), pp. 21–22.

5. Roy Medvedev, "What Awaits Us in the Future? (Regarding A. Solzhenitsyn's Letter)," in *The Political, Social and Religious Thought of Russian 'Samizdat'—An Anthology*, Michael Meerson-Aksenov and Boris Shragin, eds. (Belmont, MA: Norland, 1977), p. 77.

6. Alexander Yanov, *The Russian New Right: Right-Wing Ideologies in the Contemporary USSR* (Berkeley, CA: Institute of International Studies, University of California, 1978), p. 19; Elena Klepikova and Vladimir Solovyov, "The Secret Russian Party," *Midstream* 26 (October 1980): 12.

7. See Jerry F. Hough, *Soviet Leadership in Transition* (Washington, D.C.: The Brookings Institution, 1980), p. 65.

8. Dunlop focuses on the Russophiles' hope for a rebirth of Russia, and he calls them *vozrozhdentsy* (from *vozrozhdenie* or rebirth). I have used the term Russophile because it is most widely used in the Soviet Union. Dunlop, *Contemporary Russian Nationalism*, pp. 242–43.

9. V.I. Lenin, *Selected Works* (New York: International Publishers, 1971), p. 160. *"Sliianie"* means a "flowing together," as at the confluence of two rivers. In some notes written in German at the same time as this article, but not published until 1937, Lenin used the phrase *"Verschmelzung der Nationen." Leninskii sbornik* (Moscow: Partizdat, 1937), vol. 30, p. 128. For a more detailed analysis of Lenin's ideas and his policies in the early years of the Soviet regime, see Peter Zwick, *National Communism* (Boulder, CO: Westview Press, 1983), Chapter 3.

10. Richard Pipes, *The Formation of the Soviet Union: Communism and Nationalism 1917–1922* (Cambridge, MA: Harvard University Press, 1954), especially Chapter 2.

11. Ustrialov's article "Patriotica," was included in the collection *Smena vekh* (Prague, 1921), pp. 52–71, and it was widely read both in Russia and in the emigration; the article had originally been published in June 1920. The quotations are from *Smena vekh*, pp. 57 and 59. The origins of National Bolshevism have been described in detail in the study by Mikhail Agurskii, *Ideologiia national-bol'shevizma* (Paris: YMCA Press, 1980).

12. "On the Draft Constitution of the USSR," in Joseph Stalin, *Problems of Leninism,* 11th ed. (Moscow: Foreign Languages Publishing House, 1953), p. 687.

13. "The National Question and Leninism," in Joseph Stalin, *Works* (Moscow: Foreign Languages Publishing House, 1954), vol. 11, pp. 348–71. This article was written in 1929, but not published until 20 years later.

14. Stalin, "On the Draft Constitution of the USSR," p. 687.

15. For an English translation see *Soviet Communism: Program and Rules,* Jan Triska, ed. (San Francisco: Chandler Publishing Co., 1962). Khrushchev's principal statement on the nationalities issue will be found in a speech to the 22d Party Congress: *XXII s'ezd KPSS; stenograficheskii otchet,* 3 vols. (Moscow: Politicheskaia literatura, 1962), vol. 1, pp. 153, 215ff.

16. Brezhnev's most important statement on this topic came in a speech in December 1972 which marked the fiftieth anniversary of the creation of the USSR. Leonid Brezhnev, *Leninskim kursom* (Moscow: Politicheskaia literatura, 1974), vol. 4, pp. 41–101.

17. For a discussion of the status of the Orthodox church in the Soviet state, see the two studies by William C. Fletcher, *A Study in Survival: The Church in Russia 1927–1943* (New York: Macmillan, 1965); and Michael Bourdeaux, *Patriarchs and Prophets* (New York: Praeger, 1970).

18. Vladimir Osipov, *Tri otnosheniia k rodine* (Frankfurt: Posev, 1978), pp. 80, 84.

19. On VSKhSON see John B. Dunlop, *The New Russian Revolutionaries* (Belmont, MA: Nordland, 1976).

20. For an analysis of this incident, see Dunlop, *Contemporary Russian Nationalism,* p. 217. The *Molodaia gvardiia* episode is described by a Soviet dissident, Raissa Lert, in *An End to Silence: Uncensored Opinion in the Soviet Union,* Stephen F. Cohen, ed. (New York: Norton, 1982), pp. 189–200.

21. *Samizdat* refers to underground writing that has not been approved for publication by the Soviet censorship. Most samizdat writing circulates in manuscript form, and is widely read by Soviet intellectuals. Samizdat material that has reached the West has been reproduced by the Samizdat Archive in Munich. All their publications are assigned an archive (AS) number, and can be referenced in this way.

22. The programmatic statement of *Veche,* from the first issue of the journal, is translated in Dunlop, *Contemporary Russian Nationalism,* pp. 296–97. *Veche* is an old word denoting a popular assembly in medieval Russia.

23. Dunlop, *Contemporary Russian Nationalism,* p. 190. A collection of Dudko's sermons on religious themes has been published in English: *Our Hope,* Paul D. Garrett, trans. (Crestwood, NY: St. Vladimir's Seminary Press, 1977). Unfortunately Dudko's more political and nationalist writings have not appeared in English. These include *Veriu, gospodi* (London, Ontario: Zaria, 1978); and *Premudrost'iu vonmem* (New York: Free Word, 1980).

24. See Jane Ellis, "USSR: The Christian Seminar." *Religion in Communist Lands,* 8 (1980): 92–112; Philip Walters, "The Ideas of the Christian Seminar," *Religion in Communist Lands,* 9 (1981): 111–26; *Vol'noe slovo,* no. 39 (1980), an issue devoted to the Seminar.

25. "Deklaratsiia printsipov Seminara," *Obshchina* no. 2 (AS no. 3452), pp. 19–20.

26. Sergei Semanov, *Serdtse rodiny* (Moscow: Moskovskii rabochii, 1977), p. 27. Semanov, one of the leading National Bolshevik writers, is also the author of a biography of General Brusilov: *Brusilov* (Moscow: Molodaia gvardiia, 1980).

27. Iakovlev wrote two books denouncing Solzhenitsyn: *Solzhenitsyn's Archipelago of Lies* (Moscow: Novosti, 1974); *Living a Lie: The Anti-Soviet Activity of Solzhenitsyn* (Moscow: Novosti, 1976).

28. Aleksandr Solzhenitsyn, *Iz-pod glyb: sbornik statei* (Paris: YMCA Press, 1974), p. 129.

29. Dunlop, *Contemporary Russian Nationalism,* p. 256.

30. Semanov, *Serdtse rodiny,* p. 24.

31. See, for example, ibid., p. 43.

32. As Solzhenitsyn did in his *Letter to the Soviet Leaders,* Hilary Sternberg, trans. (New York: Harper & Row, 1974).

33. N. Iakovlev, *1 avgusta 1914* (Moscow: Molodaia gvardiia, 1974).

34. Ibid., p. 130.

35. Semanov had been chief editor of an important journal, *Chelovek i zakon.* He was dismissed from this position and rumors reached the West that he had been arrested. These rumors proved to be wrong (*Novaia gazeta,* December 11–17, 1982), but Semanov remains in semi-disgrace.

36. See Zhores Medvedev, *Andropov* (New York: Norton, 1983), p. 118.

37. Agursky, *The New Russian Literature,* p. 9.

38. *Pravda,* December 22, 1983. These words are from Lenin's *The Socialist Revolution and the Right of Nations to Self-Determination* (1916), which was cited above (see note 9).

39. *Russkaia mysl'* (Paris), July 7, 1983.

40. Konstantin Chernenko, *Human Rights in Soviet Society* (New York: International Publishers, 1982), p. 49; see Marc D. Zlotnik, "The Chernenko Platform," *Problems of Communism,* 31 (November–December 1982): 70–75.

41. *Pravda,* June 15, 1983. While Chernenko delivered an "address" (*doklad*) at this meeting, Andropov gave only a "speech" (*rech*); clearly Chernenko's address was intended to be the major policy statement on this occasion.

42. Ibid. Chernenko said this had occurred, "for example," in studies of collectivization, but he obviously had a broader context in mind.

43. Alexandre Bennigsen and Marie Broxup, *The Islamic Threat to the Soviet State* (New York: St. Martins Press, 1983), p. 125. On the demographic problem, see also the study by Helene Carrere d'Encausse, *Decline of an Empire* (New York: Newsweek Books, 1979), Chapter 3.

44. Rosemarie Crisostomo, *The Demographic Dilemma of the Soviet Union* (Washington, D.C.: U.S. Bureau of the Census, Center for International Research, International Research Document no. 10, August 1983), p. 5.

45. The problem is discussed by K. Voronov (probably a pseudonym), "Demograficheskie problemy Rossii," in Osipov's *Veche* (1973) no. 9, [AS no. 2040]. The article was republished in the emigre journal *Grani* (1975) 98: 255.

46. *Pravda,* June 15, 1983. Curiously, Chernenko spoke both of the need to "attract" (*privlech*) and to "send" (*napravit*) labor from regions of surplus manpower. It is clear from the context of this statement that he was thinking of the nationality problem.

47. In his *Letter to the Soviet Leaders.*

8

SOVIET ETHNIC POLICY IN THE 1980s: THEORETICAL CONSISTENCY AND POLITICAL REALITY

Dan N. Jacobs and Theresa M. Hill

One of the most persistent and difficult domestic issues confronting Soviet leadership in the 1980s is nationality policy. In the prerevolutionary period, Lenin only reluctantly paid attention to nationality. In the seven decades since his death, Soviet authorities have hardly considered this a primary policy area, asserting (and to a great extent, believing) that Marxism–Leninism had solved, or was well on the way to solving, all problems based on nationality differences in the USSR. Yet nationality concerns persist, and give little indication of soon going away.

Today within the Soviet Union there are still between 90 and 100 different nationalities, of whom the Russians are the most numerous, encompassing slightly over 50 percent of the total population of the USSR. In addition, there are 170 other ethnic groups. Two hundred languages and dialects are spoken. The fact is that after more than 65 years of Communist rule, the people of the Union of Soviet Socialist Republics, all Marxist–Leninist expectations to the contrary, have to a great extent held on to their ethnic identifications.

In this chapter, the authors, by examining the historical record of Soviet nationality policy, will show that the Soviet leadership has failed to create a new Soviet person and that the supposed homogeneity of the Soviet masses is nothing more than a myth. It is not unusual for the casual observer to regard the Soviet Union as a monolithic state, controlled by a party–state structure that has eradicated conflict within its borders and repressed and terrorized the Soviet citizenry until it has become an undifferentiated mass. Examination of the data on the Soviet Union will reveal important differences in such indicators as birth rates, party membership, and levels of urbanization among the ethnically diverse peoples within the various republics. An understanding and evaluation of these and other social, economic, and political indicators shed light on the range of nationality differences within the USSR. Moreover, the analysis will show how the continued vitality of traditional national and ethnic attachments creates low-level problems that have a cumulative effect, undermining plans not only for reforming the economy but also for the realization of the "New Soviet Man."

As a starting point for comprehending nationality policy in the Soviet Union, it is necessary to be aware of the process through which Russia acquired its present geographic form and multinational character.

HISTORICAL LEGACY

The Soviet Union accounts for one-sixth of the earth's land surface. It is the largest political unit in the world, with a total area of 22,402,220 sq. km., roughly twice the size of the United States. The political divisions of the state are quite extensive and reflect the distribution of national groups. The Soviet Union is divided into 15 Union republics, 20 autonomous republics, 8 autonomous provinces, and 10 national districts, all organized on the basis of nationality. As an initial introduction, Table 4 illustrates the share of nationalities that have Union republic status in the total population of the USSR. If we examine the Soviet Union today, we find that it and its predecessor state have not always been as extensive.

The formation of the Soviet predecessor began in 1462 (see Map 1) with the coming to the throne of Ivan III (1462–1505) in the comparatively minute Grand Duchy of Muscovy, or Moscow. Muscovy was able to succeed in centralizing its power first and foremost because the Mongol horde that had swept over Russia in the thirteenth century did not take physical control of the northeastern region of Russia, where Moscow was located. While in the southern steppe lands surrounding Kiev the Khans administered directly, in the northeast they ruled indirectly through the Russian princes, requiring them only to pay a tribute. In addition, the Grand Duchy benefited from its central geographic location, as well as from the political astuteness of some of its princes. Rulers like Ivan III and Ivan IV (who, in 1547, was declared "tsar of all of the Russias") understood how to penetrate the areas they wanted to acquire.

Table 4. Share of Nationalities of Union-Republic Status in Total Population of the USSR in 1959, 1970, and 1979 (percentages)

Nationalities	1959	1970	1979
Slavs			
Russians	54.60	53.40	52.40
Ukrainians	17.80	16.90	16.20
Belorussians	3.80	3.70	3.60
	76.20	74.00	72.20
Moldavians	1.06	1.12	1.13
Muslims, Excluding Azerbaidzhanis			
Uzbeks	2.88	3.80	4.75
Kazakhis	1.73	2.19	2.50
Tadzhiks	0.67	0.88	1.11
Turkmens	0.48	0.63	0.77
Kirghizi	0.46	0.60	0.73
	6.22	8.10	9.86
Transcaucasian, Including Azerbaidzhanis			
Azerbaidzhanis	1.41	1.81	2.09
Armenians	1.33	1.47	1.58
Georgians	1.29	1.34	1.36
	4.03	4.62	5.03
Balts			
Lithuanians	1.11	1.10	1.09
Latvians	0.67	0.59	0.55
Estonians	0.47	0.42	0.39
	2.25	2.11	2.03

Source: Adapted from Ann Sheehy's "The National Composition of the Population of the USSR According to the Census of 1979," *Radio Liberty Research,* 123/80, March 27, 1980, p. 14.

There are two striking features of Russian expansionism that began in the 1470s and continued for the next five centuries. First, while the state leaders have always maintained that their expansion was intended for such lofty purposes as reuniting Kievan Rus or rescuing Orthodox bretheren or extending the Revolution, in fact the state leaders were primarily interested in amassing land and consolidating their power. Second, and perhaps more

Map 1. The Growth of the Russian State*

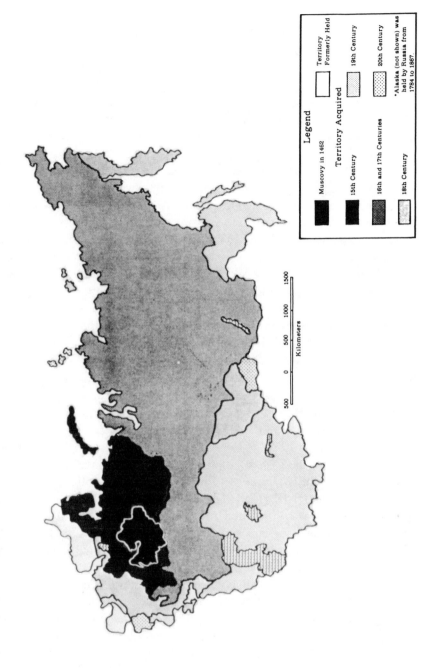

Legend

Territory Formerly Held

Territory Acquired

Muscovy in 1462

15th Century

16th and 17th Centuries

18th Century

19th Century

20th Century

*Alaska (not shown) was held by Russia from 1784 to 1867.

Kilometers

500   0   500   1000   1500

significant, while the areas Russia initially annexed were inhabited by fellow Slavs, as Russian expansionism extended in every direction, non-Slavic people fell into the Russian fold and the Russian state became a multinational empire.

The areas first annexed were those immediately around Moscow—the principalities of Rostov, Novgorod, Chernigov, and Tver. In addition, Ivan IV took full advantage of the disintegration of the empire of the Mongols to conquer the non-Slavic areas of Kazan and Astrakhan formerly held by the Mongols. Russian expansionism in the sixteenth and seventeenth centuries was primarily across the Urals and into western Siberia. The areas around the Baltic were annexed in the eighteenth century as a result of Peter the Great's victory over Sweden. Russia also acquired portions of Poland when the latter was partioned in 1772, 1791, and 1795. Finland was acquired in the nineteenth century, as were the Caucasus and the vast Central Asian regions. At the end of World War I, Russia lost Finland, the Baltic states, and Poland. The Baltic states were regained by the Soviet Union in 1940. The Soviet Union attained its current borders in the aftermath of World War II when it annexed some former East Prussian land, the sub-Carpathian Ukraine, and, in a limited sense, Poland, Hungary, Rumania, Bulgaria, East Germany, and Czechoslovakia, which became Soviet dependencies.

The basic policy of tsarist Russia toward its non-Russian peoples until 1881 was one of toleration. Despite the fact that there had been a policy of "Russification" in Poland after 1815, and measures were sometimes taken to quell Ukrainian nationalist sentiment, most areas enjoyed considerable cultural freedom. The assassination of Alexander II on March 13, 1881, however, significantly altered the Russian nationality policy. His son and successor, Alexander III (1881–1894), embarked on a serious Russification campaign that was continued by his successor, Nicholas II. The Poles, Georgians, Armenians, Finns and the Catholics, Moslems, and Jews were all subjected to the government's policy of "orthodoxy, autocracy, nationality." Attempts were made to force non-Russians to give up their language and idiosyncratic instruction in both church and state schools. The Russian language and a state-dictated curriculum took their place. The regime, viewing individualism as a danger, sought a homogeneous society. The plight of the Russian Jews illustrates the repressive nationality policy of tsarist Russia after 1881. The Jews, who unlike other ethnic groups were defined by religion, were numerous in western Russia. There they were forced to reside in the "Pale of the Jewish Settlement," not being allowed to travel, let alone live, outside it except under special circumstances. Quotas were placed on the number of Jewish students allowed to enter institutions of higher learning: "Ten percent of the total enrollment within the Pale of Jewish settlement, 5 percent in other provinces, and 3 percent in Moscow and St. Petersburg."[1] Further restrictions imposed in the late 1880s confined the movement of the Jews to urban areas, subjected their young men to long terms in the army, and prohibited their purchase of real estate. The most sinister aspect of the government's attitude toward Jews can be seen in the outbreaks of anti-Semitic violence in town and rural areas—the notorious pogroms—which after 1881 became common and were tolerated, even at times inspired, by the government.

The tsarist nationality policy of Russification did not succeed in "Russifying" nearly so much as it did in alienating many of the national groups within Russia's borders. Among each of these groups were those who concluded that the only way out for them was the establishment of their own countries, and the appropriate vehicle for achieving that objective was revolution.

The greatest force behind the push for revolution in Russia in the late nineteenth and early twentieth centuries was nationalism. To the minority nationalities (i.e., the Poles, Lithuanians, Latvians, Estonians, Ukrainians, Belorussians, and others) nationalism meant liberation from Russian domination, harrassment, and persecution. In fact, for these minority nationalities, the solution to all of their problems seemed to be independence from Russia. However, another insistent voice of revolution, Marxism, took a different position.

Marx held that nationalism was not a liberating force, but rather an integral part of the capitalist machinery for enslavement of the working masses. Within this context, nationalism was a delusion conjured up by the bourgeoisie to manipulate the working class (proletariat) and keep it in line. The phenomenon of nationalism enabled the bourgeoisie to focus the hostility of the proletariat on foreign workers rather than on the bosses at home who, Marx maintained, were the true enemies. After the revolution, when there would be a single class, nationalism would disappear.* Distinctions of nationhood (e.g., French, English, German) would evaporate. No longer motivated by considerations of nationality, individuals would lose their parochial, or ethnic, character and become truly "international."†

Along with the eradication of nationalism, Marx held, would come the elimination of national boundaries. Since the latter was an objective for

---

*Worker–master and other "class" distinctions would be eliminated by the revolution.

†Marx undoubtedly thought of himself as a thoroughgoing internationalist. However, his writings indicate that he was not devoid of nationalist impulses. He repeatedly indicated that he thought his German culture to be superior and that Slavs, in general, were hardly civilized.

Marx, he certainly did not favor the division of the Europe he knew into a still greater number of states. For Marx, in countries as in other things, bigger was better.

Though demonstrably a Great Russian chauvinist, Lenin basically accepted the Marxist attitude toward nationalism. He was convinced that ultimately there would be a single people worldwide, with one culture and one language; that the unfolding of history would disclose, in his words, "not only the drawing together (*sblizhenie*), of nations, but also their merging (*sliyanie*)."[2] However, Lenin was first and foremost a practical politician, consumed by the drive to win and maintain power, and he tailored his nationality policy to further his cause. In Russia, the chief support for revolution came from national groups like the Poles, Lithuanians, Ukrainians, and Jews, seeking to free themselves from Russian hegemony. If Lenin was to have their support, he needed a political formulation that would attract them. Saying that Polish, Lithuanian, Ukrainian, Jewish nationhood—the most fervent demand of the ethnics—was a delusion would get Lenin nowhere, even though he opposed their national aspirations, both as a Marxist and as a Russian, and considered the nationalist question, as he put it, to be a "relatively minor one."[3]

Accordingly, Lenin devised a policy that appeared to reconcile both his and the nationalists' objectives, at least until the revolution. However, because it was ultimately a pro-Russian policy, seeking the preservation of the Russian empire, Lenin sought to make it more palatable to the nationalists by presenting it as the idea of a non–Great Russian. Thus, he provided material to the Georgian Bolshevik, Joseph Stalin, and more or less stage-managed the writing of *Marxism and the National Problem,* which became the official Bolshevik policy on nationalism.

Out of *Marxism and the National Problem* came the theory of "self-determination," which in effect held that at the moment of revolution, a national group on the periphery of Russia could declare its independence and establish its own country.* While Lenin did not approve such a step, he did offer it as a possibility. It is clear that Lenin did not think that minorities would avail themselves of the possibility, because the masses would recognize the advantages of a big state and a big economy, as opposed to a small state and a limited economy. If they did not recognize the advantages, however, they could go their own way, but only if they opted for independence at the critical moment of revolution. If the nationality group on the

---

*A national group surrounded by Russians could not establish an independent state, because an independent state inside another is an anomaly.

periphery did not opt for independence at the critical moment, or if it was not on the periphery, it was to remain forever a part of the new socialist entity set up by the revolution.

The Lenin–Stalin nationality policy was attractive to the nationalists and helped to stimulate the formation of Bolshevik organizations among some of the national groups in the prerevolutionary years. However, soon after the seizure of power in October 1917, Lenin (his earlier professions and reinforcements, as late as November 1917, of the "moment of opportunity" notwithstanding) sought to keep "old" Russia together. While he recognized the danger of "Great Russian chauvinism" (the predominance of Great Russians over the other nationalities), he had his priorities. Forced to choose between Great Russian chauvinism and the disintegration of the tsarist empire, he would overlook the "principle of self-determination" and opt for the maintenance of as much of old Russia as he could keep intact.

Lenin initially enjoyed little success toward that goal. In late 1917 and early 1918, Finland, Lithuania, Latvia, Estonia, the Ukraine, Belorussia, Georgia, Armenia, Azerbaidzhan and the Transcaucasus all proclaimed independence. However, in each of these areas there were those who opposed separatism and preferred to remain part of a Bolshevized Russia. The battles for power that developed between the Bolsheviks and the nationalists became part of the civil war that divided Russia from 1918 to 1921. It has to be borne in mind that in 1917, 85 percent of the population in the borderlands consisted of peasants who were strongly nationalistic. Support for the Bolsheviks came primarily from a Russified urban population, as was the case in the Ukraine, or from an industrial population of Russians who had migrated in, as was the case in Central Asia and Armenia. The absence of an indigenous proletariat and the predominance of a highly nationalistic rural population for a time jeopardized the integrity of the empire in the borderlands. But, as the Red Army became increasingly effective, Lenin utilized it; first to prevent further dismemberment of the empire; then to regain control of the Ukraine, Belorussia,* and the Caucasus; other areas such as Finland, Poland, and the Baltic provinces, however, were able to maintain their independence.

By late 1920 then, it had become clear where the Bolshevik power prevailed. Along with Bolshevik power, however, there prevailed a general and widespread sense of dissension among all national groups, though not always for the same reasons. Lenin recognized that concessions had to

---

*Many Ukrainians and Belorussians were included in Poland, and Rumania took over Bessarabia, which included large numbers of Ukrainians. The territories involved were reincorporated into the USSR after World War II.

be made in several directions, not the least of which were toward minority sentiments. In the last years of his life he repeatedly opposed the "remnants" of Great Russian chauvinism. Beginning as early as 1921, Lenin, together with other Bolshevik leaders, sought to work out a policy for the "non-Russian peoples" of the Soviet country. This plan outlined the following "immediate tasks":

a) to develop and consolidate their Soviet statehood in forms appropriate to the conditions of the national life of these peoples;
b) to develop and consolidate in the native language, justice, administrative, economic, and governmental bodies composed of local people who know the way of life and psychology of the local population;
c) to develop a press, schools, the theatre, clubs, and cultural–educational establishments generally, in the native language;
d) to establish and develop a wide network of courses and schools, general as well as professional and technical, in the native language.[4]

Such concepts were reflected in the constitution of the Union of Soviet Socialist Republics (USSR) which gave recognition to the multinational structure of the Soviet state. The reintegration of Russia was made official in January 1924, when a new constitution establishing the Union of Soviet Socialist Republics (USSR) came into effect. The USSR was made up of six constituent republics, all nationally described: the Russian Soviet Federated Socialist Republic, the Ukrainian Soviet Socialist Republic, the Belorussian SSR, the Georgian SSR, the Armenian SSR, and the Azerbaidzhan SSR. The creation of a Federal system of national union republics did little to resolve the problems arising from the multinational character of the Soviet state, since essentially it represented only a symbolic change in the prevailing Russian attitudes toward ethnic minorities. That ethnic minorities recognized the changes for what they were is evident in their resistance efforts in the 1920s and beyond to transform the relationships between national groups.

THE DECADE OF THE 1920s:
THE ERA OF ETHNICITY

During the decade of the 1920s the regime professed its toleration and encouragement of ethnic traditions. The immediate task was to recover not only from four years of world war, but also from the civil war that followed. The economy was in a state of disarray. It is clear that Lenin, among others, believed that economic reconstruction had to be attained at any cost and that this would be hampered if national disputes erupted.

It is also clear that more than lip service was paid to the idea of administrative, judicial, and even economic autonomy. There was a special ministry for minority affairs. The Soviet regime demonstrated its flexibility with respect to cultural and regional particularism by supporting, sometimes very liberally, minority art and writing schools, theaters, drama companies, and publishing companies. There were even cases where the Soviet government created a written language for groups that had previously had none. Jewish culture in the Pale and other areas underwent a revival; theater groups sprung up and Hebrew publications were subsidized. Among Central Asia's Muslims religious schools were cultivated and there was a noticeable use of Turkic languages in local governments.

In many instances, however, the programs that were apparently designed to raise the cultural level of the general population mostly served to alienate the ethnic minorities. Old habits, old values, and old social relationships were threatened. In societies where only the priestly elite was literate, the campaign for universal education was perceived as a threat by the erstwhile aristocracy. Where multiple marriages had religious sanction and women were regarded as chattels, any attempt to limit a man to one wife and to legislate "equality" for her was bound to be regarded not as "progressive," but as a threat to fundamental principles.

Notwithstanding repeated professions of tolerance and numerous examples of support for ethnic particularism in the 1920s, the reality was that ethnic prejudices (Great Russians against minorities and vice versa) remained. There are several reasons for this. First, centuries of old animosities and suspicions could not be quickly overcome. Second, Bolshevik policies sometimes backfired or were contradicted by other policies. Finally, the primary Bolshevik concern was for the welfare and preeminence of the Great Russians.

THE STALIN ERA

The foundation of contemporary Soviet nationality policy is to be found in the principles solidified in the Stalin era. Stalin, no less than Lenin, in word denounced Great Russian chauvinism and supported internationalism. He described Great Russian chauvinism as the "principal force impeding the *sliyanie* of the republics into a single union" and declared that the "fight against Russian chauvinism had to be made the cornerstone of the national question."[5] At the same time, however, he was constructing a nationality policy on the basis of one overarching consideration: that the RSFSR enjoy a privileged position in the USSR—socially, politically, and economically—and that all other republics be subordinated to it. Clearly, Stalin passionately believed in Russian statehood, and contrary to Marxist-Leninist foundations, regarded the state as an autonomous and permanent unit. What Stalin desired was the emergence of a single culture and a single common language; a culture that was the embodiment of the Great Russian heritage.

Stalin was a Great Russian chauvinist—perhaps the greatest of the Great Russian chauvinists—and in time he became openly and then quintessentially so. The question that must be asked is: What were the reasons Stalin so fiercely pursued his "Great Russian" position? This particularly requires an explanation given the fact that Stalin was *not* a Great Russian. Certainly Stalin pursued Great Russian chauvinism for some of the same reasons Lenin did—raison d'état, ideology, and prejudice. However, Stalin was motivated by other forces as well. Many of the leaders of the opposition, with whom Stalin engaged in a brutal power struggle, were of minority extraction, specifically Jewish. He hated them because of their Jewish origins as well as because they opposed him. Moreover, it was a source of political strength and personal satisfaction for him to identify with and be identified with the majority Great Russians among the Bolsheviks against the more highly educated, internationalist and relatively few Jewish members of the opposition. Stalin was not a Great Russian, but the Great Russian Bolsheviks seemed prepared to accept him as their leader. For Stalin, who apparently suffered acute feelings of rejection and alienation throughout his life, the approbation of the majority served, among other factors, to strengthen his attachment to Great Russian dominance.

By the early 1930s Stalin was well on his way to achieving, from his point of view, the formation of a strong Soviet (read Great Russian) nationality policy. To reiterate, what Stalin sought for the USSR was the emergence of a single culture that was the embodiment of the Great Russian heritage and a single language: Russian. In such homogeneity Stalin saw strength—the image of a people united, freed of the debilitating inefficiencies of multilingual and multinational pasts.

In order to realize this vision, Stalin in the late 1920s and 1930s orchestrated a campaign against the historical, intellectual, and cultural tradition of national groups. The cultural commissar instituted a plan to reconstruct the languages of many of the peoples of Central Asia, in particular, by imposing the Cyrillic alphabet (in which Russian is written) on their languages. After Hitler's rise, the history of non–Great Russians was revised to present in a favorable light contacts with Russians antedating the Revolution, sometimes going back hundreds of years. Russians were depicted as always having been beacons of fairness for the masses, liberators, and the possessors of a higher culture. This was to be a giant step in Stalin's subordination of ethnic nationalities.

In the areas of drama, literature, and the arts, Stalin imposed the principle of "national in form, socialist in content." This meant that the Great Russians always had to be presented as friendly, generous, brave, and just, protectors of the poor and downtrodden. Non–Great Russians were free to embrace their traditional art forms; but no matter what the form, the content had to be in accord with socialist dicta. For example, the costuming in a play might accurately depict what Tadzhiks wore in the fourteenth century, but the ideas displayed had to present the Stalin–Bolshevik–Great Russian amalgam that had been developed in Russia after 1917. The "national in form, socialist in content" policy indicates the obfuscatory quality of the tolerance that the regime displayed toward local and national expression.

At the top of Stalin's policy priorities was the drive for rapid industrialization and modernization of the Soviet Union. This was necessary to fulfill the promises of the Revolution and of communism, as well as to protect the country against "capitalist encirclement." Moreover, Stalin hoped that industrialization with its exposure to urban life and the assembly line would further contribute to the socialization of a new Soviet person devoid of minority attachments.

The basis of Soviet industrialization as adopted by the Bolsheviks in the late 1920s was to be the collectivization of agriculture. Collectivization required the reorganization of the private agricultural sector and aimed at eliminating the peasants as a social class. The concept of industrialization based on collectivization depended on nationalizing the private peasant acreage and consolidating the small farms into major holdings. Although Stalin and his cohorts hoped to accomplish this through peaceful methods, bitter peasant opposition forced Stalin to resort to coercion. Resistance was strongest on the part of the Ukrainians, whose ancestors had originally fled Russia in order to escape feudalism and had held their own land for centuries. Here peasants responded to collectivization by slaughtering their animals by the tens of millions, destroying their farm implements, and burning their homes. Stalin responded by sending in the Red Army, machine-gunning thousands of Ukrainians, and shipping hundreds of thousands to camps in the north.* It was one of the first steps in the purges of the 1930s that would soon involve millions of people. A few years later Stalin attempted to force the Kazakhis to abandon their nomadic existence and settle down on collective farms. When they refused, they were shot or arrested, though thousands managed to escape across the border into China. While the Ukrainians, Kazakhis, and others who remained were "collectivized," the price was tremendous and those on the land were scarcely avid supporters of the Soviet regime. The exact number of peasants who died in Stalin's quest for collectivization is unknown, though reliable estimates range above ten million, of whom perhaps as many as three million were Ukrainian.[6]

Stalin was not only concerned with the "peasant" side of the national question. His personality and unending quest for absolute power, together with the national opposition that actually existed in areas like the Ukraine, led him to accuse minorities generally of "bourgeois nationalism." In the Great Purges that began in 1936, Stalin zeroed in on foreign-connected "spies," "wreckers," and "saboteurs" who he was convinced were undermining industrialization. He particularly suspected the minority nationalities of holding traitorous preferences vis-à-vis the Germans, whom Stalin feared were preparing to attack the Soviet Union. In the mid-1930s, Stalin carried out purges of "bourgeois nationalists" in many republics. It seems that the most usual targets among the minorities were those who served the regime as party or government officials, it being reasoned that they were the most dangerous because they were in positions of power. Thus, those who had been the most cooperative in carrying out Stalin's will were often singled out for the most intense persecution. Such leaders were sent to camps and executed by the tens of thousands. In many instances, no one among minority ethnic party organizations survived. For example, in Kazakhstan every member of the bureau of the Central Committee elected at the first congress of the CPK was shot. Of the 644 delegates to the Tenth Congress of the Communist Party of Georgia, in May 1937, 60 percent were shortly thereafter arrested, exiled, or shot. In Belorussia, party membership declined by one-half, and in the Tadzhik Communist Party, membership decreased by almost two-thirds from 1933 to 1936.[7] These figures clearly indicate the extent of the liquidation of many non-Russian official-

---

*The Ukrainians made up the vast majority of the inmates of the first mass slave-labor camp in the USSR.

doms. While it is difficult to be exact, it is reliably estimated that as many as 12 million men, women, and children perished as a result of the Stalin purges, many of whom had committed no other sin than that they were not Great Russian.*

Stalin's policy of mass terror did not end with the Great Purges. The successes of fascism only increased Stalin's already highly developed suspicions of foreigners. The onset of The Great Patriotic War on June 22, 1941, and the subsequent German occupation of many areas of the Soviet Union, such as the western Ukraine and the Volga, led Stalin to accuse several non-Russian peoples of collaboration with the Nazis. His secret police unleashed a brutal deportation campaign in which Crimean Tatars, Volga Germans, Chechens, Ingushi, Kalmyks, Karachai, and others were uprooted and dispatched to remote areas of Siberia and Central Asia. The costs in terms of life and property were incalculable. Many estimates put the total numbers of dislocated non-Russians at one million, though the actual figures may have been higher.[8]

There are continuing arguments among those interested in the subject as to whether Stalin was justified in his treatment of the minorities during World War II. Undoubtedly, there were strong pro-German sympathies among the Balts, as there were among the Ukrainians,† who by the tens of thousands welcomed the invading Germans with no less enthusiasm than in 1918. There is evidence of collaboration between the Caucasian minorities and the Nazis. However, certainly not all of the Chechens, Tatars, and other minorities were disloyal. Moreover, Soviet politics toward them after the German invasion in June 1941 were only an extension of prewar decisions, which even then were affected by Stalin's paranoia. It should also be pointed out that in the case of the one people who could in no way be sympathetic to Hitler—the Jews—their treatment by Stalin indicated no particular toleration.

After the war, Stalin's policy toward ethnic minorities did not change. Though individuals might sometimes return to their former homes, groups that had been exiled collectively could not go home. Even when exiles returned, their erstwhile houses or apartments, assuming they still stood, had been assigned to others, whom the regime refused to budge. The returnees were regarded as having no claim. Events in the communist world after

---

*Certainly, millions of Great Russians perished in the purges, as well.

---

†Evidence indicates that Stalin considered uprooting and exiling the Ukrainians as well, but he finally concluded that there were just too many of them. Gradually, it became clear to the Ukrainians that Hitler had even less regard for them than Stalin, regarding them as *untermenschen.* The great majority came to support Soviet power.

1945 reinforced Stalin's suspicions toward Russia's own minorities. The challenge from Tito's Yugoslavia, the establishment in China (which had a 4,000 mile frontier with the USSR) of the most populous communist state in the world, the visible enthusiasm of Russian Jews for the establishment of the state of Israel—all of these convinced Stalin of the imminent perils of nationalism. There is today incontrovertible proof that, at the time of his death in 1953, Stalin was planning the wholesale expulsion of Russia's three million Jews from Europe and their transport to the Far East along the Russo–Chinese frontier.

One of the great ironies of Stalinist nationality policy in operation was that, though it seemed to place great emphasis on the subordination of and suppression of minority peoples and cultures and even their ultimate *sliyanie* (merging) into the Russian people and culture, certain of Stalin's key policies tended to have just the opposite effect. The basis on which the USSR was organized (with its almost threescore Union republics, autonomous republics, autonomous regions, and national districts), despite the denial of national autonomy, preserved and even strengthened minority identification. The concept "national in form, socialist in content," while designed to curtail nationalist aspirations, in its "national in form" component actually served to keep ethnic traditions alive. And, if experience elsewhere is a criterion, the perception that there was a force for suppression and cultural extinction only helped to strengthen the determination to survive. By the end of the Stalin years, the minority nationalities in Russia were down; but they were not out.

STALINIST NATIONALITY POLICY

The basic components of Stalin's nationality policy were:

1. The primacy of Great Russian interests, as interpreted by Stalin.
2. The predominance of the Russian language and the Great Russian culture, as the highest expression of the achievements of the Soviet people.
3. The acceptance for all groups of (1) and (2) by force, if necessary.
4. Reserving the most important jobs, though not necessarily the most conspicuous ones, for Great Russians, or, in some instances, for those who are completely Russianized, especially in Central Asia, where circumstances serve to homogenize all Slavs, in their own eyes and the eyes of others.

·5. Though cultural differences in form are permitted, content must always be faithful to socialist, that is, Great Russian (as viewed by Stalin) values.

6. While some foreign cultural achievements are to be highly regarded on a case-by-case basis, it is necessary to be on guard against the class bias and corruptive influence of non-Soviet culture. Those who become overly interested in foreign cultures, especially when they have historical or family connections with the area from which those cultures spring, are politically suspect.

7. The expulsion of those groups whom the Stalin party has decided are irremediably in conflict with socialist–Great Russian–Stalinist ideals.

8. The ultimate elimination of all languages and cultures, save Russian, and the merging of all the Soviet peoples into one, with one language and one culture.

Whether Stalin ever recognized the unattainability of (8) is unknowable, but certainly it remained a goal into the last years of his life.

THE POST-STALIN PERIOD

Although the nationality policy model that Stalin established has remained the standard for Soviet society, the stage of Soviet development has not remained static, and the means available to Stalin for obtaining objectives are no longer realistically accessible in the same array. Stalin achieved his objectives—the acquiescence of the Russian peoples, majority and minority alike—through timely offerings of the carrot and liberal application of the stick.

But even Stalin recognized that his power was not unlimited and in the last years of his life, he became aware that naked force was increasingly dysfunctional: that other means were required if the regime was to win the popular support necessary for further social and economic development. Stalin's successors, while not eschewing the use of force, acknowledged its limitations and sought alternatives, but these were almost always alternative means, not objectives.

In the realm of nationality policy, the ultimate objective has been the elimination of national differences, and the adoption of the Russian language and culture by all Soviet "nations and nationalities." It is important to note, however, that these objectives have existed alongside, and in subordination to, other objectives, principally those of Soviet economic development. The minority nationalities could not be dragooned into putting forth the effort necessary to propel Soviet development forward any more than could the balance of the Soviet population. They had to be attracted to produce and inveigled to accede to Great Russian primacy and to abandon their particularism. Accordingly, Khrushchev, while advocating the basic *sblizhenie,* never specifically called for *sliyanie.* Nor did Brezhnev. Andropov mentioned it once, on December 21, 1982, on the occasion of the 60th anniversary of the formation of the USSR. He declared, "Our final goal is clear. It is, using the words of V.I. Lenin, 'not only the *sblizhenie* of nations, but also their *sliyanie.*' "[9] He never brought it up again.

In order to attract the minority nationalities, the post-Stalin leadership has used a variety of means. Research indicates that the Soviets have increased the representation of minorities in party and government ranks. Khrushchev, who had much of his experience in the Ukraine, brought some of the Ukrainians he had come to know on the way up into his Politburo (PB). Brezhnev, who had also served in the Ukraine, introduced other Ukrainians into his regime. Khrushchev seemed to make a pointed effort to include minority representation in the PB, appointing as full or candidate members one or more Belorussians, Georgians, Latvians, Uzbeks, and Kazakhis.* While Brezhnev and Andropov did not manipulate PB minority membership to the same degree, a Balt and a Central Asian were in the PB rather consistently during their eras. Of course, while these minority appointees can be pointed to as Ukrainians in the PB, they, as well as the Latvians, Belorussians, Georgians, Armenians and others who have been members of the PB, cannot be regarded as representatives of their national groups. They could achieve top positions only to the extent that they were prepared to accept and demand recognition of Great Russian primacy in language, culture, and every other aspect of Soviet life. In spite of this requirement, which would have seemed likely to make possible a still more multinational top echelon, in point of fact Great Russian representation has increased in recent years. In February 1951, toward the end of the Stalin period, PB membership consisted of five Russians, two Georgians,† one Jew,‡ and one Armenian. In February 1984, it consisted of seven Russians,

---

*Khrushchev also appointed the only woman ever to serve in the Politburo, E.A. Furtseva.

†Stalin and L.P. Beria.

‡L.M. Kaganovich, whom Stalin chose to keep around to indicate he was not anti-Semitic. No Jews have served in the PB, or any other top party post, in recent years.

three Ukrainians, one Azerbaidzhani, and one Kazakhi. On a percentage basis, Great Russian representation in the Politburo had gone up from 55.5 to 58.3 percent. Slavic representation (Russians plus Ukrainians) has gone up from 55.5 to 83.3 percent.

In the PB, other than in the Central Asian and perhaps the Baltic cases, it would appear that there was, by and large, no conscious attempt to balance PB membership according to nationality. However, if we examine the case of party membership, there seems to be much better evidence that the party really has sought wider representation, though not to the extent of eliminating Great Russian overrepresentation.

Between the end of World War II and January 1973, every major Soviet nationality remained the same or increased in party participation on a percentage basis except the Russians, Armenians, and Georgians, who had previously enjoyed disproportionately high representation (see Table 5). Between 1973 and 1983 changes were less extensive than from 1946 to 1973. However, Russian membership continued to shrink proportionally while that of the Belorussians and most of the Central Asian peoples increased. In 1983, the Russians were still overrepresented by almost 8 percent, as were the Georgians, while the Baltic and Central Asian nationalities continued to be underrepresented. It is clear that prior to the last ten years of the Brezhnev period the party leadership did attempt to broaden party membership. However, leadership has only gone part-way in equalizing percentage of party membership per nationality, either because it does not want to go further, or because members of other groups have resisted cooptation.[10]

Generally speaking, it is also true that the party has made some attempts to increase local autonomy, though more in some regions than others. For example, in Georgia and Armenia, where the regime has been more willing to rely on the local population, the leadership has become almost entirely indigenous. Elsewhere, reliance on local leadership has also increased, but in all of the most important leadership assignments, the second secretary is almost without exception Russian, or in Central Asia, Slavic. It seems apparent here, too, that the regime has attempted to adjust the balance. Judging by the widespread crackdown in the Andropov era on Georgian and Armenian party officials charged with corruption, it seems likely that in higher party circles there are doubts as to the wisdom of having permitted so much autonomy even in those supposedly reliable republics.*

---

*The appointment of a Russian, previously secretary of the Moscow City Committee, as a second secretary in Georgia, in January 1984, would seem to strengthen such a conclusion.

Table 5

Nationalities	January 1, 1946 Absolute Figures	Percent	January 1, 1973 Absolute Figures	Percent	January 1, 1983 Absolute Figures	Percent
Russians	3,736,165	67.8	9,025,363	60.9	10,809,066	59.7
Ukrainians	667,481	12.1	2,369,200	16.0	2,898,757	16.0
Belorussians	114,799	2.1	521,544	3.5	684,492	3.8
Uzbeks	61,467	1.1	291,550	2.0	428,446	2.4
Kazakhis	92,354	1.7	254,667	1.7	355,213	2.0
Georgians	107,910	2.0	246,214	1.7	302,947	1.7
Azerbaidzhanis	55,448	1.0	212,122	1.4	304,915	1.7
Lithuanians	3,704	0.1	96,558	0.7	134,866	0.7
Moldavians	2,913	0.1	59,434	0.4	98,195	0.5
Latvians	8,408	0.1	61,755	0.4	74,225	0.4
Kirghizi	14,039	0.3	46,049	0.3	70,195	0.4
Tadzhiks	13,757	0.2	58,668	0.4	80,293	0.4
Armenians	100,449	1.8	225,132	1.5	272,965	1.5
Turkmens	12,675	0.2	44,218	0.3	68,744	0.4
Estonians	7,976	0.1	46,424	0.3	58,341	0.3
Other	514,104	9.3	1,262,133	8.5	1,476,243	8.1
Total	5,513,649	100.0	14,821,031	100.0	18,117,903	100.0

Source: Partiinaya zhizn, August 15, 1983, p. 23.

Attracting Minority Support through Investment Policy

In still another dimension, the Soviet authorities have attempted to win over the "nations and nationalities" through increased investment in the development of the minority republics. In the 1980s, the standard of living in the Baltic and Caucasian republics was at the top of the Soviet scale, exceeding that of the Russian republic. The government has invested heavily in housing and medical and educational facilities outside the RSFSR. In most instances, investment on a per capita basis has been greater in most other republics than in the RSFSR. While the RSFSR standard of living is still higher than that in the Central Asian republics, principally for reasons having to do with culture, the regime has had great success in narrowing the gap between the two. There is evidence that Great Russians are aware that several non–Great Russian nationalities have been the recipients of more favorable investment treatment, and are resentful of it.

Reducing Cultural Biases

In some aspects of culture, the post-Stalin leadership has permitted a de facto liberalization. For example, it has acknowledged past errors in attempting the forcible suppression of national differences—though it has never made such an admission in the case of Jews—and it has reiterated promises that such mistakes will not be repeated. It cautions those who would continue in their efforts to extirpate the outdated values and practices of minority cultures that what is good in the past must be retained. The cultural arbiters, however, seem unable to distinguish between what is "good" and what is not. As frequently as they cite the possibility of cultural difference, they inveigh against "outdated" customs and practices, against *perezhitki,* remnants of the past, that may stimulate minority nationalism. In general though, the leadership has refrained from the use of force as an instrument for extirpating such *perezhitki*, and it has winked at their reintroduction and the consequent strengthening of local nationalism, particularly in the Caucasus and Central Asia.

The case of G.B. Garibdzhanian, former director of the Armenian branch of the Institute of Marxism–Leninism serves as an example of such tolerance. According to *Kommunist,* Garibdzhanian recently has published "numerous books and articles" exaggerating the role of Armenians as aides and disciples of Lenin, including among Lenin's alleged close supporters at least one person who was a Menshevik.[11] As early as 1958, *Voprosy istorii KPSS* called Garibdzhanian on his flagrant mistakes, but he paid no attention then, nor in later years. And in May 1983, apparently he still was paying no attention, and he was still being published.

Evidence of Continued Attempts at Russification

While the regime has sought to win over the ethnics, in order to facilitate economic growth, and has avoided direct emphasis on *sliyanie,* it has not despaired of Russification. In spite of statements by Khrushchev, Brezhnev, Andropov, and others, the Soviet goal remains the disappearance of national differences, and assimilation to Russian culture and language, though in the post-Stalin era sans physical coercion.

Despite frequent disavowals, the party maintains its Great Russian chauvinism. Its proclamation of Great Russian superiority is not so blatant as earlier, but even in the most recent times there has been a prominently featured reminder (by a Ukrainian) that the "Great Russian people by rights have been and remain the backbone of the fraternal relations of all our country's nations and nationalities."[12] While Andropov heralded the flourishing equality of peoples, on a most auspicious occasion he called as well for their *sliyanie* (merging), which is Russification.[13]

However, if coercion is under wraps, how is *sliyanie* (Russification) to be achieved? The principal instrument has been the attempted universalization of the Russian language.

In the late 1920s and 1930s, the regime instituted a plan to adjust all non-Russian languages to the Cyrillic alphabet, focusing especially on the Turkic languages of Central Asia. This in turn paved the way for the adoption of Russian as the *lingua franca.* While it is true that the republics take advantage of their freedom to teach in their national language at the primary and the secondary levels, the language of instruction in technical and scientific schools as well as in most universities is Russian. Russian is also the language of the army and republic bureaus. According to 1983 figures, 82% of all adult Soviet citizens are fluent in Russian.[14]

In further efforts to promote *sliyanie,* the Soviets have watered down population exclusiveness outside the RSFSR. At the end of World War II, when Lithuania, Latvia, and Estonia had been partially denuded of native inhabitants by the Nazi occupation, Russians were moved in and the regime dissuaded native refugees who had fled East from returning. In the Kazakh Republic, where large numbers of people migrated during Khrushchev's "virgin lands" campaign, the new settlers came under heavy pressure to remain, with the result that over 40 percent of the population is Slavic, and Russians constitute the largest ethnic group. Table 6, based on the Soviet censuses of 1959 and 1979, gives an indication of changes in the various republics brought about by migration. The data indicate that Russians constitute a substantial and growing portion of the population in the non-Russian western republics (Ukraine, Belorussia, Baltic, Moldavia) of the USSR.

Another instrument in the drive for *sliyanie* is the regime's promotion of mixed marriages among the various Soviet peoples. It tells the young that it is narrow and old-fashioned to seek "your beloved only among men of the same religion or nationality." "Look around without the blindness of . . . prejudice."[15] advises *Komsomolskaya pravda*. Statistics indicate that ethnic intermarriage has increased: from 3 million in 1959 to 8 million in 1970 and almost 10 million according to the 1979 census. While the number of families in the USSR increased from 1959–1979 by 18 percent, the number of mixed marriages increased by over 200 percent.

Above all, now as in Lenin's time, the greatest hope for *sliyanie* resides in the industrialization, education, and urbanization of the country—that is, in modernization. As the level of education of the populace increases, as peoples are brought into closer relationships with one another—in new cities, at the job, in apartment complexes—animosities and suspicions, the argument goes, will disappear and the shared experiences of the work place and the community will eliminate differences among peoples. A solidly united and undifferentiated Soviet people will appear.

Progress Report on Russification

The various means used by the regime to obtain *sliyanie* have succeeded to an extent. Eighty-two percent of all Soviets are fluent in Russian. Russians are becoming an increasingly large percentage of the population of the western republics. Intermarriage is increasingly frequent. Modernization has been widely carried out. Each one of these successes, however, must be weighed against continuing counter-indicators that have, in some instances, shown heightened (in Soviet parlance) "national self-awareness."

While it is true that there is universal Russian language instruction, the 82 percent figure is both deceiving and of doubtful validity. According to the 1979 census, 38 percent of non-Russians had little or no knowledge of the Russian language and there is reason to believe Soviet census takers are rather "liberal" in their definition of fluency.[16] Tens of thousands of Soviet youth, particularly in Central Asia, never learn Russian, with the result that when they are inducted into the army, where the officers are usually Slavs who don't know the local languages, they are of little value, for any but the lowest-level duties. The first secretary of the Central Committee of the Kirghiz party said in 1983 that special courses had been developed for military conscripts who did not know Russian. And he reported positive results: 70 percent of those called up "recently" have been able to go into "combat areas and special units."[17] But what, it must be asked, of the other 30 percent, who could not even take simple orders in Russian?

Table 6. Distribution of the Union Republics' Population by Nationality, 1959 and 1979

Republic	Percent Indigenous Nationality		Percent Russian	
	1959	1979	1959	1979
RSFSR	83.3	82.6	--	--
Ukraine	76.8	73.5	16.9	21.1
Belorussia	81.1	79.4	8.2	11.9
Uzbekistan	62.1	68.7	13.5	10.8
Kazakhstan	30.0	36.0	42.7	40.8
Georgia	64.3	74.4	10.1	7.4
Azerbaidzhan	67.3	78.1	13.6	7.9
Lithuania	79.3	80.1	8.5	8.9
Moldavia	65.4	63.9	10.2	12.8
Latvia	62.0	53.7	26.6	32.8
Kirgizia	40.5	47.9	30.2	25.9
Tadzhikistan	53.1	58.8	13.3	10.4
Armenia	88.0	89.7	3.2	2.3
Turkmenistan	60.9	68.4	17.3	12.6
Estonia	74.6	64.7	20.1	27.9

Source: *Sotsiologicheskiye issledovania*, no. 4, October–December 1982, as quoted in *The Current Digest of the Soviet Press*, 34, 49, p. 4.

Even when Russian is known, there is often a bias against using it. Many families in the Baltic and Caucasian republics who learn Russian because it provides entry into higher education and the professions, nevertheless determinedly use their native languages at home, in the streets, in shops, and in reading. In April 1978, when the republic constitutions were being revised to put them into accord with the new federal constitution, it was proposed by Moscow-inspired drafters in Georgia that Georgian be dropped as an official language, leaving Russian as the sole medium through which official government and party business could be carried out.

Demonstrations involving tens of thousands soon convinced the central regime that the Georgians were not yet ready to abandon further their national heritage. Moscow backed down. A similar attempt in Armenia was also dropped.

As for changing demographic balances, while the proportion of Russians (or those regarding themselves as such) is clearly growing in the western-oriented areas of Russia, the opposite is occurring at a much-accelerated rate in the Caucasian and Central Asian republics. Moreover, as we will see, birthrates in the latter are being maintained at a high level, or accelerating, whereas in most of the western USSR, the population is barely reproducing itself. In the matter of intermarriage, what seems more noteworthy than the extent to which it is increasing is the fact that the vast majority of citizens (80 percent according to a recent Soviet poll) opposed mixed marriages. [18]

The rapid urbanization of Soviet society has not produced the expected results insofar as the elimination of national differences is concerned, primarily because the process has been uneven. While the total percentage of the urbanized population in the USSR is 63.4 percent, there is great variation in the level of urbanization from republic to republic, with the Slavic and Baltic republics, on the average, having a greater level of urbanization than the Caucasus and Central Asian republics: (note all figures are percentages) RSFSR, 70.5; Ukraine, 62.7; Belorussia, 57.4; Moldavia, 40.9; Estonia, 70.5; Latvia, 69.4; Lithuania, 62.6; Armenia, 66.3; Azerbaidzhan, 53.4; Georgia, 52.9; Kazakhstan, 54.9; Kirgizia, 38.8; Tadzhikistan, 34.3; Turkmenistan, 47.8; Uzbekistan, 40.2. [19]

That Central Asians cling to their traditional rural way of life and resist emigration to the cities can be seen by the fact that no Central Asian republic has an urban population greater than 47.8 percent. Oddly, the regime seems to have recently developed an opposition to continued urbanization, and, in at least one instance, has ordered the "renewal" of hundreds of abandoned villages. [20]

Even more noteworthy than the failure of official exhortations, industrialization, and urbanization in bringing about *sliyanie* are indications that national differences are in fact increasing in the contemporary USSR. The Soviet press is filled with stories of the appearance of new "congregations" (which are described as being of mixed religious–national origin) and of new "holy places," particularly in Uzbekistan and Tadzhikistan, but elsewhere in the non-Russian areas of the USSR as well. The press no longer attributes such manifestations solely to elements that have not adjusted, to those still blinded by *perezhitki,* but to the present "happy time" in the life of all republics.[21] There is, the Soviet press states, a heightened "self-awareness" for Soviet nations and nationalities born of the security that an improved standard of living has provided. What a problem such an explanation provides for Soviet leadership, because it indicates that the very promise that is being used to attract the nationalities to the Soviet–Russian model, that of improved quality of life, is in fact giving rise to resistance to *sliyanie.*

The Threat of the Future

In the recent past, the regime has been willing (except primarily in the case of the Jews*) to tolerate the refusal of minority groups to yield to majority pressures and blandishments to abandon their cultural and linguistic uniqueness, and their recollections and implied dreams of independence. Because economic development has been the regime's top priority, the immediate future of the USSR has seemed to depend not on *sliyanie* but on increasing industrial and agricultural production. The belief was that the problems presented by the multinational makeup of the USSR could be handled by words of understanding and time. These have not worked, nor have concessions. Large numbers of minority nationals remain outside the mainstream of Soviet life. Not only has the problem not diminished, in the 1980s and 1990s it threatens to get worse as the regime struggles with declining economic growth and productivity and a shrinking labor pool in which non-Russians are becoming more numerous.

Soviet industrial growth slowed markedly in the 1970s† for several reasons. The labor intensive industrial and agricultural sectors of the economy no longer have an expanding reserve on tap. Furthermore, while the role of technology in production techniques has increased over the past 65 years, the Soviets have rarely been able to utilize technology to its full po-

---

*Jews in contemporary Russia are prevented from studying Hebrew, Jewish history, literature, etc., and they are restricted in their practice of Judaism. In part, Jews have been singled out for regime abuse because of their interest in the state of Israel and their expressed desire to emigrate from the USSR. However, in large part, persecution of Jews is an old Russian habit that the Communists have not only picked up but for which they have also discovered new refinements of practice and to which they have sought to give regime respectability.

---

†Under Andropov there seemed to be an indication of a reversal of the trend, but the change was slight; and even that slight improvement was thrown into doubt by the questioning of the accuracy of Andropov's figures (*New York Times*, January 4, 1984).

tential. Practically speaking, the regime has indicated that in the near future it lacks the means to achieve significantly greater efficiency in the operation of existing plants and machinery. Similarly, it has not developed technology equal to that in the West, and it lacks the resources to purchase enough Western technology to meet its goals, even assuming that it had the know-how to use that technology once acquired.

Yet, these factors, and others to be discussed, have grave implications for a Soviet leadership that sees "success" dependent on increasing production to Western levels. While the "traditional" way for the Soviet system to produce more has been to put more people on the job, the fact is that Slavic sources of labor power are drying up. This is partly because the leadership seems to feel that as many people have been taken away from agriculture as can safely be permitted, if production in that sector is not to suffer even more than it has already. Much more significantly, however, there are clear signs of demographic developments that must be extremely worrisome to those at the top.*

In the USSR in recent years, birthrates have fallen and death rates have accelerated, particularly in the Russian Republic (see Table 7). According to Feshbach, the crude birthrate in the USSR fell from 26.7/1,000 in 1950 to 18.3/1,000 in 1980. In the RSFSR, the fall was from 26.9/1,000 in 1950 to 15.9/1,000 in 1980, which was a slight increase from the 1970 figure of 14.6/1,000. The birthrate from 1950 to 1980 fell in most of the republics. The only exceptions were the Tadzhik Republic (30.4/1,000 to 37.0/1,000) and the Uzbek SSR (30.8/1,000 to 33.8/1,000). In all of the Central Asian republics, the births per 1,000 are above 29.6.

As for death rates (see Table 8), these have risen in the 30 years from 1950 to 1980, particularly in the last 20 years. In 1980, the death rate per 1,000 USSR population was 10.3. In the RSFSR it was 11.0. In Tadzhikistan it was 8.4 and in Uzbekistan it was 7.4, which were the two extremes of the Central Asian range.

What this indicates is that the birthrate in the RSFSR, the most populous republic, is far below those in Central Asia, and death rates are rising and considerably above those in Central Asia. Moreover, death rates are rising particularly among infants and among males in the 20–44-year age category, which are the prime working years. Feshbach estimates that since 1964, the life expectancy for Soviet males has dropped 5.1 years and for Soviet females 2.1 years.[22] The ramifications of these figures for the Soviet leadership are clear: they will face a domestic situation in which the Great

---

*They deny their concern, saying that Western writers, looking at the figures, "distort the reality" of the Soviet state (*Pravda,* November 29, 1983).

Russian (and more generally, Slavic) segment of the population is decreasing in size, while the Central Asian segment of the population is increasing in size.

Table 7. Crude Birth Rate, USSR and Republics, 1950–1980 (births per 1,000 population)

USSR and Republics	1950	1955	1960	1965	1970	1975	1980
USSR	26.7	25.7	24.9	18.4	17.4	18.1	18.3
Slavic Republics							
RSFSR	26.9	25.7	23.2	15.7	14.6	15.7	15.9
Ukraine	22.8	20.1	20.5	15.3	15.2	15.1	14.8
Belorussia	25.5	24.9	24.4	17.9	16.2	15.7	16.0
Moldavia	38.9	30.4	29.3	20.4	19.4	20.7	20.0
Baltic Republics							
Estonia	18.4	17.9	16.6	14.6	15.8	14.9	15.0
Latvia	17.0	16.4	16.7	13.8	14.5	14.0	14.0
Lithuania	23.6	21.1	22.5	18.1	17.6	15.7	15.1
Transcaucasus							
Armenia	32.1	38.0	40.1	28.6	22.1	22.4	22.7
Azerbaidzhan	31.2	37.8	42.6	36.6	29.2	25.1	25.2
Georgia	23.5	24.1	24.7	21.2	19.2	18.2	17.7
Kazakhstan	37.6	37.5	37.2	26.9	23.4	24.1	23.8
Central Asia							
Kirgizia	32.4	33.5	36.9	31.4	30.5	30.4	29.6
Tadzhikistan	30.4	33.8	33.5	36.8	34.8	37.1	37.0
Turkemenistan	38.2	40.7	42.4	37.2	35.2	34.4	34.3
Uzbekistan	30.8	34.3	39.8	34.7	33.6	34.5	33.8

Source: TsSU, *Nasseleniye SSSR, 1973,* pp. 69–83; and *Nar. khoz. v 1980, 1981,* pp. 32–33, quoted in Murray Feshbach, "The Soviet Union: Population, Trends and Dilemmas," *Population Bulletin,* 37, 3, August 1982, p. 17.

By the year 2000, 20 percent of the Soviet work force will be in Central Asia. At present, approximately 56 percent of army draftees (primarily

Table 8. Crude Death Rates, USSR and Republics, 1950–1980 (deaths per 1,000 population)

USSR and Republics	1950	1955	1960	1965	1970	1975	1980
USSR	9.7	8.2	7.1	7.3	8.2	9.3	10.3
Slavic Republics							
RSFSR	10.1	8.4	7.4	7.6	8.7	9.8	11.0
Ukraine	8.5	7.5	6.9	7.6	8.9	10.0	11.4
Belorussia	8.0	7.4	6.6	6.8	7.6	8.5	9.9
Moldavia	11.2	8.3	6.4	6.2	7.4	9.3	10.2
Baltic Republics							
Estonia	14.4	11.7	10.5	10.5	11.1	11.6	12.3
Latvia	12.4	10.6	10.0	10.0	11.2	12.1	12.7
Lithuania	12.0	9.2	7.8	7.9	8.9	9.5	10.5
Transcaucasus							
Armenia	8.5	8.8	6.8	5.7	5.1	5.5	5.5
Azerbaidzhan	9.6	7.6	6.7	6.4	6.7	7.0	7.0
Georgia	7.6	6.7	6.5	7.0	7.3	8.0	8.6
Kazakhstan	11.7	9.2	6.6	5.9	6.0	7.1	8.0
Central Asia							
Kirgizia	8.5	7.8	6.1	6.5	7.4	8.1	8.4
Tadzhikistan	8.2	8.9	5.1	6.6	6.4	8.1	8.0
Turkemenistan	10.2	10.4	6.5	7.0	6.6	7.8	8.3
Uzbekistan	8.7	8.2	6.0	5.9	5.5	7.2	7.4

Source: TsSU, *Nasseleniye SSSR, 1973, Nar. khoz. v 1975 and 1980,* quoted in Murray Feshbach, "The Soviet Union: Population, Trends and Dilemmas," *Population Bulletin,* 37, 3, August 1982, p. 30.

eighteen and nineteen-year-old males) come from the RSFSR and 18.7 percent from the Caucasus, Kazakhstan, and Central Asia. If current trends continue, by 1990 the RSFSR contribution will drop to 44 percent, while that from the southern republics will rise to 33 percent. Large numbers of these conscripts will in all likelihood be able to understand consistently commands in Russian little more than their older brothers did and will not be much more willing to live in cities and work in factories.

If the regime is to use its established methods of increasing production by increasing the work force, it has several ways it can go. It can crack down on the estimated one million plus parasites of working age. It can try again to discourage drunkenness, which it has been doing unsuccessfully since the 1920s. It can continue its effort to encourage Russians, Ukrainians, Belorussians, and others to increase the birthrate. It can try and induce more women to join the work force.* It can import still more *Gastarbeiters*. It can seek to entice Central Asians and Caucasians into factory jobs either in the developed areas, as it is doing, or in new facilities to be constructed in the Central Asian republics. Each of these approaches, however, has drawbacks and limited chances for success.

Central Asia: A Case Study

Central Asia contains the largest and potentially most promising untapped labor reserve in the USSR. However, the problems seem as great as the potential. As a group, Central Asians have had little interest in a factory routine they regard as confining and in conflict with traditions such as frequent prayer, feast and fast days, and other religious practices. Over the years they found other ways of making a living that were seen as more harmonious with traditional practices and less onerous than factory work: ways that the regime has frowned on but nevertheless permitted for the sake of not upsetting the apple cart and of providing services not otherwise available. Moreover, Central Asians have been reluctant to relocate to other parts of the USSR, e.g., Siberia and northern Kazakhstan. Thus, the industrial and economic potential of several regions in the Soviet Union is severely hampered by the fact that the non-Russians show little willingness to migrate permanently to those areas. When they have shown a willingness to work outside their own republics, it has generally been only for a temporary period.

Still another problem with relying on the Central Asian labor potential is the role of women in those societies. Women, for the most part, work in

---

*A new policy was implemented in 1983 that was designed to increase the birthrate, encouraging women to have children by offering them such incentives as partially paid maternity leave, added benefits for mothers with five or more children, and flexible work schedules. It is noteworthy that the policy was belatedly and apparently reluctantly introduced into Central Asia, where additional births were not desired by the regime.

the home. Though they are not kept in veiled seclusion as elsewhere in the Middle East, their function is seen as an aide to men, as the bearers of children and the keepers of the hearth, not as workers in the factory. Such a view of the proper position for women is particularly widespread in nonurban parts of Central Asia, where bride kidnapping and the bride price are still extensively practiced. Though some Central Asian women do work in factories, particularly textile plants, Tadzhik, Uzbek, and Turkmen women will not soon be working in Soviet factories in large numbers, regardless of the incentives.

There are still other impediments to employing the Central Asian reserve. Large numbers of Central Asians do not speak Russian. Among the 18 percent of Soviet citizens who are not fluent in Russian, the preponderance are Central Asian. Moreover, the problem with potential workers from Central Asia is, in addition to all else, that educational standards in Central Asia are the lowest in the Soviet Union. Supposedly, everyone, including Central Asians, completes eight years of education, but as one Soviet observer notes, a diploma in the Soviet Union does not necessarily indicate proficiency any more than it does in any other place.[23] Finally there is the widespread feeling throughout the Soviet Union that Central Asians are "different"—if not potentially subversive. While there is little evidence of organized opposition to the Soviet power on their part, they march to a different drummer; they listen to foreign broadcasts from Middle Eastern countries and wish to be united with their co-nationals and co-religionists abroad. While they may be more reliable than *Gastarbeiters*, who are not particularly welcome, it is probably just as true that *Gastarbeiters* test the bounds of Soviet tolerance less frequently than do Central Asian Soviet citizens.

It is clear that the Soviet leadership recognizes the dilemma posed by incorporating the teeming Central Asian millions into its work force and is searching for other alternatives. It has commissioned a new spot census of the RSFSR, set for 1985, to determine among other things, how many women are doing full-time housework, the ages and sex of those engaged in personal auxiliary farming, and the number of women who would enter the workforce if daycare centers were available, etc. The census will also seek to find out if the nationality makeup of the RSFSR has changed more than has been anticipated on the basis of the last census in 1979. (Are the Central Asians perhaps gaining faster, even in the RSFSR?)[24]

Whatever alternatives may be employed, the likelihood is that in the next two decades the Soviet Union is going to have to rely on Central Asians for the bulk of whatever additional labor force it recruits. If it is to attract more Central Asians to the factories, it will have to build factories in the Uzbek, Tadzhik, Turkmen, Kazakh, and Kirghizi republics (so that the native population will not have to leave); spend huge sums to improve the infrastructures in those areas; and learn to live with the holy men, holy places, foreign tracts, and the radio broadcasts to which the Central Asians have become accustomed. "National in form, socialist in content" will become more national in content as well, or the Soviets will have to eschew wider use of the Central Asian work force. And if "tolerance" becomes greater in Central Asia, it seems highly unlikely that it will be less so elsewhere.

Does Soviet leadership feel that it can permit such negation of the "Soviet way"? Can it get through the 1980s and 1990s successfully without even more frequently turning a blind eye to evidences of "national self-awareness"? A strange paradox confronts the Soviet leadership, for whatever course it chooses will entail certain sacrifices. Should the Soviet Union embark upon the path of permissiveness, ideological deterioration can only be stimulated in other areas as well. If the leadership tries to enforce *sliyanie* though, it risks its position as the leader of the international communist movement and jeopardizes the realization of its great power ambitions.

The conflict between the traditional ideology and practice in the area of nationality policy continues in the USSR. Almost from the beginning, ideology—though clearly having no intentions of permanently surrendering its claims—has yielded to necessity. If that pattern is changed significantly in the years immediately ahead, it would be surprising.

CONCLUSION

Marxism–Leninism has as one of its basic tenets the eventual merging of all peoples, languages, and cultures into a single international people, language, and culture. Even before the Revolution, however, Lenin was forced to back away from the merging concept in the name of gaining the support of minority ethnics for the Bolshevik cause. In his time, Stalin, who in nationality policy as in many other areas established the definitive Soviet policy, also recognized the need to gain minority support in order to achieve Soviet economic and political objectives and therefore gave vocal support for the postponement of merging, while often acting to the contrary. The post-Stalinist leadership has, in general, maintained the Stalinist model, though it has largely eliminated the widespread use of terror and repression to achieve the desired end.

In the 1980s and beyond, the Soviet leadership will be confronted with many problems directly related to nationality policy. The question of whether or not policy choices will be ideologically consistent with Marxism–Leninism has been resolved—since Lenin the goal of *sliyanie* has been postponed and in all likelihood that position will not significantly change. What is different, though, is that nationality policy will be operating in a new political context. On the international level, in order for the USSR to retain credibility and legitimacy as the leading Communist state, the Soviet leadership will have to avoid the danger of becoming openly Slavophile. On the domestic level, the leadership will have to consider the changing demographic composition of the USSR, which as has been shown in this essay has ramifications for many aspects of Soviet economic, social, and political policy.

Given such circumstances, it is likely that Soviet nationality policy will be constructed in such a way so as to minimize national antagonisms. The leadership will seek, within limits, to alleviate the most obvious aspects of discrimination against minorities and manifestations of Great Russian chauvinism. It will do this for a very pragmatic reason: namely, to ensure that Soviet economic and security goals can be realized. In conclusion, Soviet nationality policy will become increasingly minimalist as the leadership, even more so than in the past, seeks to "manage" nationality problems rather than "solve" them.

NOTES

1. Nicholas V. Riasanovsky, *A History of Russia,* 3rd ed. (New York: Oxford University Press, 1977), p. 437.

2. V.I. Lenin, *Polnoe sobranie sochinenii,* 3rd ed. (Moscow, 1962), 37, p. 356.

3. Ivan Dzyuba, *Internationalism or Russification?* (London: Weidenfeld and Nicolson, 1968), p. 58.

4. *KPSS v rezolyutsiyakh i resheniyakh s'yezdov, konferentsii i plenumov TsK,* 7th ed. (Moscow, 1953), I, p. 559, quoted in Dzyuba, *Internationalism or Russification?*, p. 127.

5. Stalin, *Works* (Moscow: Foreign Languages Publishing House, 1952–1955), 5, pp. 349, 272, quoted in Robert Conquest, *Soviet Nationalities Policy in Practice* (New York: Praeger, 1967), p. 53.

6. Robert Conquest, *The Human Cost of Soviet Communism* (Washington, D.C.: U.S. Government Printing Office, 1971), p. 41.

7. For further discussion of this aspect of Soviet nationality policy see Robert Conquest, op. cit., particularly Chapter IV.

8. The best discussion of this debate is found in Aleksandr M. Nekrich, *The Punished Peoples, the Deportation and Fate of Soviet Minorities at the End of the Second World War* (New York: Norton, 1978).

9. Y.A. Andropov, *Pravda*, December 22, 1982.

10. *Partiinaya zhizn*, no. 15, August 1983.

11. *Kommunist*, no. 8, May 1983, pp. 115–16.

12. N. Tarosenko, *Pravda*, December 16, 1983.

13. Y.A. Andropov, *Pravda*, December 22, 1982.

14. *Pravda*, December 16, 1983.

15. *Komsomolskaya pravda*, August 17, 1983, quoted in *The Current Digest of the Soviet Press*, 35, 34, p. 21.

16. *Sotsiologicheskiye issledovania*, no. 3, July–September 1982, pp. 11–16, quoted in *The Current Digest of the Soviet Press*, 34, 34, p. 6.

17. *Sovetskaya Kirgizia*, September 11, 1983, quoted in *The Current Digest of the Soviet Press*, 35, 42, p. 22.

18. *Sovetskaya Latvia*, July 1983, quoted in *The Current Digest of the Soviet Press*, 35, 43, p. 14.

19. Murray Feshbach, "The Soviet Union: Population Trends and Dilemmas," *Population Bulletin*, 37, 3, August 1982, p. 37.

20. *Izvestia*, August 21, 1983.

21. *Izvestia*, December 16, 1983.

22. Feshbach, op. cit. p. 33.

23. *Voprosy filosofii*, no. 2, February 1983, quoted in *The Current Digest of the Soviet Press*, 30, 46, p. 13.

24. *Sovetskaya Rossia*, October 13, 1983, quoted in *The Current Digest of the Soviet Press*, 35, 41, p. 1.

9

ECONOMIC REFORM: PROSPECTS AND POSSIBILITIES

Karl W. Ryavec

Although there has been a great deal written in recent years about economic reform in the Soviet Union, all of those writing on this subject have been in the difficult and ironic position of writing about something that does not yet exist.[1] We are in a position analogous to that of writers dealing with, for example, the "new international economic order," "stable deterrence," or a world without war. We have been writing about the idea of reform, not reform itself. So it remains here in examining what is being said and done about economic reform in the USSR since Brezhnev died in November 1982 and the significance of this for Soviet politics and economics.

In considering Soviet economic reform, we are squarely at the center of the debate and struggle between conservatives and "transformationists" or "modernizers." The Soviet economic discussion and debate mirror this confrontation between opposing philosophies and cultures. There are those in the USSR who seem to believe (since we cannot be certain what people there actually think) that the present economic system is a grand and historic achievement that is fully capable of further growth and of meeting all the standard demands made of it, while there are others (seemingly fewer but possibly a "hidden majority" constrained by the effects of Russian culture and politics) who make suggestions for change that would be transformational in effect if implemented. Although the Soviet system is conservative, a great many people in it are not. Yet we must be realistic. At the present historical moment, the conservatives in the Soviet Union are dominant and their way of doing things will continue for some time. Accordingly, the prospects of a transformational economic reform in the near future are small. Donald Kelley uses the term "cautious reform." It is the considered opinion presented here that what Soviet economic reform now actually means is getting the most out of the present economic system (even though this may well carry the danger of limiting or harming that system).[2] The reasons for this conclusion are found below.

What the Soviet economy is able to do in the near future is important to the West for several reasons. If the Soviets were to solve their economic difficulties without cutting back on defense production, they could continue their global foreign policy without change. But if the Soviets opt for economic reform, partly through reductions in their defense effort, the Soviet Union might come to have a different role in international politics. The western defense effort in the future would depend on which path the Soviet Union takes.

The word reform poses a semantic problem which, since we are discussing a political matter, becomes an ideological difficulty as well. Reform implies change many people would call significant. One reason for difficulty with the term is that several of the meanings it has had are now obsolete, that is, to renew, restore, re-establish. Its present meanings lean toward the idea of creating a better form or procedure by the removal of faults or abuses.[3] Accordingly, the term economic reform here refers to a Soviet economy made better in terms of the usual indicators of economics—efficiency, productivity, and production of quality as well as quantity.

The Soviet economic problem lies essentially in producing, at excessive cost and waste, low-quality items that arrive too late at production points with the psychological effects of fostering a managerial style of fulfilling the plan mainly in formal terms and a workers' style of working slowly, intermittently, and carelessly. The result is a per capita material standard of living equal to that of Italy. "Perhaps never before in history have such a gifted people, in control of such abundant resources, labored so hard for so long to produce relatively so little" per person.[4]

THE ESSENTIALS OF THE SOVIET ECONOMY

The Soviet economy is limited in its results because its operational principles and processes are immured in strong bureaucratic centralization, with the center ordering subordinate units to produce particular items in a specified number, in set ways, with suppliers designated as well. The terms of success are fundamentally the fulfillment of centrally set plan orders within constraints such as excessive employment and limited wage funds. Commercial criteria and the role of management and workers in decision making are quite limited, even negligible.[5] Clearly, any reform worthy of the name would have to be both wide-ranging and profound. Before we discuss the possibilities of reform, we must identify the various possible reforms of the Soviet economy, realizing, of course, that logical exercises can be undercut by politics and what the Soviets call "life itself." Logically, there seem to be only five general options, one or more of which would be only temporary:

1. The present system continued (temporary?)
2. The present system improved ("tinkering reform") (i.e., more resources and leeway)
3. A partly new system (significant additions and subtractions)
    a. "Authoritarian" (Stalinist)
    b. "Liberal" (decentralization or "socialist market" plus "East European" practices)
    c. "Technocratic" (effective though limited centralization)
4. A new system ("transformational reform")
5. Breakdown or dead end (probably temporary) (i.e., present system overloaded)

Alec Nove lists only two "serious" alternatives:

A. *A greater role for the market mechanism,* contract, commercial calculation . . . an active role for prices, the use of profits as a major managerial incentive . . . the complete or partial dismantling of administered material–technical supply.
B. *A streamlined centralized system* based on the East German "cartel" . . . in which the center's task is rendered less onerous by reducing the number of units which are the subject of planning, by merger . . . the planners allow more "slack" and reserve capacity within the plan. . . .[6]

Nove's two options correspond to the options 3b ("liberal" reform) and 3c ("effective though limited centralization"). Neither of his variants could bring about a new system (option 4) in the short term. Any reform will retain for years much of the old system (the former planning personnel, for example). Even if there is no planning in detail, old-line bureaucrats would still obstruct any reform politically. Accordingly, it is realistic to expect minor improvements at first before any change worthy of the word "reform" is born.

When the actual Soviet discussion of reform is discussed below, it will be seen that only "tinkering" is under review, at least in the press. Actual reform in the form of Nove's two "alternatives" is not yet seriously considered.

Have any reforms in Soviet history been transformational ones? Probably two have: the takeover of the "commanding heights" in 1917 (though this did not affect most of the population) and Stalin's "forced draft" industrialization and collectivization in the 1930s. The first change brought about the transfer of ownership of the means of production (plant and equipment) to the new Bolshevik-controlled state, while the second eliminated private ownership in land and moved a large portion of the peasant population into work in new urban industry. This radically changed life in the Soviet Union. But since the 1950s it has been apparent that Stalin's economic "reform" had been established too firmly. So far it has proved impervious to another transformation.

Stalin's system is unlikely to be altered significantly by those who helped build it, the present senior leaders. Stalin built a system that may be more resistant to change than is capitalism. Whereas in capitalist economies civil society is able to express its doubts about capitalism in restrictive legislation and the elevation of anti-capitalist politicians to high office, Soviet civil society is still hemmed in by Stalinism and its institutions. It is no surprise, then, that "no far-reaching economic reform has taken place since the five-year plans were originally introduced in the late 1920s."[7]

What the economists call "externalities" are crucially important in the Soviet economy. We are dealing here with a cultural–social–political system as much as or more than an economy. Culturally and politically, the USSR is in an earlier stage of development than are those systems its leaders denounce as "capitalist." Significant reform (as well as a transformational reform) requires that the Soviet Union free itself of those powerful remnants of what Trotsky called Russian *Aziatchina* (Asiatic backwardness) as well as from the present structural and procedural particularities of Soviet politics and administration.

However, just as these elements of "Sovietism" impede genuine reform, they also give the present way of producing a staying power of great though primitive strength. The population still does not expect or need, in any major sense, to live better materially. Neither do the former peasants now in the Politburo have any fundamental cultural or psychological need for a qualitatively different economy. As Alexander Eckstein once noted, "Communist and other regimes can consciously or unconsciously decide to maintain certain political arrangements and practices even if they are dysfunctional from an economic point of view. . . ."[8] It is generally agreed that the USSR is consciously maintaining an economically dysfunctional arrangement.

Even so, the Soviet economy still grows, albeit slightly, without having adopted reforms (Table 9). (And, even slight growth in an economy as large as that of the Soviet Union is significant in absolute terms.)[9] Robert Campbell expects growth to continue, even if at reduced rates. He also notes:

If output grows at 2 to 2.5 percent each year for the decade, it creates an easier situation in which to maneuver than the United States has faced during the years 1978–82, when GNP grew only 2.5 percent over four years. It is true that many problems urgently demand attention, but the situation is not beyond repair, even if the leaders are not willing to turn in their creaky old model for a radically new economic system.[10]

Table 9. Growth of Output and Productivity, 1970–1980 (average annual rates of growth, in percentages)[11]

	1970–75	1975–80	1980
Gross national product	3.7	2.7	1.4
Labor productivity	2.0	1.3	0.2
Total factor productivity	-0.5	-0.8	-1.9
Industrial production	5.9	3.6	3.4
Industry labor productivity	4.4	2.0	2.4
Industry total factor productivity	1.1	-0.6	-0.2

Source: Herbert S. Levine, "Possible Causes of the Deterioration of Soviet Productivity Growth . . .," in *Soviet Economy in the 1980s* (U.S. Congress, Joint Economic Committee, 1982), p. 154.

It is possible the Soviet leaders are gambling that better times will return in the next decade, the 1990s, which promise "some relief from at least two of the major problems—manpower and fuels."[12] In effect, it is still early for the Soviet leaders, whose lives have been linked with economic growth, to assume that the present downturn will not be overcome. We have still not seen the results of the burgeoning Soviet atomic power network, the recent importation of Western high technology, the new managerial training programs, and the beginnings of the tapping of the Moslem labor force. The slowdown of the growth rate is fairly recent and is tempered by the output of the quasi-legal "second economy," comprising at least 10 percent of the GNP. Still, despite these reasons for not changing things, there are strong forces that raise the issue of change for the Soviet economy as well as for the system as a whole.

THE SIGNIFICANCE OF ECONOMIC REFORM

Anyone who has lived in the Soviet Union has been made aware of the fact that the Soviet economy is made up of three or more economies linked together to make, overall, an economy of Byzantine complexity. There is, first of all, the general civilian economy; second, we note the military sector; third, the so-called "second" or "grey" economy comes into view (interpersonal trading and currency dealings, the state-run "commission" store, private production of items and food, and the state-supervised peasant markets); and finally, we have the "foreigners' economy," mostly in Moscow, of course, of foreign currency stores and the special establishments available to diplomats, foreign businessmen, students and scholars, and Soviets with hard foreign currency.

This chapter deals only with the general civilian economy. The military economy is an important one, of course. The USSR would not be a superpower without it. Micunović, once the Yugoslav ambassador to Moscow, recounts in his memoirs that his first impression of the USSR was, because of the multitudes of men in military uniform, of a nation at war. Such an impression is still made on foreigners. "The military sector is . . . a separate, fast-track economy with distinct organizations and a different set of rules and modus operandi from the civilian economy." Yet a reform of the civilian sector "may affect, if not alter, the balance between defense and civilian priorities and the ability of military program managers to carry out their missions."[13] Similarly left out of consideration is the second economy, "the Soviet '10 percent solution'; . . . Western economists figure its contribution to be between 5 and 15 percent of the total official GNP. And . . . it provides the kind of lubrication that allows the official system to function as well as it does."[14]

SOVIET PROBLEMS:
SOME REASONS FOR REFORM

What are the difficulties of the Soviet economy and overall system that might be alleviated or eliminated by economic reform? The general problem can be summed up by the terms "limitation," "restraint," and "repetition." It is a "self-maintenance" economy, a sort of closed system continually going over the same ground the same way despite its involvement in international trade. The Soviet economy still concentrates "overwhelmingly on the production of capital equipment for its own use," and consumer satisfaction (either for production units or individuals) has a low priority. "The thing held most important is centralized distribution."[15] Former Prime Minister Kosygin put it in Marxist terms in a way still used today by Soviet officials: "The forms of management, planning and incentive now in effect . . . no longer conform to present-day technical–economic conditions and to the level of development of productive forces."[16]

A real reform would have to change all this. Ultimately, to be a transformational reform it would have to either end the party's dominance or else transform the party, thus transforming the system. It is best to be more restrained and speak of the possible in connection with economic reform. But it must be recognized that "there is a scholarly consensus that the Soviet economy is too stagnant, the society too corrupt and degenerating, and the administrative and productive system too saddled with deferred maintenance for anything short of massive reforms to be effective." However massive reforms are out of the question for a variety of reasons, despite the fact that delay now will make reform later more difficult. As a Soviet official says, "The increased scale of production, the growing complication of economic ties and the acceleration of scientific and technical progress are enhancing the importance of every hour and every minute of working time.
. . ."[17]

The issue of national power is fundamental. Reform may be unavoidable if the country gets into an international political crisis. "Real economic reform is more likely to come because economic failure means weakness than because of an inability to supply consumer goods." It would be good for the Soviet Union to be able to avoid Indian generals saying in public, "All the Soviet Union can offer the Third World is weapons!"[18] The Soviet economy must, if the USSR wants to do better in international affairs, gain more respect abroad. Reform may help in this, particularly if it produces high-quality goods that compete on the international market.[19]

Other problems of the Soviet economy include:

Growing investment needs
Radical decline in the growth rate
Tightening labor supply (until the 1990s)
Possible end to the growth in consumption
Poor work style
Growing military burden on the economy
Low incentives for workers and farmers
Agriculture that cannot feed the country well
Energy difficulties
Defective relationship between planners and managers
Highly inefficient economic microstructures
Increasing need for Western technology[20]

Investment

Andropov said, "We are not now getting the full return on enormous capital investments."[21] This is the result of poor management and waste and of not charging enterprises for the use of land, water, and other resources.

Low Growth Rate

In 1982 industrial growth was only 2.8 percent, possibly the lowest in half a century. In 1982 and 1983 there was an actual decline of output in certain industries—coal, railroads (amount of freight hauled), wood and pulp, and ferrous metals. Although industrial production in 1983 increased 4 percent, 85 percent of the increase was due to a 3.5 percent rise in labor productivity, partly a result of the special effort of Andropov's discipline campaign. Steel production alone tells the tale. A Soviet academician notes, "Today, we are producing significantly less of the finished product from every ton of steel than the USA, Japan, and West Germany." The shortage "is now being felt in all branches of machine building."[22]

Labor Supply

Overinvestment, the maintenance of a large military (almost five million men on active duty), lack of involvement of much of the Muslim population in industry, and flagrant bidding for workers by managers produce a shortage of labor, a seller's market for labor, and a low-level upward creep of wages that outruns increases in labor productivity. Many workers are tardy or drunk on the job and often transfer from one enterprise to another.

Consumption

The level of consumer services that has been achieved does not fully meet the Soviet people's increased requirements. At present, "only 70 percent of consumer demand for leisure and household goods is being met." Light industry has not met its goals for several fabrics and the shoe industry has met only 49 percent of its plan during the first two years of the current plan.[23]

Work Style

Indifference to goals and costs and a pattern of evasion is endemic to both managerial personnel and blue-collar workers. One Moscow economist has even said that "the Americans were lucky because they did not have the problem of full employment to deal with. . . . The assurance of getting a job," he said, "is the root cause of slack effort and low productivity." Even a major official statement says, "Loafers, truants and drifters frequently feel free to do as they wish, and in terms of wages and other benefits they are on a par with conscientious employees."[24]

Military Burden

It is now generally believed that the Soviet military consumes 12 to 14 percent of the Soviet GNP, probably the highest proportion in the world among industrialized nations. Although the costs of Soviet defense grew at a lesser rate (about 2 percent in real terms) since 1976 than they had from 1966 to 1976 (4 to 5 percent), it is clear that the military burden is still increasing. Marshal Ogarkov has strong reasons for saying, "The armed forces can operate successfully only when they can rely on a powerful scientific, technical and economic base. . . ." Clearly, "the armed forces . . . have a strong vested interest in improving Soviet economic performance and expanding production and innovation capacity. . . ."[25]

Agriculture

This has been a problem area for 50 years. Even if the 1983 harvest had been 200 million metric tons and the best in five years, it would still have been below the target and less than needed. Imports will have to be about 29 million tons to provide enough grain for animals. In 1983 *Izvestia* reported: "The amount of new machinery that agriculture receives is less than the amount put out of commission by wear and corrosion."[26]

Energy

"The Soviet Union is already the least efficient producer and user of energy of any modern industrial power . . . and its energy intensiveness . . . is rising."[27] Although it may have enough conventional energy for its own use, it is forced to export much of it in order to obtain foreign currency with which to buy the high technology it cannot produce but needs.

The Planner–Plant Relationship

It is still true that the planners, Gosplan and the ministries, pretend to command and the enterprises pretend to deliver. Trust has never been established. If the plan is noticeably overfulfilled, the targets tend to be "ratcheted up" for the next year. It still happens, as Alec Nove reported many years ago, that enterprises issue "pretend" output. "Output that has been in production a long time" still is "especially attractive to the producer, while new products are undesirable" to him. They raise the risk of not fulfilling the plan and losing bonuses. Mere volume of output is still an important index of success (specified goal). Indeed, there are still too many indices. At one association of plants in Leningrad, there are "20 or more" indices compared to "eight to 10" during the late 1960s. Prices are still not rational. All this makes for a corrupting work environment, particularly since only 10 to 12 percent of the profit earned remains at the disposal of the enterprise. The "Novosibirsk paper" by the Soviet scholar Zaslavskaya points out that a rigid system of instructions from above was somewhat appropriate for the workers of the 1930s but that the "requirements and interests of contemporary workers are many times richer and wider" than those of workers of the past, and that the workers of today "are becoming significantly more complex an object of administration. . . ."[28]

Microstructures

The 20 million different items now produced by Soviet industry are made in 44,000 enterprises and associations. But this is not the total number of actual production units. Every enterprise and association has auxiliary operations (very small shops inside plants), where efficiency and labor productivity are very low and in which over one-fourth of all industrial workers are employed. This inefficient level of auxiliary production was to be done away with long ago, but as long as supplies are a problem, managers are driven by the exigencies of plan fulfillment and maximization of pay through bonuses to set up these subsidiary operations to ensure supplies. This pattern produces the "hidden reserves" about which higher authorities continually complain.[29]

Lack of Technological Innovation

The USSR has not maintained a balanced relationship with the more-developed economies. Although its economy is autarchic (independent overall), periodically it must import technologies and products from the West for further advancement. Even the great growth of the 1930s was based partly on imports of U.S. and European technology. Lend-lease, the stripping of eastern Germany and Manchuria and detente brought new borrowing. The Soviet economy is kept in partial "isolation from the ongoing industrial revolution that has made the West so hard to catch up with." Two Soviet emigrés note: "The Russians buy rapidly developing technologies but can't keep up with all the supporting technologies. They can't assimilate technology as well as they could before." Recently, voices have been raised criticizing the high rate of importing foreign technology. Although this may result in more careful importing, the fundamental dependence remains. The USSR has achieved a curious kind of limited modernity. "Modernity with gaps" and "stretched modernization" are terms that may apply. Sometimes modern equipment cannot operate because of a shortage of ordinary tools. The West's accomplishments cannot be duplicated by an "ersatz" modernity. The West and Japan continually forge ahead.[30]

Culture

Underneath all these problem areas lies that of culture (in the anthropological sense of thought and action natural to a community). The

Soviet leadership has to do more than change procedures, structures, incentives, and the atmosphere. It must get both managerial personnel and workers to adopt "universally held sociocultural attitudes that support hard work, efficiency, and professionalism." Perhaps it is even necessary to create "a new managerial elite of the Japanese type with whom political power will have to be shared."[31]

It seems clear that the USSR could profit greatly from a substantive economic reform. It may have come to one of those historical moments such as 1861 or 1905 when the need for reform is strong and apparent, even obvious, to all. All of the problems just discussed exist now and are retarding the economy seriously. They will have to be addressed. The basic question arises of whether it is too risky for the system and its elites to try a real reform. As we move on to an examination of the Soviet discussion of reform, we look for indications of realism and plans for significant change.

THE DISCUSSION OF REFORM

The post-Brezhnev discussion of economic changes in the Soviet press indicates both how some participants in the economy feel about these things and what the Soviet political elite is willing to have discussed. This discussion, then, like others in the USSR, exists somewhere between objective reality and political expediency. A standard tactic of politicians everywhere is to let discussion of a problem substitute for its solution. Luckily, however, we have some standards against which to test this "public" discussion—our past research on, and the record of, the Soviet economy, a system that has not changed fundamentally in 50 years, as well as the writings of emigrants from the Soviet Union and of samizdat and other writings not subjected to censorship. One recent and useful example of uncensored writing on the economy is the April 1983 paper of the economist and member of the Academy of Sciences Tatyana Zaslavskaya, leaked to the Western media, which deals with the nature and behavior of the Soviet worker and the politics within the state economic bureaucracy.[32]

Significantly, the present discussion deals with the same major issues that have existed for many years, namely, the stultifying effects of the ministries' running of the centralized economy, the absence of a smooth relationship between enterprises and their suppliers and their customers, the low productivity and negativistic behavior of workers,* and the disruptive

---

*A major focus of Zaslavskaya's paper.

effects of the planning agencies. But there is more intensity and directness and perhaps more realism to the discussion now. Notable is the strong criticism of the state bureaucracy and even of individual bureaucrats of prominence.[33]

Two main themes stand out in the current Soviet discussion on the economy: "What kind of economic reforms are necessary . . . and whether a reordering of scarce allocations is necessary. So far no consensus has emerged. . . ."[34] In other words, how far is the reform to go in changing the way key institutions operate and will it be necessary to cut the budgets of previously untouched projects? There is no discussion about getting the Party to move aside from its overall supervisory role in the economy. But the state bureaucracy, notably the ministries and the "planning" agencies, are being criticized. Their limitations and problems are noted in the Party-controlled press. "It is impossible to draw up at the center a plan for an enterprise that can be fulfilled without a hitch." The planners are "already overworked" and plans are incomplete and contain "holes," that is, they lack necessary items. As a result, the plans actually cause supply shortages, delays, and unutilized and demoralized labor. The excessive number of centrally set indices (goals) and their nature are under fire. One plant director gives the astounding figure of 59 goals he must meet.[35] None of this criticism is new, but it is stronger and clearer than it was.

The talk about the ministries that run industry raises the possibility of structural and procedural change and criticizes the ministries harshly. (There are now 37 industrial ministries.) It is pointed out that while there is legislation that governs the activity of industrial enterprises, there is no legislation governing accountability for the effects of plans made and imposed by higher-level organizations.[36] The party journal *Kommunist* published an exchange of articles in 1982–1983 on changes in the present ministerial setup. The economist Popov argued for change, saying that the present arrangement has mainly a historical justification and that the scientific–technical revolution now demands interbranch coordination.* He also said that new "superministerial" agencies are needed. Another economist would retain but enlarge the structure by creating the "superministry" since the actual economy is now more complex than the administrative structure. The superministries would handle branch management and long-range development, leaving the present ministries to do what they do now, "the day-to-day management of industrial subbranches." Coordination of the new superagencies would be done by a "single overall industrial management agency," perhaps a new Presidium of the Council of Ministers.

---

*Coordination among different industries and their ministries.

In opposition to such calls for improving centralization, others suggest a partial dismantling of the structure through a new system of economic regionalization which would include territorially based groupings of industries, the transfer of industrial branches based on local resources to the Union republics, and the creation of territorial construction ministries. This strategy of structural change recalls but is milder than Khrushchev's abolition of most ministries and the transfer of their functions to regional management agencies (eliminated when Khrushchev was removed in 1964). Some think more ministries are an improvement. G. Kulagin, a name prominent in the discussions of the 1960s, suggests creating new types of ministries that would manufacture all those items enterprises set up auxiliary operations to manufacture, thus making the existing ministries' work easier. But they might further overload the planners and computers.[37]

A persistent theme of the commentary about the ministries for almost two decades remains: they ought to cease detailed involvement in operations and instead become long-range overall planners and detached general regulators.[38] They ought to confine themselves to determining the proportions for branch development, make long-term capital investment decisions, and facilitate credit relations between producing units and Gosbank (the state bank), whose powers, along with those of other central agencies such as the Ministry of Finance, are also to be limited.

Despite this stepped-up campaign against the ministries, they are still defended. For example, at the same time as the warnings just mentioned appeared, a member of the editorial board of *Pravda* published a defense of the role of the "state" with hardly a mention of the party. He wrote that the state is the "economic center" and added: "The economic growth of socialist society . . . [is] inseparably bound up with the state's organizational activity. . . ." He criticizes "excessive regulation" but says "compulsion" cannot be avoided.[39]

Much of the discussion seems circular. There is talk of both stronger centralized control and decentralized production operations. Some commentators say this means new superagencies overseeing, but not actually controlling, new large regional production units which will have absorbed small industrial enterprises. Perhaps the best formulation on this issue is "centralizing the setting of goals and strategic tasks while decentralizing routine decision making."[40] But this concept has to be defined, implemented, and enforced.

Questions remain. Why, if ministries and central agencies are at the root of many of the economy's problems and are so criticized, are they not made to change or at least restricted from doing harm? There are several possible reasons. Possibly the party elite finds it most convenient to have some other group taking the blame. Possibly, too, top state bureaucrats are associated with leading members of the party bureaucracy and thus are protected from significant action. (More than 30 percent of Central Committee members are top state bureaucrats.) Possibly a decisive move against the state bureaucracy would cripple the economy, at least until bureaucrats of a new type could take their places. Perhaps what we have here is a struggle against only a faction in the ministries or just the beginnings of the real attack to be made when political conditions allow more to be done. Probably all of these factors play their roles in the party apparatus–state bureaucracy relationship.

Another focus of the discussion about reform is the enterprise directors, although this aspect of the discussion is less emphasized than that on the ministries. There seems to be doubt that the enterprise directors are ready for reform. One of the five ministers involved in a new experiment says, "Many of our economic managers have gotten out of the habit of independence, and feelings of dependence have spread among some of them. Directors have gotten used to having everything spelled out 'item by item' from above, to being mere executors." There is good reason for this. A director of a machinery plant indicates that lack of trust still permeates the economy: "Many executives are still striving for lower indices [goals] since they are not sure they will receive material resources on time and in amounts sufficient to cover the whole plan." Why should anyone in such a fluid environment take risks? The idea of management as a special skill with objective elements does not seem to be greatly emphasized, even though Western-style management programs now exist.

The related issues of consumer goods and workers' needs unavoidably come into the discussion. It is recognized that "the level of consumer services that has been achieved does not fully meet the Soviet people's increased requirements." Expanding the amount of consumer goods was discussed by the Politburo at least twice during 1983.[41] It is also recognized that workers are not working as well as they might, and ways of improving work style and increasing productivity are under discussion. Making wages relate more closely to actual work performance, but through a new small-group brigade pay system, not individual piecework, is considered, as is tightening discipline and stressing competition among workers. But it is recognized that improving workers' productivity requires providing more consumer goods. A new, long-range attempt at providing more and better-motivated workers by combining education with work and changing the educational system to introduce students to vocational training and work early on is similar to Khrushchev's reforms.[42] There is no movement toward a system of independent unions, although the talk of unions doing more for their members indicates recent Polish events have increased the leadership's concerns about possible worker disturbances.

Agriculture may be the sector in which reform is most needed, particularly since so much investment was poured into it under Brezhnev (to little result as yet) and because its low and unstable level of output is both an embarrassment and a danger to the Soviet Union. But the problem is to increase agricultural output without strengthening the peasantry as a class. Accordingly, the changes under way, though they have significance, are not radical. More personal and enterprise auxiliary farming is favored, some farmland is beginning to be assigned to small groups (though not permanently), higher prices are paid for state purchases of agricultural output, the limit on private livestock holdings has been removed, and movement has begun to increase enterprises in rural areas to process food products (integrated agro-industrial complexes in the USSR). Even though these changes were approved by the party leadership, some have complained that private agricultural activity might lead to "recurrences of bourgeois and petitbourgeois exclusiveness."[43]

Some reformers propose a major expansion of the private sector, including what might be dubbed "privatization" of some consumer goods outlets. A leading economist suggests leasing out small stores "on a contract basis." State control would remain, but a "more flexible system of incentives would provide an opportunity to raise the quality of their performance and turn loss-making ones into effective ones." There is also talk of facilitating research and the introduction of research results into production by creating private "technology input firms." Ironically, private or independent consulting firms existed in the 1960s, but they were put out of existence, probably because they might have become independent of the party and threatened the state bureaucracy's monopoly of administration. (These firms were made up of state-employed engineers working on their own time.) One economist expressly calls for "new forms" of small production organizations "based on individual initiative" and having "commodity money relations" outside the plan. All this shows how far the current discussion has come, but "privatization," however limited, would be a painful and hence radical and difficult step to take.[44]

An interesting question is whether or not the USSR will adopt changes that have been implanted as routine aspects of the economies of some of the Eastern European states. Eastern Europe has long been "an experimental laboratory in which the performance of organizational variants can be evaluated." A former Czech leader says, "I think there will be attempts in the USSR to conduct some type of economic reform like that in Hungary."[45] The Soviet press is not hesitant about printing favorable accounts of aspects of the Eastern European economies. A head of a shop in a Soviet automobile plant says of a comparable shop in the German Democratic Republic (GDR), "Things are run better there. . . ." What particularly struck him was the East German avoidance of emergencies typical in the Soviet production process and the selection of the best workers as foremen, who earn more pay than workers, unlike the situation in the Soviet shop where "a foreman, who has an enormous workload and a lot of responsibility, is paid much less than an experienced worker." The Bulgarian acceptance of low growth and the reduction of its ministries' tasks to control investment and technology, a change wanted by many Soviet economists, as well as the use of Hungarian-style free contacts among enterprises, is part of the discussion. The elimination of "tense" plans in favor of some "slack" seems to be a common feature of the Eastern European economies.[46]

Apparently the reform debate does not consider the Yugoslav and Chinese variants as relevant to Soviet needs. Yugoslavia has a free market and is tied to the Western economies. China now favors peasant private enterprise and islands of capitalism ("special administrative zones") where private enterprise will be legal. It will be a long time before we hear a Soviet spokesperson saying, as did a Chinese official recently, "To maintain capitalism in a small place is beneficial to socialism in the whole country,"[47] and certainly the USSR is not ready to discuss decollectivization (Yugoslavia and Poland).

This cursory examination of the current Soviet discussion about economic change reveals a deep reluctance to consider radical changes in the structure of the Soviet economy. Also, much of the discussion is by people of no or little political significance and much of it only calls for new laws and regulations and more of the old pressure from above. There may be a large-scale readiness for reform but this exercise, relying as it does on the output of a controlled press, cannot reveal it.

CURRENT ECONOMIC MOVES

What is actually being done in coping with "the central issue in Soviet economic affairs in the 1980s . . . adapting to economic stringency?" Is a definite "option" of the kind Western economists suggest going into effect? Or do we have a series of ad hoc measures aimed at mere "system mainte-nance" and stemming decline? Is a new economic "reservoir" being built for the Soviet Union or do we only have a series of plugs in the holes in the "dike"? Almost all Western commentators agree, in effect, with Bialer that "by far the central problem, the key to the entire emergency has to do with the need to reform the entire system of planning and management."[48]

A number of minor reform measures were instituted during the Brezhnev period (1964–1982) but, since all (even Khrushchev's 1957 de-centralization) retained detailed central planning, they were merely bureaucratic adjustments and (1) made no deep change, and (2) because of this, failed. Yet they can be said to have had a certain significance, but not as reforms. They have shown that small changes, however useful, are in-sufficient to create an improved economic mechanism. The economy of Stalin is still discernible after 30 years of tinkering.[49] Even "projec-tomania" continues, notably the development of western Siberia and the push to increase the role of nuclear energy. The resistance to reform is still strong. The head of Gosplan has said that some industries will still operate at a loss and over-full employment will continue.

The main change adopted in the organizational structure of industry in recent years is the expansion of production associations or amalgamations of enterprises. These are groupings of formerly independent industrial en-terprises producing similar items which now constitute a single enterprise under one director. By 1980 they produced 48 percent of industrial output and employed 50.1 percent of industrial workers. In addition, there are now some territorial–production complexes (large regional groupings of enterprises). Yet there are complaints that the ministerial apparatus has given up little to them.[50] The ministries still have the last word. Since they have not been transformed in nature, they retain the tendency to inter-fere in industrial operations, thereby inhibiting managerial initiative. Few ministries are financially self-supporting, as reformers want.[51] Nor is any ministry yet financially liable for the errors it makes for factories. Unless the factions that emerge on top from the current long-term succession pro-cess want industry to be run in a new way, the ministerial structure will re-tain its present position. Even the most recent experiment extending the rights of associations and increasing their responsibilities operates within the ministerial context. In July 1983 the Politburo approved a new mode of operation for the enterprises under five ministries, granting them more lee-way in the use of funds, profit retention, and higher bonuses for technical personnel. This experiment is beginning to deal with the problem of unrealistic prices by allowing enterprises to set, by themselves, "temporary prices" for new products they produce.[52] It will be interesting to see if this experiment is later extended.

Along with structure and prices, a central feature of any effective reform must be the introduction (as long as central planning is retained) of a major indicator of enterprise success that does not cause economic distortions or allow the covert reintroduction of the old index of gross output, a simple indicator favored in the past. All success indicators introduced to replace gross output have been criticized for their own distortions.[53] New success indicators continue to be tried, however. In order to make more concrete the Politburo's idea of giving consumer goods production a bigger place in the Twelfth Five-Year plan, a new index for consumer goods production was introduced in 1983. It is to have a payoff, if met, in managerial bonuses.[54] Another new managerial requirement is the index for the fulfillment of plans for the development of science and technology which, if not met, will reduce bonuses by at least 25 percent.[55] But loading different indicators on managers, however progressive the goal, can become a continuation of the old practice of measuring success by quantitative quotas.

The problem of low worker motivation and productivity is being addressed in a limited way. A discipline campaign with teeth in it has been introduced. In addition, an attempt is being made to: (1) talk more in the media about workers (probably to try to give them a higher sense of self-worth and thus improve their motivations); (2) have party organizations observe the workers' situation more closely (an effect of the Polish events); and (3) begin to displace payment by individual piecework in favor of payment by the results of small group output ("contract brigades"). But only a beginning has been made on this last element, one which workers may not like. It does seem, however, that the campaign to increase discipline is being implemented. One party–state resolution specifies that violators of labor discipline will lose vacation days and can even be transferred to lower-paying jobs for periods of three months. An attempt is even being made again to link poor work at one job with the bonus rate at the next job. This seems to suggest the reinvigoration of the old labor book* and a toughened environment for the Soviet worker.[56] The question, however, is whether the persisting labor shortage will force managers to ignore poor work discipline in order to have the required labor, however poorly it works. Moscow can issue resolutions, but managers have to get the work done somehow, particularly if their goals are not relaxed.

---

*A record of work performance workers must take from each job to the next. The labor book system was allowed to lapse, in effect, under Brezhnev.

Agricultural workers, too, are being affected by change from above, the main element of which is the agricultural contract brigade, a small group that contracts to farm a particular plot. On one state farm in Altai Krai, land, plus equipment and seeds, was turned over to small teams of six to eight persons or families for a five-year period. These teams did better than the state farm in a number of ways. A similar plan is being implemented on some collective farms, with a level of guaranteed pay in case of natural calamity. But not many of these contract brigades have been formed. Only 8 percent of all plowland in the Russian Republic has been transferred to them, and even when it is, the old problem of consumer goods shortages creates pressures for more significant change. One Soviet commentator asks, "What good is big money to a worker if he can't spend it as he would like in his own settlement? . . . The organization of teams . . . should be accompanied by growth in the supply of goods and services in rural localities." Other changes include paying higher prices to farms and 50 percent higher bonuses on high deliveries of agricultural products. Although we may be seeing an attempt to adopt aspects of the Hungarian private agricultural system, the Soviet leadership has not adopted the "far-reaching changes within the . . . system as a whole . . . necessary to allow private agriculture . . . to operate as effectively as it does in Hungary."[57]

Even with these changes, the Soviets are still in a pre-reform phase. They seem to be actively and realistically trying to make their present economic system work better, but in a small-scale way. They are not yet trying to create a new economic arrangement. If they do start to think in transformational terms, it will be only after the results and failures of the present changes are generally apparent. This may well take years and depend heavily on non-economic factors. A key word may be "intensification"—of what exists; that is, keep the current principles and arrangements but make them operate more smoothly and faster to more material effect. One specialist puts it this way: "The Soviets have failed to fashion a comprehensive approach. . . . Rather, a myriad of innovative approaches to industrial decision making has emerged which diversifies the traditional administrative model dating back to Stalin."[58]

MODELS AND REALITY

Western economists have devised various potential models of Soviet economic change. Certainly neither a "radical" nor a "liberal" model is now operative. No market economy is coming into existence and no large-scale and legal private economy exists; this would be called a "liberal" approach. And it is clear no significant participation by workers in decision making is contemplated; this would be in the Marxist tradition. Perhaps we see a combination of what Robert Campbell calls the "conservative" and "reactionary" models—a retention of most of the standard Soviet features of an economy plus a stress on discipline and a threat of stern action. One exception to this combination of models is the new contract brigade system in farming. However, since agriculture has long been in crisis, an exception here is understandable. In any case, the centrally planned economy remains. Neither of Alec Nove's two alternatives, of marketization or streamlined centralism, has been adopted. Of George Feiwel's three possibilities of Soviet reform ("market socialism, indirect centralism, and modified centralism") it looks as if modified centralism with a technocratic approach is appearing. No Western model fully applies. Igor Birman is correct in seeing "a sort of hybrid," with movement toward decentralization and an increase in incentives, "while maintaining state property and overall state direction."[59]

LIMITS TO REFORM

There are several factors that have dictated this limited direction, pace, and amount of change. First of all, a huge economy itself produces innumerable limitations on change—fears of crippling what exists, a degree of comfort in present arrangements, and the reluctance to undertake the awesome task of changing something big that is moving. And any slowdown or decline is relative. The economy will still be huge and Soviet power great. Zero or near-zero economic growth may be the new norm for all industrial societies. Second, any reform is risky. Would a decentralized reform work now, after 50 years of directive planning? Once "there were capitalists with at least some capital, skills, and connections. Peasants knew how to work and wished to do so." Hungary, the shining example of Soviet-style socialism, was under Stalinism for only a decade; people retained the old ways. How, if at all, does one recreate the habits of the market? And, if efficient centralism is followed instead, how does one get efficient bureaucrats? Does it mean the social base has to be changed first? Can a really new centralism be forged? Russians are adept at getting around rules. A proverb says, "Russians will always find an antidote to the poison of the law." This takes us to society's base—culture, which tends to outlast mere political regimes and their dreams. Westerners are often open to change, partly because they have mastered it, taken the sting out of it, or so they may think. But a Russian leadership has to be leery of change. Consider 1917–1921, 1929–1938, and the post-Stalin thaw. An entire new chief directorate of the KGB had to be established to deal with the last big social change in the USSR. A Russian leadership is more inclined to political "maintenance" than political change.

Third, there are the dangers and costs of reform. Whichever model is picked, large numbers of people will be adversely affected. Nove cites the "casualties" of the market. Bialer notes that the initial period of any reform is "immensely costly" and "disorganization is inevitable," as is the "disruptive effect" on production. Unemployment and higher inflation may result. Why go through this? The dangers are serious. Decentralization in a multiethnic country implies devolution of power to different peoples. Russians might only lose in this. Brzezinski says, "A genuinely far-reaching decentralization of the Soviet system, even if only economic, would pose a mortal danger to Great Russian imperial control, and thus, . . . to the security of the Great Russian people. . . ."[60] What effects would Soviet reform have on Eastern Europe, which could take the cue to go further? What would it mean for the international image and stature of the "socialist" USSR?

Finally, politics is involved. Heavy politico-bureaucratic resistance to reform is inevitable whichever model is followed. Other important limiting factors are the unstable international situation, particularly the anti-Soviet stances of the United States and China, and the fact that the succession process has not yet stabilized fully. Economic reform is not possible without a lower arms budget, and that requires a better relationship with the United States.[61] Although an improvement may be possible, it will take time. If, as is likely, the succession is multistage and awaits the emergence of a younger long-term general secretary, reform could be stalled for several years. Its rate can even slow down or stop completely while the full succession works itself out. Chernenko, because of his advanced age, is unlikely to have the time required to obtain the sort of political power required to introduce new initiatives, even if he were inclined toward them.

A fundamental political limitation is the lack of a pro-reform "public," much less one social group with the power to force reform. "In-house" critics and economists cannot do much without political support. The Soviet expert "is clearly on tap, not on top. . . ." Another fundamental barrier is the Soviet ideology which, even if not believed in, is still professed in Marxist language. According to it, production for use is superior to production for exchange. As long as this language is politically useful, it cannot be ignored. Not only is no powerful group clearly for reform, most groups would oppose or be suspicious of aspects of it. Party officials, managers, white-collar workers, central bureaucrats, the officers corps—all would oppose some effects of decentralizing reform.

The state bureaucracy is a real impediment. There is no way now to make a "clean cut" through it, purging it at one fell swoop in order either to effect a new Stalinism or any other kind of transformational change. Stalin had it easy. He could fire all the "bourgeois specialists" and, indeed, anyone else. Now Chernenko cannot even fire all the bureaucrats over age 50 (an act that might make real change possible?). It is exactly these people who are most closely tied to the existing economy.

THE NEW LEADERSHIP AND REFORM

Successful reform of any kind demands leadership, a political base, and a supportive rationale. A successful reform or even a significant attempt at reform demands a decisive and active leader who, like Peter the Great, can implement great projects. He will need a political base. The factional politics common in a succession struggle may make reform an issue. A pro-reform coalition could be put together—people from the high-technology field, the defense ministries, the military, the party apparatus, younger and newly trained engineers, scientists, and economists. The contender for reform has to be willing and able to remove large numbers of people from certain structures and replace them with people who think as he does and who are also loyal to him. The potential for a reform coalition is present, and certainly the political culture favors strong leaders.

In addition, since the USSR is an ideological political system, an ideological justification will have to be developed, promulgated, and inculcated. The reform has to be more than a tactic. It has to be a new departure in fact or appearance and justifiable in Marxist–Leninist terms.[62] The reform that comes out of this will be, of course, both Russian and Soviet and may well not match any of the Western models of economic reform. No doubt the reformers will try to isolate the pressures for economic reform from those of political reform.

Soon after he became general secretary in November 1982, Andropov indicated he favored certain aspects of economic reform, such as the expansion of the powers of production units and learning from other socialist countries, but that everything must be done "circumspectly." At the Central Committee meeting of June 1983, he spoke of "discipline and order" and "organization and responsibility," and emphasized "ensuring the well-adjusted, uninterrupted operation of the entire economic mechanism." However, he had little time as general secretary (only half a year of relatively good health) and accordingly he only barely began the process of change.

Although Konstantin Chernenko became general secretary soon after Andropov's death, he does not occupy that office as firmly as did Brezhnev or Andropov. Chernenko, who was Brezhnev's top aide for three decades, has never administered a major institution or region of the USSR. He did, however, learn how the system works from his vantage point as head of the Politburo "office," the General Department, under Brezhnev. But this experience had not been sufficient for him to get Brezhnev's job at his death in 1982. Andropov got it instead, and during his year in office promoted a number of persons allied with him to positions of prominence, including a few to Politburo membership. Accordingly, Chernenko came to his present post weaker than Andropov. It is generally thought that the Politburo old guard of Ustinov, the defense minister, and Gromyko, the foreign minister, both (like Chernenko) over 70 years of age, were able to use their own and their subordinate institutions' and their supporters' influence to install Chernenko as against someone from the younger faction who might have been close to Andropov and his policies. It seems, then, that Chernenko is a compromise figure who is more a coordinator of a divided Politburo than a genuine leader. In addition, he probably cannot move much toward economic reform since his two old-line supporters, Gromyko and Ustinov,* are both, as far as can be discerned, opposed to such reform.[63] More importantly, having been a central cog of the Brezhnev administration from its beginning, he himself is very unlikely to want reform but instead will tend to be a political "maintenance man" of the existing system. Only absolutely necessary and non-destabilizing changes are likely to be made in the short run.

The question is how long can he and his conservative associates (the "Brezhnev group," in effect) dominate the Politburo. Although it would not be realistic to suggest the younger people on the Politburo are strongly pro-reform, yet it does seem some of them are more favorably inclined toward it than the older Politburo members. For example, Romanov, while first secretary in Leningrad, "sponsored a number of pioneering ventures in management" and particularly emphasized the introduction of new technology, though with an "emphasis on toughness and discipline in organization."[64]

It is possible that Gorbachev may be the "Andropov heir" in the Politburo. In his election speech of February 1984, he listed many of the

---

*Ustinov died December 20, 1984.

priorities Andropov had emphasized—modernizing technology, improving management, strengthening labor discipline, fighting corruption, and increasing agricultural output.[65] He is also seen in the West as the leader of the younger Politburo faction and as a future general secretary. He may already be functioning, as one Soviet official said in October 1984, as a sort of second general secretary. But, dynamic as he may be to have become a Politburo member when only a few years older than 50, his specialization area of agriculture makes him vulnerable. Since Soviet agriculture is so prone to bad harvests, he may have to take the blame for the next one. On the other hand, his risky position drives him to try for improvements and reform in agriculture.

Chernenko's statements on the economy are a mixture of continuity and change. This is natural for a man new to his job and limited by a conservative support base. Although he has raised the prospect of reform by calling for the "restructuring of the entire economic mechanism," for "bold action" on the economy, and for solving "the problems of the intensive development of the economy in a far more energetic way," he has not called for an economic reform as such and has more than balanced his mention of change with conservative references to increasing labor productivity, efficiency, and hard work and the "strengthening of order, organization and discipline" at the work place. In addition, he tends to sound like the ideological specialist he has been by equating the ideological "elevation" of people with the improvement of their standard of living. This moralistic orientation is revealed by his words favoring the new educational program: "We must teach our children not what is easy . . . but what is hard."[66] By this he means work, and particularly manual work.

Chernenko may come to favor an economic reform but, if he does, it will most likely be a centralizing one in which typically Soviet values are upheld. In any case, Chernenko can try nothing in the realm of reform until, and if, he either controls the Politburo or has its firm support. This will take time, political maneuvering, and even luck. The further progress of reform may have to wait until Chernenko and his conservative associates pass from the scene and the succession process opens up new political possibilities.

CONCLUSION

In essence, the argument here has been that, although a number of small steps of change are being taken in the economy, in some cases steps that have not been seen since before Stalin's time, these changes do not add up to one big change that can be called an economic reform. It has also been argued, however, that the discussion about the economy and the mood surrounding it are of some realism and vitality, suggesting that if certain conditions were to exist, it would be possible to begin a reform. Yet, these conditions, a settling of the succession process and the emergence of a decisive leader, a reaching of a palpable economic dead end and the coming to power of a younger generation, do not yet exist. Hence, instead of reform there is a series of correctives and tinkering. As a result, the steps being taken will not make the Soviet Union stronger, though they may be making it less weak and so better able to undertake and undergo a reform in the future under new leaders and new conditions.

NOTES

1. Here is a partial listing of major Western writings important for the study of Soviet economic reform.

Books: Abram Bergson and Herbert S. Levine, eds., *The Soviet Economy: Toward the Year 2000* (London: Allen & Unwin, 1983), particularly the articles by Joseph Berliner and Seweryn Bialer; William J. Conyngham, *The Modernization of Soviet Industrial Management: Socioeconomic Development and the Search for Viability* (Cambridge: Cambridge University Press, 1982); Michael Ellman, *Economic Reform in the Soviet Union* (London: Political and Economic Planning, 1969); Marshall I. Goldman, *The USSR in Crisis: The Failure of an Economic System* (New York: Norton, 1983); Thane Gustafson, *Reform in Soviet Politics: Lessons of Recent Policies on Land and Water* (Cambridge: Cambridge University Press, 1981); Erik P. Hoffmann and Robbin F. Laird, *The Politics of Economic Modernization in the Soviet Union* (Ithaca: Cornell University Press, 1982); Holland Hunter, ed., *The Future of the Soviet Economy: 1978–1985* (Boulder: Westview Press, 1978); Abraham Katz, *The Politics of Economic Reform in the Soviet Union* (New York: Praeger, 1972); William Kaizer, *The Soviet Quest for Economic Rationality: The Conflict of Economic and Political Aims in the Soviet Economy, 1953–1968* (Rotterdam: Rotterdam University Press, 1974); Moshe Lewin, *Political Undercurrents in Soviet Economic Debates: From Bukharin to the Modern Reformers* (Princeton: Princeton University Press, 1974); Karl W. Ryavec, *Implementation of Soviet Economic Reforms: Political, Organizational, and Social Processes* (New York: Praeger, 1975); Nicolas Spulber, *Organizational Alternatives in Soviet-type Economies* (Cambridge: Cambridge University Press, 1979); Daniel Tarschys, *The Soviet Political Agenda: Problems and*

Priorities, 1950–1970 (White Plains, NY: M.E. Sharpe, 1979); J. Wilczynski, *Socialist Economic Development and Reforms: From Extensive to Intensive Growth under Central Planning in the USSR, Eastern Europe, and Yugoslavia* (New York: Praeger, 1972); Eugene Zaleski, *Planning Reforms in the Soviet Union, 1962–1966: An Analysis of Recent Trends in Economic Organization and Management,* Marie-Christine MacAndrew and G. Warren Nutter, trans. and ed. (Chapel Hill: University of North Carolina Press, 1967).

Articles and sections of books: Joseph S. Berliner, "Managing the USSR: Alternative Models," *Problems of Communism,* 32, 1 (January–February 1983): 40–55; Seweryn Bialer, "The Politics of Stringency," in Seweryn Bialer, *Stalin's Successors* (Cambridge: Cambridge University Press, 1980), Chapter 15; Daniel Bond and Herbert Levine, "The 11th Five-Year Plan, 1981–85," in *Russia at the Crossroads,* Seweryn Bialer and Thane Gustafson, eds. (London: Allen & Unwin, 1982), Chapter 4; Robert W. Campbell, "Economic Reform and Adaptation of the CPSU," in *Soviet Society and the Communist Party,* Karl W. Ryavec, ed. (Amherst: University of Massachusetts Press, 1978), pp. 26–40; Robert W. Campbell, "The Economy," in *After Brezhnev,* Robert F. Byrnes, ed. (Bloomington, IN: Indiana University Press, 1983), pp. 68–124; Paul Cocks, "Administrative Reform and Soviet Politics," in *Soviet Economy in the 1980s,* U.S. Congress, Joint Economic Committee (Washington, D.C.: U.S. GPO, 1982), Part 1, pp. 46–64; Paul K. Cook, "The Political Setting," in ibid., pp. 10–29; M. Elizabeth Denton, "Soviet Perceptions of Economic Prospects," in ibid., pp. 30–45; Herbert S. Levine, "Possible Causes of the Deterioration of Soviet Productivity Growth in the Period 1976–80," in ibid., pp. 153–68; George R. Feiwel, "Economic Performance and Reforms in the Soviet Union," in *Soviet Politics in the Brezhnev Era,* Donald R. Kelley, ed. (New York: Praeger, 1980), pp. 70–103; Marshall Goldman, "Economic Problems in the Soviet Union," *Current History,* 82, 486 (October 1983): 322–25, 339; P. Hanson, "Economic Constraints on Soviet Policies in the 1980s," *International Affairs* (London), 57, 1 (Winter 1980–1981): 21–42; John P. Hardt, "Imperatives of Economic Reform and Communist Political Systems," in *Perspectives for Change in Communist Societies,* Teresa Rakowska-Harmstone, ed. (Boulder, CO: Westview, 1979), pp. 71–80; Ed. A. Hewitt, "Economic Reform in the Soviet Union," *The Brookings Review,* 2, 3 (Spring 1984): 8–11; Hans-Hermann Hoehman and Gertraud Seidenstecher, "Soviet Economic Policy: Reform Measures but No Reform," *Osteuropa* 11 (1979): 936–42; Nancy Nimitz, "Reform and Technological Innovation in the 11th Five-Year Plan," in *Russia at the Crossroads,* Bialer and Gustafson, eds., pp. 140–55; Alec Nove, "Alternative Models," in *The Soviet Economic System,* 2nd ed. (London: Allen & Unwin, 1980), Chapter 11, and "The Politics of Economic Reform," in *Political Economy and Soviet Socialism* (London: Allen & Unwin, 1979), Chapter 9; Bruce Parrott, "Innovation and the Politics of Bureaucratic Change," in *Politics and Technology in the Soviet Union* (Cambridge: MIT Press, 1983), pp. 278–93; Henry Rowen, "Central Intelligence Briefing on the Soviet

Economy" (statement before the Subcommittee on International Trade, Finance, and Security Economics, December 1, 1982, mimeo); Blair Ruble, "Muddling Through," *The Wilson Quarterly* (Winter 1981), reprinted in *Comparative Politics, 83/84,* Christian Soe, ed. (Guilford, CT: Annual Editions, Dushkin Publishing, 1983), pp. 207–11; Gertrude E. Schroeder, "Soviet Economic 'Reform' Decrees: More Steps on the Treadmill," in *Soviet Economy in the 1980s,* Part 1, pp. 65–88, and "The Soviet Economy on a Treadmill of Reforms," in *Soviet Economy in a Time of Change,* vol. 1, U.S. Congress, Joint Economic Committee (Washington, D.C.: U.S. GPO, 1970), pp. 312–40; Robert Wesson, "Productivity," in *The Aging of Communism* (New York: Praeger, 1980), pp. 53–58. The numerous relevant reports of Radio Liberty researchers are not included above although several are cited below (as RL plus number and date).

2. "The improvement of our economic mechanism will take place on the basis of the already existing mechanism." Eduard Shevardnadze, First Secretary of Georgia, on Budapest Television, October 6, 1983. Quoted in *Soviet Nationality Survey,* 1, 3, (March, 1984): 4.

3. *The Shorter Oxford English Dictionary,* 3rd ed., vol. 2 (Oxford: The Clarendon Press, 1973), p. 1778.

4. Zbigniew Brzezinski, "The Soviet Union: World Power of a New Type" (address to the 25th Annual Conference of the International Institute for Strategic Studies, Ottawa, September 8, 1983, mimeo), p. 13.

5. See Alec Nove, *Political Economy and Soviet Socialism* (London: Allen & Unwin, 1979), p. 156.

6. Nove, *Political Economy,* pp. 156–57. Nove rejects the idea "control by the direct producers" (the workers) as "nice" but utopian.

7. Marshall I. Goldman, *The USSR in Crisis: The Failure of an Economic System* (New York: Norton, 1983), p. 339. See also Timothy J. Colton, *The Dilemma of Reform in the Soviet Union* (New York: Council on Foreign Relations, 1984).

8. Alexander Eckstein, "Economic Development and Change in Communist Systems," *World Politics,* 22, 4 (July 1970): 475–76. Eckstein's central hypothesis is that "the stage of economic development imposes certain imperatives of its own on any . . . system, including Communist ones" (p. 475).

9. The analysis of this paper covers the period through mid-1984.

10. Robert W. Campbell, "The Economy," in *After Brezhnev,* Robert F. Byrnes, ed. (Bloomington, IN: Indiana University Press, 1983), p. 120.

11. Herbert S. Levine, "Possible Causes of the Deterioration of Soviet Productivity Growth . . .," in *Soviet Economy in the 1980s,* U.S. Congress, Joint Economic Committee, p. 154. Definitions of the terms used are given there.

12. M. Elizabeth Denton, "Soviet Perceptions of Economic Prospects," in ibid., p. 45.

13. Veljko Micunović, *Moscow Diary* (Garden City, NY: Doubleday, 1980); address by Kenneth W. Dam, Deputy Secretary of State, October 31, 1983,

U.S. Dept. of State, *Current Policy,* no. 525, p. 2; Paul Cocks, "Administrative Reform and Soviet Politics," in *Soviet Economy in the 1980s,* U.S. Congress, Joint Economic Committee (Washington, D.C.: U.S. GPO, 1982), Part I, p. 61. This issue seems to have figured in the ouster of Marshal Ogarkov in September, 1984. See the *New York Times,* September 13, 1984.

14. Blair Ruble, "Muddling Through," *The Wilson Quarterly* (Winter 1981), reprinted in *Comparative Politics, 83/84,* p. 211. And see, for example, Gregory Grossman, "The 'Second Economy' of the USSR," *Problems of Communism,* 26, 5 (September–October 1977): 25–40; and Dennis O'Hearn, "The Consumer Second Economy: Size and Effects," *Soviet Studies,* 32, 2 (April 1980): 218–34. Grossman notes that "the second economy . . . is a kind of spontaneous surrogate economic reform that . . . represents a de facto decentralization" that may make a formal reform more difficult (p. 40).

15. Francis Seton, "Economic Planning in Communist Societies," in *The Soviet Union and Eastern Europe,* George Schöpflin, ed. (New York: Praeger, 1970), p. 282; and A. Aganbegyan, quoted in *Bandiera rossa* (Rome), July 1965, p. 6; U.S. Joint Publications Research Service, 31, 814 (September 1, 1965): 16. For recent comments on Aganbegyan on the economy and the need for reform, see his articles in *Trud,* August 28 and August 29, 1984, p. 2.

16. A.N. Kosygin, "Ob uluchshenii upravlaniya . . .," *Pravda,* September 28, 1965, p. 2.

17. From a speech by the vice-chairman of the Trade Union Council, *Izvestia,* August 18, 1983, p. 3.

18. Robert Wesson, *The Aging of Communism* (New York: Praeger, 1981), p. 95. Professor Alexander Erlich made the same point to me in 1968. The Indian general made the remark at a conference of the Philadelphia Council of World Affairs in May 1982.

19. Zdenek Mlynař (a former secretary of the Czech CP), interview, *RUSSIA,* 5–6 (1982): 145.

20. This list is based on Bialer, "The Politics of Stringency," pp. 287–93; and Campbell, "The Economy," pp. 81–121.

21. *New York Times,* August 8, 1983; *Washington Post,* November 12, 1983; *Pravda* and *Izvestia,* April 24, 1983, p. 1; John F. Burns, "Soviet Economic Data Indicating '83 Rebound," *New York Times,* December 26, 1983; *Izvestia,* December 27, 1979, and *Sotialisticheskaya industriya,* March 16, 1982, quoted in Andreas Tenson, "The Fate of Soviet Steel . . .," RL 435/83, November 17, 1983, p. 1; Ann Sheehy, "Union-Republic Plan Results for 1983," RL 62/84, February 8, 1984. I am indebted to Marshall Goldman for noting that some of the Soviet figures may be overstated.

22. *Kommunist,* no. 3, 1983, p. 13.

23. *Pravda,* March 30, 1983, p. 1; Tenson, "Soviet Efforts to Boost Consumer Goods Production Make Little Progress," RL 259/83, July 7, 1983, pp. 1–2.

24. *Pravda*, May 7, 1982; quoted by Tenson, "Obstacles to Scientific and Technological Progress in the USSR," RL 281/82, July 12, 1982, p. 1; *Pravda* and *Izvestia*, August 7, 1983, pp. 1–2; Leonard Silk, "Russian Economy Gives Andropov Huge Problems," *New York Times*, June 12, 1983, p. A12; *Pravda*, July 1, 1983, pp. 2–3.

25. U.S. Congress, Joint Economic Committee, *Soviet Defense Trends*, staff study, September 1983, p. 2; Hedrick Smith, "Soviet Arms Spending Said to Slow," *New York Times*, November 19, 1983; N. Ogarkov, "Victory and the Present Day," *Izvestia*, May 9, 1983; and Cocks, "Administrative Reform," p. 61. On the differing methodologies and estimates of the CIA and Defense Intelligence Agency (DIA), see, for example, *New York Times*, August 7, 1983.

26. *New York Times*, November 17, 1983; *Izvestia*, September 30, 1983, p. 3. Marshall Goldman informs me the 1983 harvest was slightly over 190 million tons. It seems the 1984 harvest too was undistinguished.

27. Gustafson, *Reform in Soviet Politics*, p. 159. Energy intensiveness may now be dropping.

28. D. Valovoi, *Pravda*, March 21, 1983, p. 2; *Sotsialisticheskaya industriya*, March 1, 1983, p. 2; G. Kulagin, *Pravda*, July 12, 1983, p. 2; and Tatyana Zaslavskaya, "Doklad o neobkhodimosti bolee yglublennogo izucheniya v SSSR sotsial'nogo mekhanizma razvitiya ekonomiki," AS no. 5042, Vypusk no. 35/83, August 26, 1983, p. 8. Zaslavskaya's paper has been much discussed in the West. See, for example, *New York Times*, August 5, 1983, pp. A1 and A4; and Philip Hanson, "Discussion of Economic Reform in the USSR: The 'Novosibirsk Paper,' " RL 356/83, September 23, 1983.

29. *Ekonomika i organizatsiya promyshlennogo proizvodstva*, no. 8 (August 1983) (the figure 44,000 does not include 32,000 construction organizations); *Izvestia*, November 18, 1983.

30. Igor Birman, "The Economic Situation in the USSR," *RUSSIA*, 2 (1981): 15; Hunter, *The Future of the Soviet Economy*, p. 174; Bruce Parrott, *Politics and Technology in the Soviet Union* (Cambridge, MA: MIT Press, 1983), pp. 47–48; Feiwel, "Economic Performance," p. 100, referring to R. Amann et al., *The Technological Level of Soviet Industry* (New Haven: Yale, 1977); and Joseph Berliner, *The Innovation Decision in Soviet Industry* (Cambridge, MA: MIT, 1976); Jon Zonderman, "Emigrés' Doctrine on US/USSR Trade," *Boston Business Journal*, July 18–24, 1983, p. 25; *New York Times*, July 24, 1983; RL 308/80, August 29, 1980, citing *Stroitel'naya gazeta*, September 2, 1979.

31. Gordon B. Smith, "Prognosis for Soviet Administration," in *Public Policy and Administration in the Soviet Union*, Gordon B. Smith, ed. (New York: Praeger, 1980), p. 213; and Alexander Yanov, *Detente after Brezhnev* (Berkeley: University of California, Institute of International Studies, 1977), p. 14; and see Feiwel on the "indelible adverse repercussions" the "system" (the party) has had on work culture. "Probably the system's greatest failure was that it depressed the will to produce, to create, to 'do a good day's work' " ("Economic Performance," pp. 100–101).

32. Zaslavskaya, "Doklad a neobkhodimosti," pp. 21–22. She indirectly upholds a Western scholar's judgment that Soviet thinking on the economy is quite diverse, even ambiguous. See Richard F. Vidmer, "Soviet Studies of Organization and Management: A 'Jungle' of Competing Views," *Slavic Review,* 40, 3 (Fall 1981): 421.

33. Leonard Silk, "Andropov's Economic Dilemma," *New York Times Magazine,* October 9, 1983, p. 100. Foreign observers and Soviet participants have, in effect, been in some agreement for a long time.

34. Elizabeth Teague, "Andropov's First Six Months: Policy Disagreements Emerge," RL 206/83, May 25, 1983, p. 1.

35. *Izvestia,* July 13, 1983, p. 2; *Pravda,* December 8, 1982 and March 17, 1983; and *Sotsialisticheskaya industriya,* March 1, 1983, p. 2.

36. *Ekonomika i organizatsiya promyshlennogo proizvodstva (EKO),* no. 8 (August 1983): 16–49.

37. Ibid.: 50–69; *Pravda,* May 5, 1983, p. 2; *Pravda,* December 8, 1982, discussed in David Dyker, "Scale and Specialization in Soviet Industry: A New Policy Initiative?" RL 11/83, January 5, 1983.

38. For outline history of Brezhnev's statements against the state bureaucracy, see Erik P. Hoffmann, "Changing Soviet Perspectives on Leadership and Administration," in *The Soviet Union Since Stalin,* Stephen F. Cohen et al., eds. (Bloomington, IN: Indiana University Press, 1980), p. 79; and Donald P. Kelley, "The Communist Party," in Kelley, *Soviet Politics in the Brezhnev Era,* pp. 32–34.

39. *Pravda,* May 12, 1983, pp. 2–3.

40. Karagedov, *EKO,* no. 8 (August 1983): op. cit.

41. *Pravda,* March 30, 1983, p. 1; and April 30 and September 24, 1983, p. 1. Under Andropov and Chernenko, *Pravda* carries on the front page a weekly statement of some of the topics dealt with by the Politburo at its meetings. Not all likely topics are mentioned. For example, no coverage of the Korean airliner incident of 1983 appeared.

42. *Pravda,* October 3, 1983, p. 2; RL 410/83, November 4, 1983, p. 2; and *Sovetskaya Rossiya,* September 21, 1983, p. 3.

43. Jerry F. Hough, "Andropov's First Year," *Problems of Communism,* 32, 6 (November–December 1983): 61–62; the articles by Schoonover, Johnson, and Lane in *Soviet Economy in the 1980s,* U.S. Congress, Joint Economic Committee (Washington, D.C.: U.S. GPO, 1982), Part 2; the quotation is in Ann Lane, "USSR: Private Agriculture on Center Stage," ibid., p. 39; *Pravda,* April 19, 1983, p. 1.

44. *Trud,* December 12, 1982, quoted in Andreas Tenson, "More Leeway for the Private Sector?" RL 16/82, January 10, 1983, p. 1. In this way the second economy could be legalized and then taxed and regulated. On the previous existence of independent consulting firms (in Leningrad and, interestingly, Novosibirsk), see Ryavec, *Implementation of Soviet Economic Reforms,* p. 171; and see Tenson, "A Call to Legalize Proscribed Technology Input Firms," RL 181/

83, May 4, 1983, who doubts they will be resurrected; and R.G. Karagedov in *EKO*, No. 8 (August 1983), op. cit.

45. Holland Hunter, "The Soviet Economy and the Challenge of Change" (review article), *Problems of Communism,* 28, 2 (March–April 1979): 48; see Ryavec, *Implementation of Soviet Economic Reforms,* pp. 118–119 (Romania and the GDR), and 134–135, 232–233 (Bulgaria); Mlynař, op. cit. Zaslavskaya also refers to Bulgarian practices.

46. *Pravda,* April 18, 1983, p. 2; *Ekonomicheskaya gazeta,* November 27 and 31, 1983, p. 20, and *Voprosy ekonomiki,* 5 (1983): 119–128. Discussed in David A. Dyker, "Soviet and East European Planning: A New Convergence?" RL 433/83, November 15, 1983. See also Allen Kroncher, "What Reforms Does the Soviet Economy Need?" RL 442/82, November 4, 1982.

47. *New York Times,* January 18, 1984, p. A6. China is allowing foreign firms to operate within the country, as does Yugoslavia, and is even investing in capitalist firms abroad, e.g., in a computer firm in New Hampshire. For a sense of the official Soviet view of the Yugoslav economy, see David Dyker, "Market Socialism and Economic Performance—a Soviet Assessment," RL 54/83, January 28, 1983. Books on the Hungarian and Chinese economic reforms include: Paul Hare et al., eds., *Hungary: A Decade of Economic Reform* (London: Allen & Unwin, 1981); George C. Wang, *Economic Reform in the PRC* (Boulder: Westview, 1982); and Lin Wei and Arnold Chao, eds., *China's Economic Reforms* (Philadelphia, PA: University of Pennsylvania Press, 1982). Bertsch notes that the Hungarian reforms "may in some cases have been borrowed from the Yugoslav experience."

48. Robert N. Campbell, "Economic Issues in the USSR" (review article), *Problems of Communism,* 32, 1 (May–June 1983): 65; Bialer, "The Politics of Stringency," p. 291.

49. Franklin D. Holzman, *The Soviet Economy* (New York: Foreign Policy Association, 1982), p. 52; J. Wilczynski, *The Economics of Socialism* (London: Allen & Unwin, 1977), p. 25; Gustafson, *Reform in Soviet Politics,* p. 160. A list of the main features of the post-1957 reforms can be made by using the list in Wilczynski, *Socialist Economic Development and Reforms,* pp. 26–27 (to 1976) and then using Nimitz, "Reform and Technological Innovation," pp. 147ff, or seeing also Allen Kroncher, "The Economic Policies of the Brezhnev Era," RL 463/83, November 22, 1982, an excellent analysis.

50. Michael Kaser, "Economic Policy," in Archie Brown and Michael Kaser, eds., *Soviet Policy for the 1980s* (Bloomington, IN: Indiana University Press, 1982), pp. 198–99; *EKO,* August 1983, op. cit.

51. By 1980 only five all-Union ministries were on *khozraschet.* Kaser, op. cit., p. 198. "The changes in economic management . . . are instruments of a command economy. . . ." Ibid., p. 200.

52. *Pravda* and *Izvestia,* July 26, 1983, p. 1; and *Pravda,* November 23, 1983, p. 2. It was discussed in the *New York Times* on July 27, 1983, pp. A1, A4.

53. See Campbell, "Economic Issues in the USSR," 1983, p. 68.

54. *Pravda,* September 24, 1983, p. 1; *Izvestia,* May 19, 1983, p. 2.

55. *Pravda,* August 28, 1983, p. 1.

56. *Pravda,* August 7, 1983, p. 1; and various research reports of Radio Liberty, e.g., RL 337/83, September 7, 1983; RL 476/83, December 20, 1983.

57. *Izvestia,* March 27 and 28, 1983, p. 2; Andreas Tenson, "Organization of Agricultural Labor Under the Eleventh Five-Year Plan," RL 210/83, May 27, 1983; and Lane, *Soviet Economy in the 1980s,* U.S. Congress, Joint Economic Committee, p. 24.

58. Blair A. Ruble, a review of Conyngham, *Revue Canadienne des Slavistes,* 25, 2 (June 1983): 320; *New York Times,* November 19, 1983, p. 6.

59. Joseph S. Berliner, "Managing the USSR Economy: Alternative Models," *Problems of Communism,* 32, 1 (January–February 1983): 40–56; Eckstein, "Economic Development and Change," p. 492; Nove, *Political Economy and Soviet Socialism,* pp. 156–57 (a pair of models accepted almost literally by the Soviet economist Ignatovsky in 1983); Feiwel in Kelley, *Soviet Politics,* p. 99; and Birman, "The Economic Situation in the USSR," p. 23.

60. Ruble, "Muddling Through," p. 211; Birman, "The Economic Situation in the USSR," p. 23; *Wall Street Journal,* July 21, 1983, pp. 1, 21; Nove, *The Soviet Economic System,* pp. 299, 317–318, 320; Bialer, "The Politics of Stringency," pp. 291, 303; and Brzezinski, "The Soviet Union," p. 8.

61. Smith, *Public Policy and Administration,* p. 209; and Hough, "Soviet Politics under Brezhnev," *Current History,* 82, 486 (October 1983): 333.

62. The example of Tito in 1950 is a case in point. Workers' self-management was presented as a step forward in Marxism.

63. Wolfgang Leonhard quoted in *Die Welt,* September 8, 1983. Translated in *The German Tribune,* 1100, September 18, 1983, p. 8.

64. Peter Taylor, "Romanov's Promotion," RL 288/83, July 29, 1983, p. 4. Romanov was promoted to the central party Secretariat in 1983. See also A. Ruble, "Romanov's Leningrad," *Problems of Communism,* 20, 11, 6 (November–December 1983). Romanov has endorsed industrial associations strongly.

65. *New York Times,* March 1, 1984, p. A15.

66. *Pravda* and *Izvestia,* March 3, 1984, pp. 1–2. For a discussion of the Chernenko succession, see Marc D. Zlotnik, "Chernenko Succeeds," *Problems of Communism,* 33, 2 (March–April 1984): 17–31. Chernenko's earlier statements have appeared in various collections, e.g., *Zabota partii i pravitel'stva o blage naroda* (Moscow: Politizdat, 1974); and *Voprosy raboty partiinogo i gosudarstvennogo apparata* (Moscow: Politicheskaya literatura, 1982), especially pp. 390–440 in the latter, "The Main Field of Activity Is Economics."

10
SOVIET FOREIGN POLICY
SINCE BREZHNEV

Joseph L. Nogee

Soviet foreign policy, like domestic policy, is in a state of transition. Leonid Brezhnev's death in November 1982 did not lead to any major change in foreign policy. Yuri Andropov and Konstantin Chernenko have pursued essentially the same policies they inherited from their predecessors. Looking back at Soviet policy since the Revolution, one can see that generally the accession to power of a new leader did not immediately result in a shift in direction in Soviet foreign policy. The one exception to this generalization is Soviet policy following the death of Stalin in 1953.[1] Leonid Brezhnev, though operating with quite a different style (less flamboyant and impulsive) than Khrushchev, pursued for a number of years the same general line of his predecessor. Sharp demarcations in a state's foreign policy usually reflect more fundamental changes than just a change of administration.

Soviet foreign policy during the Brezhnev administration can be conveniently divided into three periods. The first, 1964–1968, marked a broad continuity with Khrushchev's policies. During these years an intensified build-up of military forces took place, particularly of naval and nuclear forces; economic reform was initiated and abandoned; and a reform government in Czechoslovakia was overthrown by military force. The second period was that of detente, which lasted from 1969 to 1979. Third, there was the period from 1979 through 1982, which witnessed the collapse of detente. For analytical purposes the important demarcation in recent Soviet foreign policy is that between detente and the collapse of detente at the end of the 1970s. Thus, the latter years of Brezhnev's administration and those of Andropov and Chernenko together are a part of an emerging period in Soviet foreign policy characterized by a high degree of tension between East and West.

In order to understand the basis of current East–West tension, we must briefly review the origins of detente and the reasons for its collapse. Three factors were particularly important in the Soviet decision to push for detente in the early 1970s. One was the emergence of China as an independent actor in international politics, coupled with a deepening of the Sino–Soviet schism. Increasingly, China came to be viewed not just as a rival in the Communist world but as a serious threat to Soviet security, a threat that might become more menacing were China and the United States to engage in collusion against Soviet interests. Thus, a principal Soviet objective of detente was to forestall a political rapprochement between its two major adversaries. This goal reflected classic balance of power behavior.

A second factor behind detente was the new military balance that developed between the two superpowers. By the beginning of the 1970s, the Soviet Union achieved a military position of approximate parity with the United States. For the first time the Soviet Union was not constrained in its relationship with the United States by being in a position of military inferiority. The political implications of this were significant. It meant, *inter alia,* that in arms control negotiations Moscow could negotiate from a position of equality and would not be frozen in a position of permanent inferiority by any agreement that might freeze the status quo. Furthermore, the nuclear inventories of both sides had reached levels beyond that necessary for deterrence, providing an incentive for both sides to take seriously the idea of arms control. Specifically, the Soviet Union was particularly interested in stopping the development of a U.S. defense against ballistic missiles. An arms control agreement was also appealing to the Kremlin because it would constitute tacit recognition by the United States of Soviet Russia's emergence as a global superpower of equal status.

A third factor moving Moscow toward detente had to do with the state of the Soviet economy. In a word, it was bad. Productivity as measured by gross national product steadily declined throughout the late 1950s and 1960s. Reforms introduced in the Eighth Five Year Plan (1965–1970) intended to increase economic efficiency and improve the quality and quantity of goods available to the Soviet consumer had by the end of the plan period proven to be a failure. The Brezhnev administration was faced with essentially two alternative approaches to increase productivity. One was to restructure the economic system radically; the other was to modernize Soviet industry by importing technology from the industrialized West, particularly the United States. Both approaches posed political problems for the party leadership, but the latter was chosen as the least disruptive to the domestic political structure. The need for trade with the United States as a means to import technology was an important consideration in the Soviet shift toward detente.

Why did detente collapse? There are several explanations. One has to do with the failure of both the Soviet Union and the United States to achieve the specific goals each had sought. Detente did not prevent the collusion between China and the United States so feared by Moscow. Richard Nixon saw an opportunity to strengthen Washington's position vis-à-vis Moscow by means of a rapprochement with China, and he took it. The benefits from arms control also proved to be less than expected. SALT I, in itself a significant accomplishment, was expected to be the first of a series of arms control agreements. Not only did SALT II take more than twice the time to negotiate than SALT I, it failed to be ratified by the government that signed it. And, third, Soviet–American trade made only modest gains during the 1970s. The 1972 Trade Agreement which was to be one of the economic pillars of detente was repudiated by the Soviet Union because of amendments imposed by the U.S. Congress which Moscow found objectionable.

It should be noted that Washington was no more successful than Moscow in achieving its foreign policy objectives through detente. The Nixon administration assumed a linkage between U.S. concessions in trade and technology and Soviet restraint in the Third World. In particular, the United States sought assistance in pressuring North Vietnam to compromise its terms for ending the war in South Vietnam. The conquest of Vietnam in 1975 was only one of several extensions of communist power in the Third World by military means in the 1970s. After Vietnam came Cambodia and Laos in 1975, Angola in 1976, Ethiopia in 1977, South Yemen in 1978, and Afghanistan in 1979. These extensions of Soviet power or influence violated the American, though not the Soviet, conception of what was to be achieved via detente.

On a more general level detente collapsed because the balance of power on which it rested changed during the decade. A general equilibrium existed at the inception of detente which shifted to the disadvantage of the West. Western decline became evident during the oil crises of 1973 and 1979 which exposed the economic vulnerability of the industrial democracies. U.S. weakness was manifested by the disunity and paralysis of will caused by the Vietnam War, the Watergate scandals, and the inability to confront the Iranian government during the hostage crisis. As Soviet military power grew steadily the perception of a changing balance of power apparently tempted the Kremlin to act with less restraint.

Though Soviet behavior contributed to the collapse of detente, Moscow never ceased to proclaim its desire to see detente restored as the hallmark of its relations with the West. At the Twenty-Sixth Party Congress, which met in the winter of 1981, Leonid Brezhnev reaffirmed Soviet interest in "continuing and deepening detente," even going so far as to endorse the idea of a summit meeting with President Reagan. The fact was that in the 1980s Moscow found itself even less secure—notwithstanding its greater military power—than it had been a decade earlier. The crisis in Soviet–American relations coincided with several other foreign problems whose solutions came no easier to Andropov or Chernenko than they had to Brezhnev. When Brezhnev died on November 10, 1982, he bequeathed to his successors unresolved problems in Afghanistan, the Middle East, Eastern Europe, and with China and the United States.

Afghanistan, after almost half a decade of Soviet occupation, is no more pacified than it was when the invasion began in late 1979. In 1984 Soviet forces numbering approximately 105,000 sustained the puppet government of Babrak Karmal, but could not suppress a guerrilla insurgency which was supported by widespread popular forces (though themselves bitterly divided) who sought to replace the Marxist regime in Kabul with an Islamic republic. Repeated Soviet offensives in strategic valleys in different parts of the country have inflicted heavy casualties on the Afghan population and have led to the migration of several million refugees into Pakistan and Iran. But Moscow has yet to see the light at the end of the tunnel which would permit the withdrawal of Soviet forces without the collapse of Karmal's government. On the other hand, neither is there evidence that Soviet forces can be driven out of the country by the *mujahedeen*, or guerrillas. Moscow has demonstrated that it is prepared, if necessary, to fight a long war of attrition. From the beginning, the Soviets have justified their presence in Afghanistan on the grounds that "foreign" elements (principally American, Pakistani and Chinese) were behind the Islamic insurgency. Late in 1983 *Red Star* claimed that 300 U.S. instructors in Pakistan were training the Afghan rebels. "Moreover," charged the official organ of the Red Army, "they are no longer limiting themselves merely to training the bandits, but are, to all intents and purposes, directing their military operations."[2]

For Moscow the price for its invasion of Afghanistan has been substantial. Politically, it formalized the death of detente. At the United Nations the action was condemned in the Security Council and by the General Assembly. Censure by the United Nations has little credibility these days, though clearly Moscow was discomfited by the strong anti-Soviet reaction in much of the Third World. It is more difficult to describe the tangible costs of Afghanistan because the number of Soviet casualties has never been revealed. Western sources estimate that as of the beginning of Andropov's administration somewhere between 10 and 15 thousand Soviet troops were killed or wounded. Chinese estimates of Soviet deaths are higher. Chernenko, in his first half-year in office, has been no more successful than his predecessors in incorporating Afghanistan into the Soviet system (à la Mongolia). It may require the kind of prolonged campaign that it took the Soviets in the 1920s and 1930s to end Moslem resistance to their rule in Central Asia.

The Middle East, perhaps more than any other region in the world, illustrates the difficulty of the superpowers to control events that affect the outcome of their foreign policies. Soviet influence in the Middle East reached a nadir following the Israeli invasion of Lebanon in the summer of 1982 and the poor performance of Syria—supplied with Russian arms— against Israeli armed forces. Moscow was able to influence neither the outcome of events during the war nor the diplomacy of the postwar period. Several months before he died Brezhnev proposed a plan for peace in the Middle East which was simply ignored.

Soviet influence in recent years has increased less because of what Moscow has done than because of the failures of U.S. policy in Lebanon and the inability of Israel and the Western powers to control outcomes in the region. Yuri Andropov proceeded to rebuild Syria's military forces, and as Syria's influence gradually re-emerged during 1983 and 1984, Soviet prestige rose with it. But the Kremlin understands very well the fragility of its influence, for it no more controls Syrian domestic politics than does Syria control the political forces at work in the region.

The war between Iraq and Iran was another of those events whose outcome was important to Soviet interests but beyond its control. Moscow, torn by its desire to avoid offending Iraq, a former ally and important Arab state, or Iran, a large oil-rich state in the throes of an anti-Western revolution, cautiously avoided siding with either openly. Behind the scenes, however, the Kremlin tilted first toward one side, then the other. Initially, the Soviet Union supported Teheran, in part because of dissatisfaction with Iraqi President Saddam Hussein's purge of communists after taking power in 1978 and in part because of the greater long-term potential of Iran. The Andropov administration moved gradually toward a more neutral position and then shifted back to its former ally. Moscow was presumably motivated by its failure to make any significant impact on the government of the Ayatollah Khomeini. In 1983 the Iranian government banned the Tudeh (Communist) party, arrested many communists, and expelled 18 Eastern bloc diplomats. Publicly, the Soviet Union continues to take the position of urging a peaceful settlement, but under Chernenko Iraq has received large quantities of Soviet-built tanks, artillery, and missiles. Soviet vacillation is a demonstration of the extent to which its policies in the Middle East often are forced to react to events rather than dominate them.

The revolution that erupted in Poland in the summer of 1980 was the most serious crisis to confront Moscow since the Czechoslovakia crisis in 1968. Poland is the linchpin of Russia's Eastern European empire. Its population of 36 million people is the largest in Eastern Europe, giving it the second largest military force in the Warsaw Pact. Of the non-Soviet Warsaw Pact states, only the German Democratic Republic has a larger economy. Equally important to its size is its location. Poland not only links East Germany to the Soviet Union, it provides the most direct route for an invasion of European Russia (historically one frequently used). For these reasons the Solidarity movement which threatened to end Communist party rule in socialist Poland constituted a challenge Moscow could not ignore. Nor did it do so. Repeatedly, throughout 1980 and 1981, the Kremlin threatened to take military action unless Polish authorities put their house in order. In December 1981 they did. Wojciech Jaruzelski, who took over control of Poland's Communist party, proclaimed martial law, arrested thousands of Solidarity activists, and put the powers of government in the hands of a supreme military council headed by himself. During the 19-month period of martial law, Jaruzelski systematically destroyed the power of Solidarity as an organization. Though an underground movement continued to exist, Jaruzelski established sufficient control that he could permit Pope John Paul II to make a potentially destabilizing visit to his native country in the summer of 1983. All in all, Moscow emerged from the crisis of the early 1980s much better than Brezhnev dared to hope for when the revolution began. Without the use of Soviet military forces Communist power in Poland had been preserved. The Brezhnev doctrine remained in tact without the costly consequences of having to engage Soviet and Polish armed forces.

Nevertheless, the Polish issue has hardly been solved permanently. The underlying causes of Polish discontent remain: economic mismanagement, food and consumer goods shortages, corruption among the ruling elite, the stifling of intellectual and political freedom, and nationalism smothered by Soviet domination. Periodically, the Poles have rebelled against their communist masters and there is every possibility that the revolution of 1980 has not been crushed but deferred. Widespread protests on May Day, 1984, exposed the hostility to the Jaruzelski regime that lies behind the facade of acquiescence.

Moscow's strategy to deal with the problem involves political and economic techniques. Under Chernenko the Soviet Union has taken steps to bind the country more tightly into the Soviet economic orbit. On May 4, 1984 the two governments signed a 15-year economic pact providing for economic, scientific, and technological cooperation to the year 2000. Chernenko described the agreement as "a document of major *political* importance."[3] The Soviet leadership has often claimed that the rise of Solidarity was linked to the economic ties between Poland and the West. It does not seem likely that the Soviet Union can afford to pump into the Polish economy the resources necessary to overcome popular dissatisfaction. And, even if it could, that would not meet the noneconomic, nationalistic sources of popular discontent with Soviet domination. In the long run what will be required will be a more fundamental change in the relationship between the Soviet Union and the countries of Eastern Europe, a change that is hardly likely to come from the conservative leadership in power, or for that matter from the generation waiting in the wings to assume power.

Sino–Soviet relations continue to be a major source of concern to the Kremlin. Yuri Andropov, following the path of his predecessor, sought to normalize relations between the two states. He demonstrated this by the warm reception he gave to the Chinese representative on the occasion of Brezhnev's funeral. Negotiations to improve relations were resumed in 1983. Though a number of cultural and trade agreements were signed during the Andropov period, the two countries were unable to compromise on the three basic Chinese demands for a normalization, *viz.*, (1) the withdrawal of Soviet forces from Afghanistan, (2) the withdrawal of Vietnamese troops from Cambodia, and (3) the reduction of Soviet forces along the Sino–Soviet border.

Though the Chinese remained deeply suspicious of the Soviet Union there was evidence that they wanted some improvement in Sino–Soviet relations. Very likely the Chinese desire was stimulated by their dislike of the pro-Taiwan position of the Reagan administration. On February 10, 1984 (one day after Andropov's death), China and the Soviet Union signed a $1.2 billion trade agreement providing for an increase of trade (which was approximately $800 million in 1983) by about 50% in 1984.

Chernenko, however, has so far been unable to develop any new momentum in dealing with the Chinese. Early in 1984 Zhoa Ziyang visited Washington, the first time a Chinese premier visited the United States and the first visit by a top-level official since Deng Xiaoping came to the United States in 1979. This visit paved the way for Ronald Reagan to make his first visit to China, which he did from April 28 through May 1. Though on balance Sino–American relations were strengthened by the visit, the Chinese made clear their unwillingness to join in Reagan's anti-Soviet crusade.

They insisted on censoring remarks critical of the Soviet Union that the U.S. president had wanted to make on Chinese television. Clearly, Peking was trying to position itself into a more middle posture between the superpowers. For Moscow, however, the Zhoa–Reagan exchange visits were menacing. *Pravda* saw in the visit by the Chinese premier some "political–strategic" purpose.[4] In the aftermath of Reagan's visit Moscow suddenly and unexpectedly postponed indefinitely a visit to China by First Deputy Premier Ivan Arkhipov. The Soviet first deputy premier would have been the highest-ranking Soviet official to visit China since 1969. Probably the postponement was intended as a rebuff to Peking for the warm reception accorded to President Reagan during his visit. Both China and the Soviet Union are looking for ways to improve their relationship, but the incentive for change is greater on Moscow's than Beijing's part. In July 1984 the authoritative journal *Beijing Review* contained the observation that "It is unrealistic and impossible for Sino–Soviet relations to return to what they once were in history."[5] In other words, China will be a problem for a long time to come.

No problem confronting the Soviet Union is more important than its relationship with the United States. Indeed, since World War II the security interests of each power have focused on the other. All other relationships, however vital, have been secondary. This does not mean that every problem confronting each superpower has its origins in the activities of the other; far from it. But it does suggest that each state is capable (as no other state is) of destroying the other, and that the most dangerous crises for both are those which could escalate into a military conflict with the other. Thus, the general state of Soviet–American relations is a major factor in the security of each as well as in international peace and global security. The foremost foreign policy problem facing Konstantin Chernenko and his colleagues is the antagonistic character of Soviet–American relations in the mid-1980s. The principal symptom and cause of that problem has been the arms race and the collapse of arms control negotiations.

The two SALT agreements reached during the period of detente (SALT I, 1972 and SALT II, 1979) reflected the mutual recognition that a general condition of parity existed between the armed forces of the United States and the Soviet Union. Though SALT I had expired in 1977 and SALT II was never ratified, each government agreed to observe the basic terms of the treaties so long as the other did so also. Unfortunately, even the general observance of both agreements did not stop the arms race. That was because only strategic weapons (principally launchers) were covered, and the primary restrictions were quantitative rather than qualitative. Thus it was possible for each side to develop more powerful and accurate weapons so long as they remained within the quantitative restraints of the treaties.

Actually the central issue during the period under consideration involved not strategic (i.e., intercontinental) weapons, but theater (i.e., European) weapons. At stake was a NATO decision to modernize its intermediate nuclear force (INF) in the face of determined Soviet opposition. It was by far the bitterest issue in contention during the latter years of Brezhnev's administration and the post-Brezhnev period. The immediate origin of the issue was the decision by NATO in 1979 to deploy 572 Pershing II and cruise missiles in Germany, Britain, Italy, the Netherlands, and Belgium by the end of 1983 unless the Soviet Union agreed before that date to withdraw a new intermediate-range missile known as the SS-20 which it had begun to deploy in 1977. The SS-20 was the successor to older (SS-4 and SS-5) missiles which were becoming obsolete and which the Soviet Union considered to be vulnerable to NATO's "forward-based systems", particularly submarine-launched missiles. The SS-20 was more powerful and accurate than any land-based missile under NATO's control. It had three warheads, was mobile and solid fueled, and could strike at any target in Western Europe.

To NATO the SS-20 created serious military and political problems for the alliance. Militarily, the Warsaw Pact was seen as upsetting the balance of power because NATO had no comparable weapons. The power and accuracy and survivability of the SS-20 made it potentially a first-strike weapon, particularly if the Soviet Union were to deploy them in large numbers. There were two possible political consequences of this perceived Soviet superiority which concerned the West. One was that Moscow would use its nuclear superiority to pressure Europe to maintain a foreign policy compatible with Soviet interests much as Finland is required to do. The other potential consequence of the SS-20 was the European fear that it would erode the credibility of the U.S. nuclear guarantee which many Europeans (particularly the Germans) saw as the ultimate source of their security. The presence of Pershing II and cruise missiles, it was believed, would guarantee that United States nuclear forces would be engaged in the event of a nuclear war in Europe.

Moscow, not surprisingly, saw the issue differently. From its perspective the planned Pershing II and cruise missile deployment would upset the balance of power in NATO's favor. Soviet authorities argued that parity already existed between the Warsaw Pact and NATO, with each side having approximately 1,000 delivery vehicles. The Soviet calculation included U.S. and German Pershing I missiles, allied fighter-bombers capable of hitting targets in the Soviet Union, as well as all British and French nuclear forces comprising land- and sea-launched missiles and intermediate-range bombers. Though Britain and France considered their nuclear forces to be "national" deterrents only and not a part of the NATO defense, from Moscow's perspective any weapon that could strike at Soviet soil had to be counted as a component of NATO.

NATO, then, was willing to abandon its planned deployment of the INF only if Moscow disbanded its SS-20s. The Soviet Union wanted to stop the INF but not at the expense of its SS-20s. Presumably NATO would be willing to scale down its INF numbers in return for a Soviet reduction of SS-20s. Negotiations to establish acceptable levels did not commence until late in 1981, and it quickly became apparent that both sides were more interested in influencing public opinion than in reaching an agreement. President Reagan proposed what he called the "zero option": NATO would cancel the INF deployment if the Soviet Union would dismantle all of its SS-4s, SS-5s, and SS-20s. Moscow clearly was not willing to dismantle what it already had in place for a United States commitment in effect to do nothing. The Soviet counter-offers were hardly more generous. Brezhnev proposed a mutual freeze on the deployment of any new missiles while negotiations continued. Yuri Andropov made a significant concession in December 1982 when he agreed to reduce the number of SS-20s in Europe to the total size of the British and French forces, then numbering 162 missiles, providing the proposed NATO force was abandoned completely. This was unacceptable to the West not only because Britain and France refused to consider their missiles as a part of the NATO deterrent but also because the SS-20s were newer, more accurate, and carried three times the number of warheads than the Anglo–French launchers. In the spring of 1983 Andropov agreed to meet one of these objections by accepting a level of SS-20s whose warheads would equal the combined number of warheads in the British and French forces; but again, the price was a total abandonment of the NATO INF deployment. This political gamesmanship reached a climax in late 1983 when the United States began installing cruise missiles in Britain and Germany as scheduled. Andropov reacted quickly and sharply by breaking off the INF negotiations. His position, maintained by his successor, was that the Soviet Union would not resume talks on reducing intermediate nuclear forces in Europe until the United States removed the cruise and Pershing II missiles that had been put in place. Late in 1984 INF negotiations had still not resumed.

An important factor in Soviet calculations was the possibility that public opinion in the West might pressure the NATO governments not to deploy the Pershing II and cruise missiles. In Europe and the United States a strong antinuclear movement opposed the INF deployment, particularly in several of the countries slated to receive the missiles. Soviet pressure on Germany was particularly intense. Leonid Brezhnev visited Bonn to encourage the antinuclear peace activists and to put pressure on the German government. In the relatively short period of his rule Andropov showed considerable skill and determination in appealing to European public opinion, but ultimately that strategy failed. Three critical elections in 1983—Helmut Kohl's Christian Democratic victory in March, the Italian elections in June, and Margaret Thatcher's Conservative party defeat of Labor in June—virtually guaranteed that deployment would proceed as planned. Andropov's failure to modify the NATO deployment was the biggest foreign policy failure of his administration.

When the Soviet negotiators walked out of the INF talks Moscow also ceased negotiating the separate but related issue of strategic arms. These are nuclear weapons delivered by intercontinental ballistic missiles (ICBMs), submarine-launched ballistic missiles (SLBMs), and intercontinental bombers or cruise missiles. Cruise missiles are air-breathing drones that fly close to the earth's surface and can be controlled after launch. Since the beginning of the SALT talks in 1969, strategic arms limitations have been the main focus of arms control efforts. This has not been so since the collapse of detente. After the U.S. failure to ratify the SALT II treaty and the inauguration of a Republican administration which was clearly skeptical about strategic arms control, the central forum for negotiations centered around the NATO INF deployment. The observation made above regarding the gamesmanship employed in the INF talks applied even more to the strategic arms negotiations, which were labeled by the Reagan administration as START, for strategic arms reduction talks.

The substantive goals of both sides can be identified briefly. For the United States the central objective was to reduce the Soviet inventory of medium and heavy ICBMs (the SS-17s, SS-18s, and SS-19s) which were viewed as capable of destroying most of the United States land-based ICBMs in a surprise attack. Moscow had several concerns: to prevent the United States from building a first-strike capability; limiting the development of United States cruise missiles; and inhibiting the modernization of U.S. nuclear forces. These objectives were translated into specific proposals around which the two sides negotiated. Ronald Reagan attempted to bring about "deep cuts" in Soviet heavy missiles with a proposal to reduce all nuclear warheads to a maximum of 5,000 (from approximately 7,500) with no more than half to be deployed on ICBMs. He also sought a ceiling of 850 for all ICBM and SLBM missiles. Andropov countered with a proposal to reduce Soviet strategic arms by 25%, in effect reducing Soviet ICBMs and SLBMs to a total of 1,800. Throughout 1983 modest further concessions were made by both sides, but the gap remained unbridgeable. Moscow had no intention of restructuring its nuclear deterrent away from large ICBMs to sea-based missiles as desired by Washington. As mentioned above, in December 1983 the Soviets terminated all arms control negotiations.

The bitterness that developed in Soviet–American relations in the early 1980s was in part a consequence of the new leadership that came to power during that period. The election of Ronald Reagan brought to the U.S. presidency the most strident anti-communist since the cold war began. Though anti-American polemics were standard fare in Soviet propaganda, Soviet leaders in general cautiously avoided being the spokesmen for the sharpest criticism of the United States and its leaders. Ronald Reagan in an unprecedented way gave full vent to his revulsion for the Soviet system as typified by his famous "evil empire" speech before a group of evangelicals in March 1983.

Ronald Reagan's anti-communism was considerably more than just rhetoric. He backed up his strong words with a military build-up which convinced the Soviets that the Reagan administration was committed to restoring the superiority that the United States once possessed vis-à-vis the Soviet Union. In measure after measure Reagan made known his determination to challenge the Soviets on every possible front: in imposing economic sanctions against Poland, in pressuring Europe not to exchange technology and credit for Soviet natural gas, in giving military assistance to anti-communist forces in Central America. Nothing illustrated more clearly the depth of Soviet–American antagonism than the mutual recriminations that followed the Soviet shooting down of a Korean civilian airline that had strayed over Soviet territory on September 1, 1983. Andropov and his colleagues were deeply stung and outraged by the charges of "uncivilized" behavior and "barbarism" made by U.S. leaders. The Soviet accusation that the airliner was an American spy plane and the refusal of Moscow to assume any responsibility for the tragedy (269 lives were lost) only added to Western indignation.

Under Chernenko's leadership the Politburo has chosen to reciprocate the Reagan administration's hard line. One of the architects of that line is Soviet Foreign Minister Andrei Gromyko. At the 35-nation Stockholm Conference on Confidence and Security-Building Measures and Disarmament which began in January 1984 Gromyko claimed that "a drastic turn for the worse" had occurred in international relations. He accused the

United States of "engaging in secret, subversive activity and terrorism against other states." Of the Reagan administration he said that "lasting confidence cannot be achieved while the preaching of hostility, hate and boneheaded 'crusades' and the pinning of ignorant labels on whole countries' peoples continues."[6]

Soviet behavior also matched its rhetoric. In the spring Defense Minister Dmitri Ustinov announced an increase in the number of missile-carrying submarines off the coast of the United States. In a not-so-subtle allusion to the Pershing II missiles he warned the United States that Soviet SLBMs could now strike at U.S. targets within 8–10 minutes from launch. U.S. sources also reported an increase in the number of Soviet SS-20 missiles to 378. Another expression of Soviet policy was the decision not to participate in the summer Olympics in Los Angeles. The USSR National Olympic Committee acknowledged the political basis behind the decision:

> It is known that, from the first days of preparations for these Olympics, the American administration has steered a course aimed at using the Games for its own political purposes. Chauvinistic sentiments and anti-Soviet hysteria are being whipped up in the country.

Marat V. Gramov, the chairman of the Soviet committee, explained the reason for the Soviet action very frankly: ". . . the Olympic problems are in the overall context of President Reagan's policy."[7] By pulling out of the summer Olympics, Moscow sought to minimize the use of the games in Los Angeles by the administration to enhance its prestige.

Soviet behavior in 1984 undoubtedly reflected the fact that 1984 was an election year in the United States. Moscow has occasionally had its preferences in U.S. presidential elections, though rarely did it attempt to influence the outcome. In 1984 there was not the slightest doubt which side the Kremlin wanted to win in November. *Izvestia,* the official government newspaper observed in March: "But on the whole, the Democrats are countering R. Reagan's bellicosity and adventurism with a foreign policy that is based on common sense and an understanding that America will be secure only when the Soviet Union is secure."[8] Soviet understanding of U.S. politics combines considerable information with a substantial lack of insight. But the leadership recognizes the limits of what can be done to influence public opinion. Nevertheless, Moscow was clearly determined to avoid doing anything that might assist the political fortunes of the Reagan campaign. That included avoiding any significant concession to the United

States or even giving credence to the White House claim that the Reagan strategy for dealing with the Russians was the soundest. This factor may explain the brusqueness bordering on rudeness of the Chernenko administration in the spring and summer of 1984.

Considerations of style aside, the differences between the Soviet and U.S. systems are profound and the clash of interests real. Though Soviet behavior may have triggered the military build-up of the Reagan administration, Chernenko and his colleagues are convinced that the objective of U.S. policy is global military supremacy. They view communism and capitalism as fundamentally antagonistic. At the same time they recognize the supreme necessity of preventing a nuclear war. Therein lies the basic dilemma of Soviet foreign policy, and U.S. foreign policy as well. The problem is to keep the cold war from getting hot.

NOTES

1. See Marshall D. Shulman, *Stalin's Foreign Policy Reappraised* (New York: Atheneum, 1965).
2. *Current Digest of the Soviet Press (CDSP)*, 35, no. 52 (January 25, 1984): 15.
3. *New York Times,* May 5, 1984. Emphasis added.
4. *CDSP,* 36, no. 3 (February 15, 1984): 13.
5. *Beijing Review,* 27, no. 28 (July 9, 1984): 32.
6. *CDSP,* 36, no. 3 (February 15, 1984): pp. 1, 3.
7. *CDSP,* 36, no. 19 (June 6, 1984): 2, 6.
8. *CDSP,* 36, no. 12 (April 18, 1984): 10.

INDEX

absenteeism, campaign against, 97–98
advertising, in Soviet media, 37
Afghanistan: and detente collapse,
    219–220; reform of media
    system, 36
age, and media consumption, 58
agitation, by oral media, 44–45
agriculture: collectivization of,
    161; contract brigades, 202;
    and economic reform, 192, 198
Aliev, G., 94, 140–141
All-Russian Social Christian Union
    for the Liberation of the People
    (VSKhSON), 135, 137
All-Union Agency for the Protection
    of Authors' Rights (UARP), 40
Americanism, vs. Soviet ideology,
    115–116
Andropov, Y.: authority-building
    strategy, 28; and controlled
    change, 26; as disciplinarian,
    26; disappearance of, 29;
    domestic problems of, 86;
    legacy of, 101; legal policy
    under, 85–101; legislation
    by, 93–100; power struggles of,
    10; reform program of, 27;
    rise of, 25–31; and Russian
    nationalism, 140–142;
    succession of, 10–11
arms control: and detente, 218;
    and expansionism, 75; Soviet
    policy, 223–224; strategic vs.
    European weapons, 224; of
    strategic missiles, 226
army, *see* military

assimilation, Stalin's definition, 129
audience opinion: of newspaper
    readers, 46; and political com-
    munication, 45–49
authority: of Andropov, 25–31;
    building of, 19–23; in elite
    politics, 15–31; hegemonial,
    77–79; vs. power, 19–20, 24–25

Berdiaev, N., 135
birth rates, 175–177
Borodin, L., trial of, 141–142
Brezhnev, L., 2; authority building
    by, 23; foreign policy of, 216;
    military attitudes toward, 81;
    passing of generation, 1–13;
    political leadership, 1–13;
    problems of, 86–87; protracted
    succession and military, 79–82;
    "stability of cadres" policy, 9;
    successors to, 8–9
Brezhnevite accommodation, with
    military, 73–74
bride kidnapping, 179
British Broadcasting Corporation,
    56

capitalist countries, media treat-
    ment of, 54
censorship: and ideology, 110; of
    media, 39, 41
Central Asia: anti-urbanization ef-
    forts, 173; education of workers,
    179; importance of, 178–180;
    labor problems in, 178–179;
    language problem, 179

231

ABOUT THE EDITOR
AND CONTRIBUTORS

Joseph L. Nogee is professor of political science and director of the Russian Studies Program at the University of Houston. In 1984–85 he was the Henry L. Stimson Professor of Political Science at the Army War College. He has also taught at New York University, Vanderbilt University, and Rice University. He is the author, coauthor or editor of five books including *Soviet Policy Toward International Control of Atomic Energy* and the coauthor of *Soviet Foreign Policy since World War II*.

George W. Breslauer is associate professor of political science at the University of California, Berkeley and Chair of the Berkeley-Stanford Program on Soviet International Behavior. He is currently involved in research on Soviet elite politics and Soviet views of the Third World. He has authored or coauthored four books including *Khrushchev and Brezhnev as Leaders: Building Authority in Soviet Politics*.

Robert H. Donaldson is the president of Fairleigh Dickinson University. Previously he held administrative and academic positions at Vanderbilt University and Herbert H. Lehman College, City University of New York. He has served at the Department of State as International Affairs Fellow of the Council on Foreign Relations and at the Strategic Studies Institute of the Army War College. He is the coauthor of *Soviet Foreign Policy since World War II*.

Darrell P. Hammer is professor of political science at Indiana University. He is the author of *The Politics of Oligarchy*, now in its second edition. He has been a Fulbright fellow and in 1977 studied in Moscow as an academy of science exchange scholar. His numerous articles have been published in such journals as *Problems of Communism,* the *Slavic Review* and *Soviet Studies.* His current research involves the study of Russian nationalism.

Theresa M. Hill received her B.A. from Saint Mary's College, Notre Dame, Indiana. She is currently a doctoral candidate and teaching fellow in political science at Miami University, Oxford, Ohio.

Dan N. Jacobs is professor of political science at Miami University, Oxford, Ohio. He has authored numerous books of which the most recent are *Borodin: Stalin's Man in China, Studies of the Third Wave: Recent*

Migration of Soviet Jews to the United States (coauthor), and *Comparative Governments* (senior author). He is currently working on a political biography of Nikita S. Khrushchev.

Roman Kolkowicz is professor of political science at the University of California, Los Angeles, where he was the founding director of the Center for International and Strategic Affairs from 1975–81. He is currently codirector of the Project on Arms Control and International Security, which is sponsored by former presidents Jimmy Carter and Gerald Ford under the auspices of the Carter Center at Emory University.

Alfred G. Meyer is professor of political science at The University of Michigan. He has taught at a number of universities including Michigan State University and Harvard University. His numerous books and articles deal with Marxist and Leninist ideology, with Soviet domestic and foreign politics, and with general communist studies. His most recent book, a biography of Lily Braun, a noted German feminist and socialist, will be published in 1985.

Ellen Mickiewicz is dean of the graduate school and professor of political science at Emory University. Her current research on the Soviet media system includes issues of elites and their functions and the role of feedback in media theory and policy. This research has been published in the *Journal of Communication* and the *Slavic Review*. She has also published in *The Soviet Union in the 1980s*, published by the Academy of Political Science.

Karl W. Ryavec is professor of political science at the University of Massachusetts at Amherst. He is the author of *Implementation of Soviet Economic Reforms* and the editor of *Soviet Society and the Communist Party*. He has published in *Soviet Studies* and the *Slavic Review*. He was a consultant to the Arms Control and Disarmament Agency. He is currently doing research on U.S.-Soviet relations and the Soviet state bureaucracy and politics.

Robert Sharlet is professor of political science at Union College. A specialist on Soviet and East European politics and law, he has published four books including *The New Soviet Constitution of 1977* and *The Soviet Union since Stalin* (coeditor). His current research focuses on Soviet legal history and the emergence of "contra-systems" in Eastern Europe and the Soviet Union.